PAGAN
CELTIC
IRELAND

BARRY RAFTERY

PAGAN CELTIC IRELAND

The Enigma of the Irish Iron Age

With 223 illustrations

THAMES AND HUDSON

Tairgím an leabhar seo i ndil-chuimhne m'athar
Seosamh OReachtabhra
le gean agus le buíochas

AUTHOR'S NOTE

In writing this book I have drawn extensively on published works, on my own
research and on material, as yet unpublished, which was generously made
available to me by colleagues. For ease of reading, however, there are no
acknowledgments in the text, nor are there any bibliographical references.
Special thanks for information on unpublished sites are due to C.J. Lynn,
E. Grogan, S. Caulfield, C. Donaghy, C. Foley, E. Rynne, A. Moloney,
E.P. Kelly, C. Newman, G. Eogan, H. Roche, R.B. Warner, T. Condit and
M. Gibbons. I am also indebted to R.B. Warner for supplying the radiocarbon
calibrations, to Professor J. O'Meara for translating the Latin inscription on the
oculist's stamp from Golden, Co. Tipperary, and to Professor P. MacCana for
assistance with the earliest recensions of the *Táin*. Thanks are due, too, to
A. Maloney, D. Jennings, C. McDermott and M. Keane for much technical
assistance with computer discs. And I am particularly indebted to my wife
Nuala for compiling the index and to the editorial staff at Thames and Hudson.
Finally, I would like to record my thanks to Dr Patrick Wallace, Director of
the National Museum of Ireland, for help and generosity in providing
illustrations and to the staff of the Antiquities Division of that institution for
their courtesy and assistance over many years.

© 1994 Thames and Hudson Ltd, London

First published in the United States of America in 1994 by
Thames and Hudson Inc., 500 Fifth Avenue, New York, New York 10110

Library of Congress Catalog Card Number 93-61274

ISBN 0-500-05072-4

Printed and bound in Slovenia

Contents

Preface   7

1 Introduction   9

A land of gods and heroes 13

2 From Bronzesmith to Blacksmith   17

The Late Bronze Age background 17   The Hallstatt Iron Age 26
The crannóg at Rathtinaun, Co. Sligo 32   The end of the
Bronze Age 35

3 Hillforts   38

The typology of hillforts 38   Function 48   Chronology and
culture 58   The Spinans Hill complex 62

4 King and Tribe   64

Royal sites 64   Tara 65   Cruachain 70   Dún Ailinne 71
Emain Macha 74   Function and significance 79   Places of
assembly 81   Linear earthworks 83

5 The Road to God Knows Where   98

The associated wooden artifacts 101   Cultural significance 103
Chariotry and horses 104   Travel and transport 110

6 The Invisible People   112

Hearth and home 113   Domestic crafts 117   The production
of food 121   Personal adornment 127   Weapons and
warfare 141

7 Technology and Art   147

Iron technology 147   The craft of the bronzesmith 150
Techniques of bronze production 151   The art of repairing 158
Goldworking 161   Stoneworking 162   La Tène art styles 162

8 **Cult, Ritual and Death**   178

Ritual sites 180   Standing stones 181   Wet sites: rivers,
lakes and bogs 182   Human and animal forms 185   Bog
bodies 187   Burials 188

9 **Beyond the Empire**   200

The burials at Lambay 200   Ireland and the Classical
authors 203   Ptolemy's map 204   Romans in Ireland 206   The
sacred mound at Newgrange 210   Roman finds at occupation
sites 212   Scattered evidence of Roman presence 214

10 **Celts, Culture and Colonization**   220

Definition and terminology 220   Archaeology and
philology 223   The invasion problem 224   The introduction
of La Tène 225   The enigma of southern Ireland 226   In
conclusion 228

Appendix: Radiocarbon Dates Used in the Text   229
Notes to the Text   231
Further Reading   231
Sources of Illustrations   235
Index   235

Preface

Significant advances have taken place in recent years in our understanding of the Irish Iron Age. These have involved new discoveries and a range of new dates, both radiocarbon and dendrochronological, all of which have contributed to a wider understanding of the period. The present volume attempts to bring together the new information in order to provide a synthetic overview for the general reader. The work is not concerned with the minutiae of typological or chronological argument so beloved of modern archaeologists, but seeks rather to present a coherent and readable picture of life and death in the Irish Iron Age. This picture is based essentially on the available archaeological evidence; the written sources have been used, with some circumscription, to add colour to the picture.

Studies of the annual growth rings of trees ('tree-ring dating' or 'dendrochronology') have shown that radiocarbon dates are increasingly too young, the further back in time one goes before the Christian era. The correlation of radiocarbon years with true calendar dates has been one of the success stories of chronometric studies over the last decade. In this book I shall follow the correlation or 'calibration curve' of Stuiver and Pearson (1986). Thus, all radiocarbon dates in the text will be given in calendar years, calibrated to two standard deviations in a range of 95 per cent probability. Where there are several dates from a site, the earliest and latest dates are given to indicate the probable chronological range. In the appendix, however, all the individual dates are given, both as BP ('before present', i.e. before 1950) and in calibrated form. It should be noted that the actual date can lie anywhere within the calibrated range.

It goes without saying that this book could not have been written without the patience, help and support of my family. To Nuala, Sara and Tilly I record with pleasure my deep thanks. The greatest debt of all, however, I owe to my father, the late Joseph Raftery, who paved the way which I all too inadequately follow. It is to his memory that this book is dedicated.

I Map of Ireland with counties and principal placenames mentioned in the text.

CHAPTER 1

Introduction

Qui ipsorum lingua Celtae, nostra Galli appellantur.
'In their own language they are called Celts, in our tongue Gauls.'
GAIUS JULIUS CAESAR (100–44 BC)

July the 18th in the year 387 BC was not a good day for Rome. On the left bank of the Tiber on that date Roman forces were disastrously defeated at the battle of Allia by hordes of fearsome barbarian invaders pouring southwards across the Alps from central Europe. The marauders advanced rapidly on Rome and found, to their astonishment, the gates open and unguarded. What remained of the Roman fighting force cowered on the Capitol. There followed widespread massacre and pillage and most of Rome was reduced to a smouldering ruin. After a lengthy siege of the Capitol the invaders were finally bought off and Rome, though humiliated, survived to rise again.

Who were the barbarians that devastated Rome in the early fourth century BC? The Roman historian Livy, who described the events in graphic detail, referred to these people as Gauls and, more specifically, as members of a Gaulish tribe known as the Senones, led by a certain Brennus. It is common today to refer to the Senones, and to the Gauls in general, as Celts.

The origins of the Celts can be traced back long before the migrations to Italy. From the melting pot of the central European Bronze Age, a people emerged in the later eighth century BC whose distinctive material culture has been termed the Hallstatt culture, after an important cemetery discovered near the salt-mining town of Hallstatt in upper Austria. Salt was certainly an important element in the economy of these people, but more important was their development for the first time of an effective ironworking industry in Europe north of the Alps. It was the Hallstatt culture which played a significant role in the widespread dissemination of iron technology across Europe. Greek writers in the sixth century BC refer to the existence of *Keltoi* in central Europe. It may well be that there is overlap between the *Keltoi* and the archaeologically known Hallstatt culture.

The development of Hallstatt civilization across Europe can be clearly traced as, with time, its ruling dynasties became increasingly wealthy and powerful. From the sixth century BC onwards, and particularly in the early fifth, trading contacts with Greek colonies on the Mediterranean coast and with Greeks and Etruscans on the Adriatic greatly increased the prosperity of the Hallstatt rulers. These chieftains had a particular taste for wine, and they naturally

9

began to accumulate the appropriate utensils for its proper consumption. Their ostentatious burials, such as at Vix in eastern France and Hochdorf in southwest Germany, were filled with the exotic produce of the Mediterranean: great bronze cauldrons and mixing bowls, painted drinking goblets, flagons and strainers. Sometimes delicate Chinese silk found its way into these royal tombs and at Hochdorf the dead chieftain reclined on a wheeled settee of bronze, as he had doubtless done in life, aping the customs of refined Mediterranean society. In such burials a four-wheeled cart generally accompanied the deceased noble to the grave.

Around the middle of the fifth century BC Hallstatt society appears to have suffered a crisis, and rapid decline set in. There followed a phase of major population movements across Europe. Entire tribes appear to have criss-crossed the Continent seeking land and plunder. It was such migrations which brought the Celts to Italy, Greece, Asia Minor and deep into eastern Europe as far as the Carpathian Mountains. And it was such movements which brought Rome to its knees, led to the sack of Delphi, and generally shook the Classical world to its very foundations.

fig. 2   The people of this second phase of Celtic expansion are known by various names. Classical commentators generally refer to them as *Galli* (Gauls) or *Galatae* (Galatians), but Caesar interestingly suggests that they described themselves as Celts (see quotation above). Archaeologists, studying the physical remains, refer to their material culture as the La Tène culture. The name derives from a major, presumably votive, deposit of more than 2000 artifacts, which was discovered in 1846 on the western edge of Lake Neuchâtel in Switzerland. Weapons figured prominently in this find, and especially striking were the numerous highly ornate iron scabbards in which many of the swords were carried. The fine curvilinear art featured on the scabbards is one of the most distinctive and widely dispersed aspects of this La Tène culture.

With the appearance of these people we move from the shadows of prehistory towards the light of the written record. For while they themselves left no written accounts, the writings of Mediterranean authors give us an often vivid picture of the Celts, which amplifies considerably the evidence of archaeology. Thus they appear to be fearsome yet naïve, courageous yet foolhardy, vain, deeply religious and with a well-defined social hierarchy.

'Physically', we are told by Diodorus, 'the Gauls are terrifying in appearance, with deep-sounding and very harsh voices. The nobles shave their cheeks but let the moustache grow freely so that it covers the mouth. And so when they are eating, the moustache becomes entangled in the food, and when they are drinking the drink passes, as it were, through a sort of strainer.' Another account states that 'nearly all the Gauls are of lofty stature, fair, and of ruddy complexion, terrible from the sternness of their eyes, very quarrelsome, and of great pride and insolence.'

Certainly their belligerent character is repeatedly emphasized by the Classical authors. Cato the Elder, for example, wrote that in Gaul there were only two main passions: 'war and loquacity'. And, according to Strabo, 'The

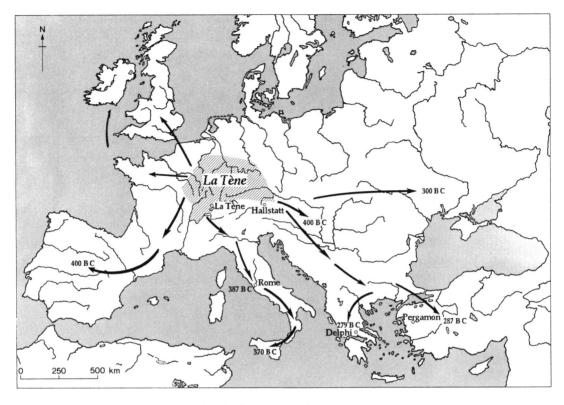

2 *Map to show the spread of La Tène cultural influences across Europe.*

whole race is madly fond of war, high-spirited and quick to battle . . .' They were recklessly brave and impetuous, often rushing naked into combat. Personal honour and individual valour were of paramount importance and in fighting there was considerable emphasis on man-to-man confrontations. Thus, in the words of Diodorus, we are told that:

> When the armies are drawn up in battle array they are wont to advance before the battle-line and to challenge the bravest of their opponents to single combat, at the same time brandishing before them their arms so as to terrify their foes. And when someone accepts their challenge to battle, they loudly proclaim their own valorous quality, at the same time abusing and making little of their opponent and generally attempting to rob him beforehand of his fighting spirit.

Celtic women, according to Ammianus Marcellinus, were every bit as ferocious as their menfolk.

The Celts were known to be cruel victors, decapitating their enemies and suspending the heads from the necks of horses, or displaying them in sacred places; some may even have retained the heads at home, as trophies. They were also reputed to be skilled horsemen, and the Classical writers speak admiringly of their expert use of the chariot. But the aggressive qualities of the Celts were not confined to the battlefield. Athenaeus tells us that at meals 'when the hindquarters were served, the bravest hero took the thigh-piece, and if another man claimed it, they stood up and fought in single combat to the death.' In the later Irish epic tales we encounter a similar scene.

The importance of religion in every aspect of daily life is clearly evident from the Classical sources, and the Druids were particularly powerful (see below p. 179). They were consulted on all important issues and young men flocked to them for training. 'It is said' according to Caesar 'that they memorize immense amounts of poetry, and so some of them continue their studies for twenty years. They consider it improper to commit their studies to writing . . .'

The Celts settled acoss a vast area of Europe, and while the different groups never formed one, politically unified society, they did share many aspects of material culture, language and religion. It is just this overlap between the language or ethnicity of these peoples and La Tène material remains that justifies the use of the term 'Celtic' as a convenient cultural label.

One of the most striking witnesses to the spread of La Tène cultural traditions across Europe is to be found in the characteristic burials, often in cemeteries, which are widely dispersed across the Continent. The rich and powerful were interred with their chariots, now light two-wheeled vehicles as opposed to the more cumbersome four-wheeled wagons of the Hallstatt period. Such burials are concentrated for instance in the Marne region of France, in the Ardennes area of Belgium and in southwest Germany along the valley of the Moselle River. A few have been found further east. Such exceptional burials are often lavishly bedecked with weapons, ornaments and domestic items as well as Mediterranean imports which continue the traditions of the late Hallstatt phase. The vast majority of the burials, however, are of the more humble warriors and their womenfolk, laid out individually in inhumation cemeteries. These graves are often surrounded by a square-ditched enclosure but generally lack a covering mound. The deceased was usually accompanied *fig. 3* by a sword and spears and covered by a large oval shield. Females were laid to rest with their personal possessions and their finery. The many fine artifacts of iron, bronze and gold contained in these burials afford us detailed insights into the technical and artistic sophistication of the Celts. In the working of metals in particular, the Celts were at least the equals of any contemporary peoples. In the creation of a new abstract, curvilinear art form, however, they left a legacy which was to endure (see p. 162).

The Celts in Europe lived in open settlements and fortified hilltop sites. The latter – better documented because of the often imposing defences which survive to the present day – changed with time from defended villages to full-scale towns. In the last century BC, Caesar referred to such settlements in Gaul as *oppida* (towns), clearly acknowledging their urban status. These well-planned, highly fortified settlements could accommodate thousands of people, often in streets of rectangular houses, with centres of commerce, administration and religion. They were truly tribal capitals, the first towns of transalpine Europe. In keeping with the increasing importance of trade and commerce among the Celts, coinage now came into widespread use and the major tribes minted their own currency.

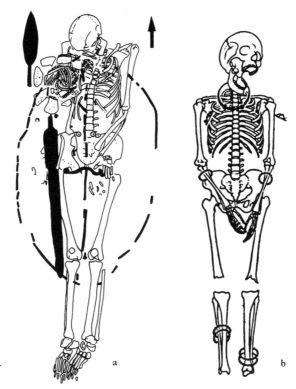

3 Typical burials from early La Tène inhumation cemeteries in Europe. (a) Warrior burial at Sobocisko in Poland; (b) female burial, Andelfingen, Switzerland.

a   b

The Roman conquest of Europe brought change. Caesar's Gallic wars in the fifties BC were the beginning of the end for the Gauls. By the birth of Christ the Celts were defeated, the oppida were forcibly depopulated and *pax romana* extended to the English Channel. Within just over half a century most of Britain had been taken. Apart from highland Scotland it was Ireland alone which remained free of Roman domination. It was in Ireland, especially, that the old ways continued.

A land of gods and heroes

Ireland retained its largely undiluted Celtic ethos well into the medieval period. A long oral tradition stretching back, at least in part, to the pre-Christian Iron Age was committed to writing in the early Christian monasteries. This material, in contrast to the accounts of the Classical authors, does not purport to document historical people or events, or at least if it does we have no way of knowing that this was so. Instead the Irish sources present us with an immense body of material combining fact and fantasy, myth and legend, ancient lore, Classical interpolation, pan-Christian fables and medieval folk tradition. As a source of information on the Irish Iron Age it provides us with a challenge of exceptional complexity.

The oldest and most extensive of the early Irish sources is the so-called

Ulster Cycle. This consists of about eighty separate tales. The longest is the *Táin Bó Cuailnge* (The Cattle Raid of Cooley). The other stories are either foretales (*remscéla*) which set the scene for the main events or explain elements of the principal drama, or side-tales loosely connected with the principal characters. In all, the tales of the Ulster Cycle are preserved, in varying degrees of completeness, in some ten manuscripts.

The oldest surviving version of the *Táin*, the so-called Recension I, is preserved in two principal manuscript compilations, neither of which preserves a complete text of the story. The first, known as the *Lebor na hUidre* (The Book of the Dun Cow), was compiled towards the end of the eleventh century in the monastery of Clonmacnoise and is the earliest extant Irish manuscript devoted to Irish vernacular literature. It is now housed in the Royal Irish Academy in Dublin. The second is the Yellow Book of Lecan, a late fourteenth-century manuscript compilation. A fuller version of the *Táin* (Recension II) was written in the second half of the twelfth century in the volume known as the Book of Leinster, which is kept in Trinity College. It was originally called *Lebor na Nuachongbála* (The Book of Nuachongbáil) after a place in Co. Laois in Leinster now known as Oughavall and which was, in early times, the site of a monastic establishment. This second redaction of the *Táin* aims to provide a unified, coherent telling of the tale, by eliminating the duplications, variants and interpolations which are a feature of Recension I and by adopting throughout a relatively consistent, if somewhat inflated, narrative style.

Recension I of the *Táin* is believed to be a conflation of two lost ninth-century versions, and the tale was undoubtedly known as early as the first half of the eighth century. Some scholars feel that it was already recorded in the seventh century. The *Táin* displays an obviously Ulster bias and this has led modern commentators to think of an Ulster source for the long-lost original recension, possibly the monastery of Bangor in Co. Down. Indeed, it has been suggested that the production of the tale had political undertones, extolling Ulster's former greatness at a time when the province had been reduced to little more than a territorial rump east of the River Bann. In fact, an eleventh-century writer stated disparagingly that 'these stories did not happen at all as they were told, but it was to ingratiate themselves with the rude Ulster race that the smooth-tongued poets invented the lying fables.'

The Ulster Cycle depicts a heroic society of kings and queens, of warrior champions and Druids. The masses are scarcely mentioned. The tales are primarily concerned with the Ulaidh, a people who ruled an Ulster then comprising the entire northern half of Ireland from Donegal in the west to Antrim, Down and Louth in the east. Their king, Conchobhar mac Nessa, resided at the royal centre at Emain Macha (Navan Fort) in modern Co. Armagh. Under the king the principal heroes were Conall Cernach, Fergus mac Roich and, of course, the redoubtable Cú Chulainn. Other prominent characters were the Druid Cathbhadh, the wise Sencha mac Ailella and the trouble-making Bricriu.

The principal action revolves around a great conflict between the Ulstermen on the one hand and the Connachtmen – under their warrior queen Medbh and supported by the rest of Ireland – on the other. The pretext for the invasion of Ulster by the armies of Medbh was the desire to capture a special bull, the *Donn Cuailnge* (the Brown Bull of Cooley), to match the white-horned bull (*Findbennach*) in the possession of Medb's husband, Ailill. In their time of crisis the Ulstermen are laid low by a debilitating sickness because of an ancient curse, and only Cú Chulainn, who is uniquely immune to the malady, stands between the enemy and Ulster. In a series of single combats Cú Chulainn holds the Connacht army at bay until in a great, tragic climax he meets his foster-brother, Ferdia. After an epic encounter Ferdia is killed, but Cú Chulainn is himself mortally wounded. By now, however, the men of Ulster have recovered and they rise to defeat the Connachtmen. The *Donn Cuailnge* had, in the meantime, been captured by Medb and brought to Connacht. The tale ends in a mighty conflict between the two bulls. The Connacht bull is killed but the Bull of Cooley dies from its exertions.

The Ulster Cycle is an epic saga of considerable literary quality. Its primary purpose was to entertain, and there can be little doubt that it began in oral form. Thus arose the exaggeration and bombast, the grand descriptions, the often outrageous hyperbole and the larger-than-life characters. It is not difficult to envisage an enrapt audience, protected from the damp and gloom of a winter's evening by a blazing log fire, listening enthralled as the great tale unfolded. It would have been delivered in suitably theatrical style, shouted or whispered as the mood changed and filled with dramatic pauses to heighten tension.

The tales of the Ulster Cycle thus give us interesting insights into the early Irish mind, not merely of the story-teller but also of the listeners. But the tales also provide us with clear evidence of the wide erudition of the medieval redactors. For, in its surviving form, the *Táin* is a consciously conceived prose narrative based in part on an oral tradition but deriving in large measure from the contemporary literate culture of early Ireland. The literary experience of the compilers included a direct knowledge of Latin literature and of Greek epic, a knowledge of the Scriptures, of apocryphal works and of the fathers of the Church. Direct imitation and borrowing from Homer may also be recognized and, indeed, the early redactors may have been attempting to create their own native version of a Homeric epic. It has even been suggested that in the original version Cú Chulainn's part was incidental but that this was expanded enormously in the twelfth century to transform him into an Irish Achilles. The original *leitmotif* of the story may, in fact, have lain in the rivalry between two divine bulls, perhaps reflecting an underlying memory of an ancient bull cult. However, as the philologist David Greene wrote, 'once it had been established as the national epic, it became the common property of saga-writers who remoulded it to the taste of their period'.[1]

While much of the extant saga material, therefore, derives from sources which are neither Celtic nor Irish, there seems to be an underlying, pre-Christian, preliterate, oral Celtic tradition, and it is this which is of most immediate concern for a study of the Irish Iron Age.[2] We do not know exactly when the *Táin* first took shape, although we have several clues. One is that it contains a pre-Christian base, suggesting a date before the fifth century. Similarly, the political division of Ireland which pervades the tales (with a large, dominant Ulster and no apparent institution of a High Kingship) points to a date before the dismembering of Ulster and the establishment of the kingdom of Midhe in the middle of the fifth century AD. The Ulster Cycle seems, therefore, to have been in existence by about AD 400. How long before this is uncertain. Another point to bear in mind is that the *Táin* need not necessarily have been simply a mirror of the contemporary way of life of the people – it may have been an invocation of an idealized past.

Despite these uncertainties, the Ulster Cycle is of great importance in studies of philology and of early Irish poetry and prose, and it obviously sheds considerable light on aspects of pagan Celtic religious practices and beliefs. For the archaeologist, however, the key question to be addressed is the extent to which it is relevant to the study of the material remains. Is it, in fact, legitimate to regard the tales as a 'window on the Iron Age' as philologist K.H. Jackson suggested? More specifically, are they a 'window' on the Irish Iron Age and, conversely, is it possible to detect an archaeological horizon in the country which we can equate with the culture of the *Táin*?

As will emerge in the following chapters, the archaeological material associated most closely (but not, of course, exclusively) with the Irish Iron Age displays the same La Tène characteristics as those artifacts associated with the Celts of Poseidonius and Caesar on the European mainland. In addition, La Tène material in Ireland has significant concentrations in Ulster and Connacht, the very areas which figure prominently in the events of the *Táin*. Thus, there has been a not unreasonable tendency to regard the Irish La Tène horizon as the physical evidence of the society of the Ulster Epic Cycle.

However, if we examine the La Tène objects found in Ireland and set them against the descriptions in the tales we find there is no detailed correspondence. In fact a systematic search through the sagas suggests that in no single instance can it be assumed that material descriptions reflect the reality of Irish Iron Age archaeology. Nowhere can we be certain that such descriptions do not derive from the contemporary world of early medieval Ireland. For instance, the archaeologist J.P. Mallory's detailed study of the sword as mentioned in the *Táin* has shown that there are scarcely any areas of similarity between the short-bladed weapons which survive from the Iron Age in Ireland and the great and ornate slashing swords so frequently referred to in the literature.[3] He concluded that the sword as described in the *Táin* is likely to have been an implement of Viking rather than of Iron Age type.

The early tales, however, paint a vivid and lifelike picture. While we must quibble with the specific, there can be no doubt that the overall ethos is pagan, and the gods and heroes who stride so dramatically across the pages of the Ulster Cycle form a striking backdrop to Iron Age archaeology. The written sources add colour to our reconstruction of Iron Age Ireland but, inevitably, we must turn to archaeology to determine the details.

CHAPTER 2

From Bronzesmith to Blacksmith

To bronze Jove changed Earth's golden time;
With bronze, then iron, stamped the age.
                                    HORACE (65–8 BC)

The Late Bronze Age background

Ireland at the beginning of the last pre-Christian millennium was on the threshold of her first Golden Age. Though situated on the periphery of Europe, the country was in the mainstream of European cultural developments. Long-standing links with Britain were maintained and there was direct contact with France and north Germany. Connections with Iberia and with the Mediterranean world may also have existed at this time. Above all, however, it was the Baltic, whence came the precious amber, which was increasingly important as a source of technical inspiration for the Irish metalworkers. Ireland, to judge by the wealth of her archaeological remains, reached a peak of prosperity between the eighth and sixth centuries BC. As well as absorbing much from abroad, the country was also an exporter of goods and perhaps also of expertise. At Jarlshof in the Shetland Islands, for example, sunflower pins of Irish type were being produced for the local community, possibly by an Irish bronzesmith. Clearly, therefore, Ireland was far from being a cultural backwater. Her bronzesmiths and goldworkers were at least the equals of any in contemporary Europe.

The country in the early centuries of the last millennium BC was covered extensively by forests and vast tracts of soggy marshland. Sporadic forest removal had been going on since Neolithic times and there were by now many clearings, but much of the older agricultural land, abandoned after the onset of soil exhaustion, must have been recolonized by secondary woodland. The forests abounded in game, notably the red deer and the wild pig which were, it seems, occasionally hunted to supplement the diet of the people and to provide skins, antlers, tusks and other useful commodities. Indeed, a wooden deer-trap, which may date as early as the Late Bronze Age, has been found at Drumacaladerry, Co. Donegal. Wolves, no doubt a menace to the flocks in winter, stalked the forests. The wild cat (*Felis silvestris*) was also present, and the brown bear (*Ursus arctos*) – recorded from late Neolithic/Early Bronze Age levels at Lough Gur, Co. Limerick – may well have survived in remote areas of the country into the Late Bronze Age. Certainly in Scotland the bear persisted into the early part of the last millennium BC. Smaller animals such as the badger, otter and hare have been recorded from native Late Bronze Age sites,

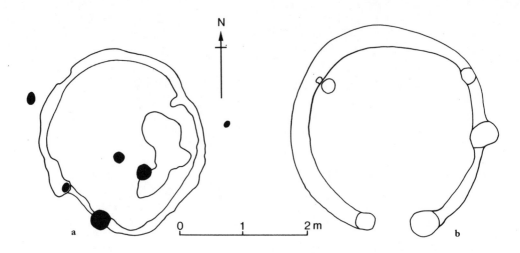

N

0   1   2 m

a   b

*4 The Late Bronze Age hut sites of Rathgall, Co. Wicklow (a) and Curraghatoor, Co.
Tipperary (b).*

and these too were most likely hunted for their hides. There was a wide range of
bird-life in Late Bronze Age Ireland, including species such as the crane and
the sea eagle, now extinct there. The rivers must have been teeming with fish.
We have little information concerning fish in the diet of the people, however,
for even under the most favourable conditions fish remains are difficult to
detect in excavations. At Island MacHugh, Co. Tyrone freshwater mussels
were eaten by the occupants of a lakeside settlement.

The country was probably tolerably well settled at this time and population
was doubtless on the increase. A network of routeways by now existed, hacked
through the forests and extending along river valleys and natural ridges. To
traverse the endless bogs, trackways of varying type (sometimes of quite
considerable sophistication) were laid down. These were of branches, hewn oak
planll. 2 planks or carefully woven brushwood rods cut from coppiced hazel stands. The
tracks were sometimes several kilometres in length and provided local links in a
chain of communications which were spreading tentacle-like across the
country. The high degree of technical and typological homogeneity displayed
by the surviving artifacts over wide areas of Ireland indicates the relative ease
with which ideas and commodities could move across the country.

The available evidence suggests that the mass of the population in Late
Bronze Age Ireland lived in small, scattered homesteads, probably for the most
part in single family groups. The majority are likely to have been isolated,
undefended sites and are thus difficult to detect archaeologically. Such a
settlement existed on the southern slopes outside the hillfort at Rathgall, Co.
pl. 4   Wicklow; and at Curraghatoor, Co. Tipperary there was a small undefended
fig. 4 village with up to twelve structures.

More concern for personal safety was displayed by the people who built the
small lakeside settlements known as crannógs. Several examples have been

excavated, including Knocknalappa, Co. Clare, Ballinderry No. 2, Co. Offaly, Rathtinaun, Co. Sligo and Moynagh, Co. Meath. In such structures considerable effort was involved in piling up stones, timber and brushwood on the marshy lake shores to provide dry and level platforms upon which to construct the dwellings. Stoutly woven wickerwork fences, in addition to the wet and muddy surroundings, gave a measure of security to the occupants of these sites. At Clonfinlough, Co. Offaly, a palisade of ash posts backing on to a tiny lake provided an oval enclosure some 55m in greatest internal diameter. *fig. 5* Within this there were at least three circular huts of wickerwork walling, each with a central hearth and floors of planks and stone slabs. Uniquely among the Irish Late Bronze Age settlements, timbers from this important site have yielded dendrochronological dates of 908 BC and 886 BC.

5 *Plan of the palisaded Late Bronze Age bog settlement at Clonfinlough, Co. Offaly. The timber remains of three huts have been exposed in the excavated areas.*

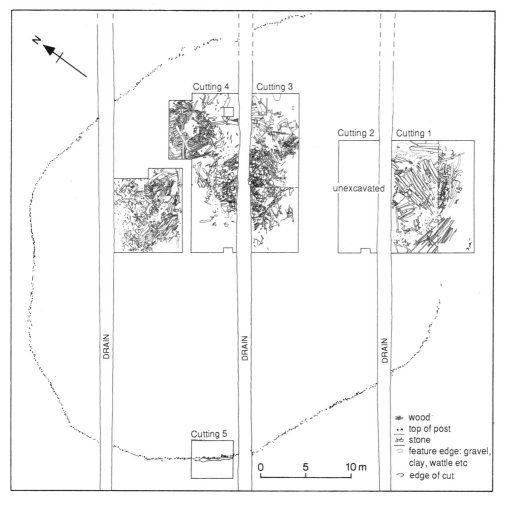

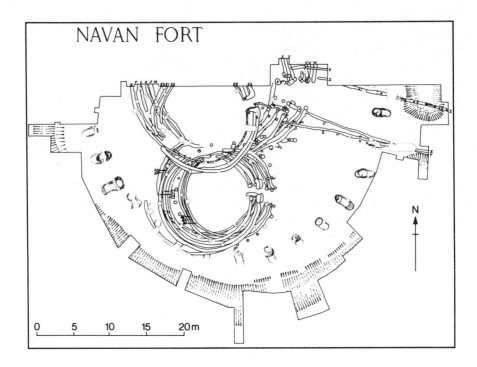

NAVAN FORT

N

0   5   10   15   20m

6,7 *The Late Bronze Age settlement at Navan Fort, Co. Armagh. (Above) The overlapping rings each represent a single, free-standing timber hut, which was frequently replaced over the centuries. (Below) Reconstruction of one of the Late Bronze Age occupation phases at the site.*

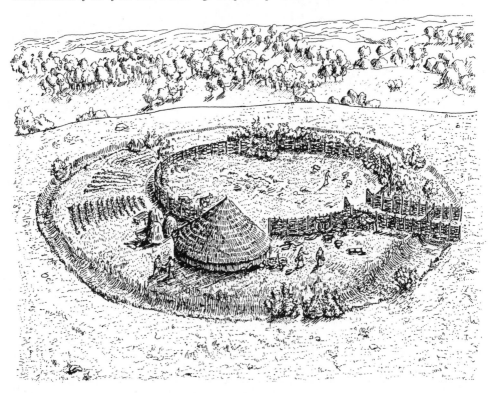

On dry land, too, small enclosed settlement sites existed. At Aughinish in
Co. Limerick, for example, two circular stone enclosures of Late Bronze Age
date have been found, each with a single central hut. Hilltops were also
occupied at this time, as they had been earlier, but now there are indications
that the hills were being defended. This was not, however, the case on
Cathedral Hill, Downpatrick, Co. Down, where the Late Bronze Age
occupation, contrary to what was once believed, seems to have been
undefended. At Navan Fort, Co. Armagh, however, a small, stockaded
enclosure, circular in plan, protected a settlement which at various times in its
long history comprised either one or two round, timber-built houses.   *figs. 6, 7*

True hillforts may well have appeared at this time (see p. 58). At Rathgall in
Co. Wicklow, for example, an extensive settlement of Late Bronze Age date has
been discovered on the hilltop, which is in all probability contemporary with
the massive bank-and-ditch defences surrounding it. At Haughey's Fort in Co.   *pl. 5*
Armagh, a large hilltop enclosure of Late Bronze Age date has also recently
been investigated. Excavation will undoubtedly reveal other hillforts of Bronze
Age times but evidence is not yet sufficient to determine if such extensive
hilltop enclosures indicate the existence of sizeable population centres.

Evidence for both cultivation and animal husbandry during the Late Bronze
Age has been found. No ploughs of this period are known from Ireland but it is
reasonable to assume that the wooden ard was in use, probably drawn by a pair
of oxen. The corn was harvested by means of a short-bladed, socketed sickle
and later ground to flour on a saddle quern. It may have been eaten as a
porridge-like substance but at Rathgall, Co. Wicklow, charred remains of what
could have been bread have been found.

All the common domesticated animals have been recognized from Irish Late
Bronze Age settlements and the indications are that cattle were dominant. At
Haughey's Fort, Co. Armagh, dogs of considerable size were present; these
animals were probably slaughtered for their meat by the inhabitants. The
horse, already noted from levels dating to the early second millennium BC at
Newgrange, Co. Meath, is clearly attested to in the country during the Late
Bronze Age: horse bones have been found at several settlement sites. In
addition, a textile fragment from Cromaghs, Co. Antrim had horse-hair tassels
and several settlements have produced horse-trappings of various kinds.
Despite the discovery of probable cheek-pieces of bone from two occupation
sites, however, we cannot be certain that the horse was ridden. It might have
been used in traction only, for wheeled vehicles were already in existence by
this time. Block-wheels from Doogarymore, Co. Roscommon and Timahoe,
Co. Kildare – which date to the Bronze Age/Iron Age transitional phase – are
doubtless typical of the wheels in general use during the Later Bronze Age (see
p. 104). Vehicles with such heavy wheels could never have travelled along the
narrow, brushwood trackways in the bogs and must have been intended only
for dryland travel. Furthermore, they must have been unsuitable for travelling
long distances, so they were probably heavy-duty vehicles made to serve the
needs of the local farming communities. Extended journeys were probably

done mainly on foot, although dugout canoes were used to cross rivers and lakes and it is not unreasonable to assume that skin-covered boats of coracle type were also widespread. The possibility that vessels of some substance existed in Ireland during the Late Bronze Age is suggested by the discovery at the bog settlement of Clonfinlough, Co. Offaly of two large, carefully carved oars, each more than 2m long.

Clues to the physical character of the people in Late Bronze Age Ireland remain elusive: no skeletons from this period have been discovered, because the few known burials are cremations. Razors *have* been found, however, indicating that shaving was practised by some members of the community. There is only one surviving fragment of Late Bronze Age textile from Ireland. This comes from Cromaghs, Co. Antrim, and had been used to wrap a hoard of bronze objects. It may have been a piece of a cloak. Thus the Late Bronze Age folk evidently knew how to weave; archaeologists assume they used horizontal rather than vertical looms since no loom-weights have been found in Ireland. Leather shoes were worn: a single example has come from a Late Bronze Age crannóg at Rathtinaun, Co. Sligo.

At home, the normal containers used by the Bronze Age people were crude, bucket-shaped vessels of clay, seemingly made with little regard to aesthetic

pl. 6 considerations. Wooden containers assembled from staves or carved from a single block were also known, and buckets and cauldrons of sheet-bronze existed, fabricated with a skill which sharply contrasts with that of the other containers. These may not, however, have been for normal domestic use as none has shown evidence of burning or charring.

A feature of the latest Irish Bronze Age is the extraordinary increase in the number and variety of metal artifact- types within the country. In the surviving archaeological record it is the achievements of the bronzesmith and the goldworker which are pre-eminent. Many new tools appear, including thousands of looped and socketed axeheads, chisels, gouges, hammers, knives, sickles, and many more. New, too, are the cast-bronze horns or trumpets which have been shown by recent technical examination to represent a quite exceptional level of bronzeworking skill. The bronzesmiths were equally adept at sheet-metalworking and casting. Stone moulds had become virtually obsolete by this time, and clay moulds were now in general use. A whole range of new tools associated with fine metalworking was developed and new techniques were learned, such as annealing, soldering and the manufacture of lead-alloy bronze.

Novel forms of personal ornament also appeared during this period, many showing direct inspiration from Nordic Europe. Most common were disc-headed pins of varying type, especially the so-called sunflower pins: these represented an essentially Irish development. Beads of presumed Baltic amber were in widespread use and were probably highly prized; glass beads made their appearance in the country at this time too. Other substances such as jet or lignite were also used occasionally, for beads, bracelets or decorative mounts.

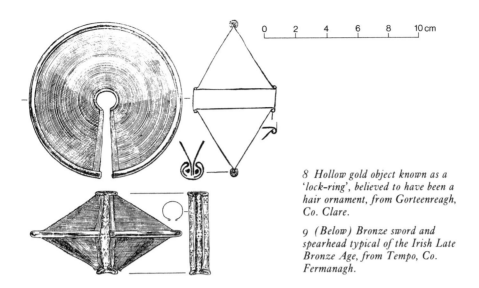

8 Hollow gold object known as a 'lock-ring', believed to have been a hair ornament, from Gorteenreagh, Co. Clare.

9 (Below) Bronze sword and spearhead typical of the Irish Late Bronze Age, from Tempo, Co. Fermanagh.

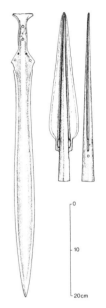

But it is of gold that the most spectacular items of personal adornment were made. During the Late Bronze Age there was a dramatic increase in the use of this metal in Ireland. Pennanular, trumpet-ended objects, variously described as dress-fasteners or bracelets, are numerous (see pl. 3) and there are other bracelet forms, neck ornaments (including the magnificent gorgets), pendants, pins, 'sleeve fasteners' and ornaments which might have adorned the hair. Occasionally, gold was used for other purposes such as for the manufacture of decorative discs, boxes and large, hollow balls. The outstanding technical skill of the Irish goldsmiths is often breathtaking. This is particularly so in the case of the so-called 'lock-rings' – hollow, biconical objects which appear at first glance to be made of ribbed sheet gold (see *fig. 8*). Under magnification, however, it becomes apparent that the 'sheet' is created by soldering together hundreds of tiny gold wires. These objects display a virtuosity which is scarcely surpassed in ancient goldworking anywhere.

Some metalsmiths seem to have worked at specialist goldworking centres. One such was in the lower Shannon area where there is a notable concentration of gold objects, including all the known gorgets. Undoubtedly there were also other centres. But the source of the gold is uncertain. It appears not to have come from Wicklow, once regarded as the only source of native gold, and, indeed, there is a noticeable lack of gold artifacts in the very areas where Wicklow gold was to be found. We must assume that other sources of natural gold were exploited in the country during the Late Bronze Age.

The archaeological evidence thus points to a considerable degree of material prosperity in the country. This doubtless had some bearing on the ominous escalation of violence, which is indicated by the dramatic expansion in the number of lethal, death-dealing weapons. Now, increasingly it seems, power came from the point of a sword. Well over 600 such weapons have been found, *fig. 9* and there are spears, too, in abundance. Shields also appear. These are always round, decorated (and strengthened) by ribs and bosses, and are made of wood,

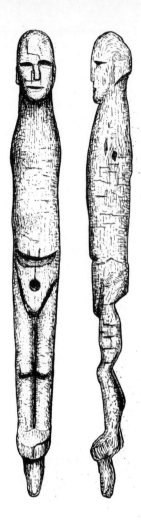

10 *Carved human figure of yew wood from Ralaghan, Co. Cavan. Radiocarbon evidence now indicates a date for this in the Late Bronze Age.*

0   10   20   30 cm

pl. 7   leather and bronze. The last, however, of thin sheet metal, are non-functional, ceremonial objects. It is to the wood and the leather that the Late Bronze Age fighters entrusted their lives in battle.

It seems reasonable to assume that some, at least, of the fine gold objects were made for ritual or ceremonial purposes. The same might be suggested of the cauldrons or even the horns, but votive or ritual intent is virtually impossible to prove archaeologically. There can be little doubt, however, about the votive nature of the 113.5-cm high wooden figure from Ralaghan, Co. Cavan
fig. 10   (radiocarbon-dated to around the beginning of the last millennium BC). A similar function was probably served by a small artificial pond in Tray townland, Co. Armagh, which is known as the 'King's Stables'. Some 800 m from Navan Fort, the site was constructed in the early centuries of the last millennium BC and contained a high proportion of dog bones, red deer antlers and a cut human skull, along with clay mould fragments of Late Bronze Age type. The great increase in the number of hoards of metal objects at this time – over 150 examples are now known – has also been taken as evidence of ritual deposition. Not every hoard may signify a ritual deposit, but the dramatic spread of the custom across western Europe, at a time of political uncertainty and seeming climatic deterioration, may not be entirely coincidental. Among

the most extraordinary of the Irish hoards are the so-called Great Clare Hoard from Mooghaun North, which contained in excess of 146 gold items, and the Dowris, Co. Offaly hoard, which consisted of a minimum of 218 bronze objects including weapons, tools, buckets, cauldrons, 'crotals' and some 26 trumpets.   pl. 1

The most obvious evidence of ritual practices, the disposal of the dead, is poorly represented in the archaeological record of the Irish Late Bronze Age. As far as we know, cremation was the exclusive rite and the remains were simply interred in pits, sometimes contained within upright pots of the type used in domestic contexts. At Rathgall a circular ditch enclosed three cremation deposits, and at Ballybeen, Dundonald, Co. Down a small circular   fig. 11
ditch enclosed a simple pit-cremation. A ringbarrow with central cremations excavated at Mullaghmore, Co. Down may also belong to the Late Bronze Age. There are a few other possible examples.

In summary, the archaeology of Late Bronze Age Ireland is dominated by metalwork which survives in very considerable quantities. It is clear that the inhabitants established a complex industrial organization to meet the increasing demand for products. They not only expanded the range of artifact types available, but developed new techniques and began to experiment with the manufacture of copper and gold alloy. Full-time, specialist craftsmen evidently existed. Some were, perhaps, itinerant but the technical sophistication of much of the material indicates that permanent workshops were in operation. Society was structured and hierarchical, and strong ruling dynasties must have emerged both to create the ordered and stable conditions in which

11 A Late Bronze Age ring-ditch with central cremation deposit at Ballybeen, Co. Down.

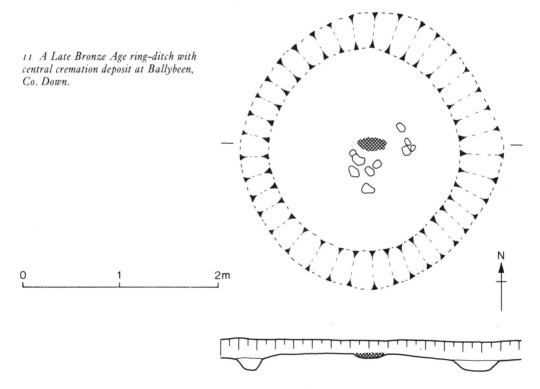

0   1   2m

N

metal-working could thrive, and to plan and co-ordinate the complex processes of the metal industry. We know nothing about the nature of native mineral exploitation, but this had to be organized and the products transported throughout the country. The distribution of imported raw materials, notably tin, also required elaborate organization involving middlemen, transport agencies, the use of ships and a network of foreign contacts. Clearly, those who controlled this organization would have enjoyed high status within the country. We can take it that competition for such control led to inter-tribal tensions, thus contributing to the development of weaponry and the trend towards defended settlements.

The Hallstatt Iron Age

As Ireland was approaching her Bronze Age climax, significant cultural innovations – which mark the conventional beginning of the European Iron Age – were spreading across Europe. The use of iron, even on occasion iron-smelting, was known sporadically in various parts of Europe throughout the second millennium BC, but it was only from the late eighth century BC that its exploitation on a significant scale began. It can hardly have been a sudden event, however. In the early stages of production, quenching to harden the metal was probably not yet known and carburization (the absorption by the iron of a small quantity of carbon to produce steel) would have been haphazard. Thus, the advantages over bronze of the poor-quality iron produced at this stage would not have been readily apparent. But the widespread availability of iron ores, combined perhaps with pressure on the resources needed to produce bronze, would have encouraged persistence with the new metal and the gradual perfection of manufacturing techniques. It could be, too, that the new metal was associated with prestige and power. It was the Hallstatt people who presided over the westward dissemination across Europe of iron technology. It is not clear how far this was brought about by population movements or by the gradual diffusion of new ideas through acculturation. No doubt both mechanisms played a part. But the spread appears to have been rapid for, within a few generations, iron manufacture had reached the islands on the Atlantic fringe of Europe.

By the seventh century BC, iron smelting was already being practised in different parts of Britain. Tap-slag from a settlement at All Cannings Cross in Wiltshire, England could date as early as this, as could a corroded lump of iron from Sompting in Sussex (found adhering to one of seventeen bronze axeheads discovered in a hoard with an early Hallstatt (i.e. Hallstatt C) phalera and a cauldron). Small finds of iron, all from seventh- or sixth-century BC native contexts, include rings from Staple Howe in Yorkshire and Balashanner in Angus, and a stud from Sheepen Hill, Colchester, Essex. Iron artifacts have also been found in recent excavations on a Late Bronze Age settlement at Potterne in Wiltshire. A group of iron looped and socketed axeheads (distributed from Midlothian in the north to Wiltshire in the south) may be

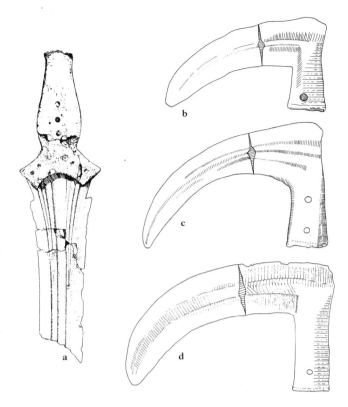

12 Items from the metalwork hoard of indigenous Late Bronze Age and intrusive Hallstatt C material, found at Llyn Fawr in Wales. The sword (a) is an imported Hallstatt weapon of iron. The sickles, however, are of local manufacture – two are of bronze (b,c) while the third (d) is an iron copy. 1/3.

early attempts by indigenous bronzesmiths turned blacksmiths to imitate in iron long-established Late Bronze Age types. An interesting pin from Fengate, Cambridgeshire, could also be interpreted as a transitional piece, since its pin of iron echoes the Hallstatt 'swan's neck' form, while the added bronze disc is more reminiscent of the insular disc-headed pins of the later Bronze Age.

Most instructive, however, in the context of early British iron-working, is the famous hoard of metal objects found on the bed of a former lake at Llyn Fawr, Glamorgan in Wales. This yielded tools and a cauldron all typical of the insular Late Bronze Age. Along with these was a variety of metal objects (some imported, others based on foreign prototypes), and several objects of iron – all unequivocally Hallstatt C in character. They include horse-trappings of different types, an iron spearhead and an iron sword of clearly Continental manufacture. But the most interesting item of all is a socketed sickle of iron. This is one of three such implements from the deposit and is similar in every way to the other two examples apart from the fact that the latter are of cast bronze. The find illustrates again how local craftsmen, though evidently masters of iron technology, nonetheless continued to produce the old forms. The association of such a clearly transitional piece with imported Hallstatt C objects is an obvious indication of European inspiration. Furthermore, this influence seems to have been at work by the seventh century BC.

fig. 12

While the general impression is of a gradual and peaceful acquisition of iron-smelting techniques by the Late Bronze Age inhabitants of Britain, it has been

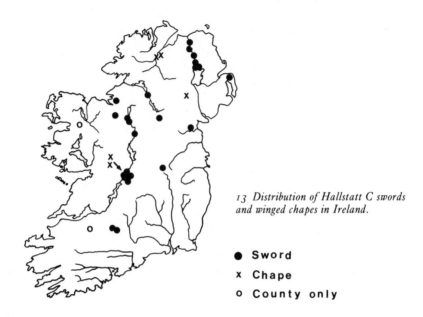

13 Distribution of Hallstatt C swords and winged chapes in Ireland.

● **S w o r d**

x **C h a p e**

o **C o u n t y   o n l y**

suggested that the innovations might have been brought by groups of Hallstatt invaders entering the country in the seventh century BC. The Hallstatt artifacts from Llyn Fawr are undoubtedly the trappings of a mounted aristocracy and one scholar has wondered if they were transported to south Wales as loot from a Hallstatt settlement which existed somewhere in the area of the Severn estuary.[4] The presence of immigrant Hallstatt C groups in Britain has also been suggested on the basis of a scatter of bronze swords and chapes which are concentrated mainly in eastern and southeastern Britain. All are stray finds and the majority are from riverine or coastal contexts. These objects are clearly derived from Hallstatt C forms on the Continent but, with a few exceptions, they are of demonstrably insular manufacture. Their significance continues to be debated. Undoubtedly there must have been a few visitors from the European mainland, but – lacking contemporary burials and related settlements – it is difficult to find any unequivocal evidence of immigration on a significant scale. Other Hallstatt C artifacts from Britain, such as razors, pins, brooches and horse-trappings, are either stray finds or from recognizably native contexts, thus lending little support to the invasion hypothesis. Moreover, recent work has clearly shown that the majority of these objects are copies of foreign models rather than actual imports.

Locally made bronze swords of Hallstatt derivation were also appearing in Ireland in the seventh century BC and it may well be that iron smelting was already beginning there at this time. But this period in Ireland's prehistory is particularly problematical for the quantity of relevant material is small and relevant objects are rarely found in associated groups. Hallstatt bronze swords from Ireland now number almost fifty and there are eleven contemporary chapes. As in Britain, these are found mainly in rivers or a short distance from the coast. Particular concentrations occur in the Shannon and the Bann Rivers.

fig. 13

Few such swords have been found in eastern and southern areas of the country. The only find from an archaeological context is a chape fragment from a native Late Bronze Age horizon at Navan Fort, Co. Armagh.

These swords (classified by George Eogan as Class 5 swords) reach a *fig. 14* maximum length of 77 cm and are on average 15–20 cm longer than those of the developed Late Bronze Age group (Class 4). A characteristic feature is the possession of divided, 'fishtail' tang-ends. In several examples the edges of the blades are defined by grooves or ridges, and a number possess rivets with hollow heads and tiny central projections. The grips were fitted with plates of bone or horn and to judge by the wooden replica found in a bog at Cappagh, Co. *fig. 14* Kerry, flattened-oval pommels, probably again of bone or horn, existed. The swords are likely to have been carried in scabbards of wood or leather at the ends of which bronze chapes were fitted. The latter are hollow and of hammered sheet-bronze; they are of either 'boat-shaped' or 'winged' forms. *fig. 14* These Irish swords have the same ultimate Continental antecedents as the British weapons, and typological examination by the archaeologist J.D. Cowen has shown that they, too, are clearly of insular manufacture.[5] The Irish winged chapes are also quite distinct in detail from those on the Continent. Though sharing certain features with the swords and chapes of the mainland European groups, the Irish objects have more in common with examples from southern England. They cannot, however, be regarded as imports from Britain for there are important differences, particularly in blade form, which distinguish the two insular sword groups from each other.

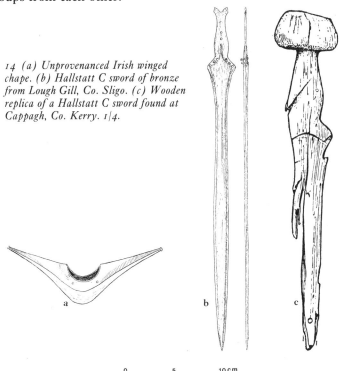

14 (a) Unprovenanced Irish winged chape. (b) Hallstatt C sword of bronze from Lough Gill, Co. Sligo. (c) Wooden replica of a Hallstatt C sword found at Cappagh, Co. Kerry. 1/4.

a   b   c

0   5   10 cm

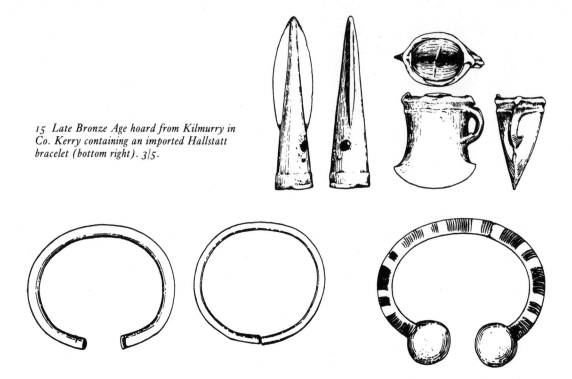

15 Late Bronze Age hoard from Kilmurry in Co. Kerry containing an imported Hallstatt bracelet (bottom right). 3/5.

As with the corresponding British evidence there are differing views as to how the presence of these Hallstatt swords in Ireland should be interpreted. Some scholars believe that the fact that Class 4 swords of the Late Bronze Age continued to be made after the appearance in Ireland of the Hallstatt weapons (the latter influencing in certain detail the later sword developments), along with the absence of Hallstatt swords from native Late Bronze Age hoards, indicates cultural distinction between those responsible for the manufacture of the two sword types. They suggest that local sword smiths would not have been making two quite distinct types of sword at the same time. Some furthermore explain the Irish distribution as indicating the presence of incoming warrior bands: the archaeologist Colin Burgess described this distribution as a 'classic raiding pattern'.[6] It has been pointed out, however, that the distribution of the Hallstatt swords overlaps with that of the native Class 4 swords.

Clearly the distribution pattern can be explained by other mechanisms unconnected with warrior intrusions. For example, as the archaeologist Timothy Champion pointed out, the absence of Hallstatt swords from hoards need mean only that the custom of depositing hoards had largely ceased by the time Hallstatt influences had arrived in the country.[7] Or perhaps the manufacture of two different sword types by contemporary native workshops implies that the swords were to serve different functions: the distinction might simply be that the Hallstatt weapons were for cavalry warfare whereas the Class 4 swords were used by infantry.

Apart from the swords and chapes there is little else from Ireland of Hallstatt C character. Important, however, is a penannular, knob-ended bronze bracelet of eastern French origin found, like the Navan Fort chape, with *fig. 15* native bronzes in a hoard at Kilmurry, Co. Kerry. A few pins of simple swan's-neck type which may be of Hallstatt derivation are known from Ireland. There are also some brooches of fibula or safety-pin type which are undoubtedly Hallstatt imports, but it is difficult to prove that these were ancient imports: they could derive from recent antiquarian activities. A 'fleshhook' from Dunaverney, Co. Antrim, elaborately adorned with separately cast swan and raven figures, is undoubtedly an ancient import, probably from central Europe, but its background may be Late Bronze Age rather than Hallstatt C. A few other stray items such as cup-headed pins, sunflower swan's-neck pins and certain bronze axe types reflect ultimate Hallstatt influence, but they are not necessarily evidence in every case of direct contact between Ireland and the Hallstatt world.

The Hallstatt finds from Ireland indicate changes in weaponry and, perhaps, in fashions of dress-fastener, but do they represent the beginning of an Irish Iron Age? There are hints that iron-working was already beginning at this time but the evidence for this is not extensive. Two looped and socketed axeheads of iron are known, one from Lough Mourne, the other from Toome, in Co. *fig. 16* Antrim. As has been noted above for the corresponding British axeheads, it is not unreasonable to see the two Irish examples as transitional pieces forged by indigenous smiths in the new metal but retaining the form of the bronze

16 (Left) Looped and socketed iron axehead from Lough Mourne, Co. Antrim. The type appears to reflect Bronze Age traditions of axe manufacture. 2/5.

17 (Right) Riveted sheet-iron cauldron found at Drumlane, Co. Cavan. 1/8.

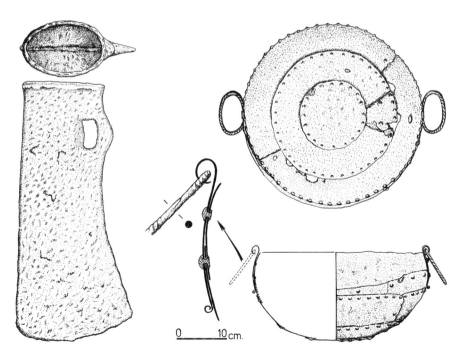

axeheads with which they had been familiar for generations. Another iron object from Ireland which is often taken to be a similarly transitional piece is a
fig. 17 globular cauldron of riveted sheets from Drumlane, Co. Cavan. Though differing in form from the cauldrons of the Late Bronze Age the method of manufacture is similar.

Apart from these stray finds which could point to an embryonic iron industry in northeasterly parts of the country, there are two excavated settlements which have produced iron objects of presumed early date. The first of these is at Aughinish, Co. Limerick, where one of two small, enclosed habitations produced a range of coarse, domestic pottery, saddle querns, a portion of a tanged chisel of Late Bronze Age type and corroded iron remains of what may be part of a horse-bit. Recent unpublished radiocarbon determinations for the level confirm a dating for it in the first half of the last millennium BC.

The second site to produce iron, and by far the most important in the context of the Irish Bronze Age/Iron Age transition, is that at Rathtinaun, Co. Sligo.

The crannóg at Rathtinaun, Co. Sligo

fig. 18 The site is crannóg 61, one of nearly 400 crannógs which were exposed around the shores of the small lake, Lough Gara, when drainage in 1952 had lowered its level by as much as 2.5 m. Due to the discovery of some Late Bronze Age artifacts close by, the crannóg was selected for excavation by Joseph Raftery of the National Museum and was totally excavated between 1952 and 1955. A complex stratigraphical sequence was uncovered which extended from the Late Bronze Age to the early historic period.

Before investigations commenced, the crannóg consisted of an oval mound of stones about 2.5 m high with maximum dimensions of 29 m by 36 m. Arcs of wooden piles projected from the lake mud in its immediate vicinity. Excavation showed that there was a slight rise in the lake bed with a central hollow which had been levelled by piling timbers and brushwood within it. On top of this the crannóg was built by heaping further layers of timber and brushwood so that a level occupation platform above the water and the mud was created. Most of the structural remains of occupation had been removed by water action and by the activities of later inhabitants. However, an arc of a circle 9 m in diameter, formed by the stumps of upright planks, was thought by the excavator to represent the remains of a hut. A roughly laid corduroy path of logs led from the entrance. Seven fire baskets were also found and these may indicate that other huts had once existed on the site.

The finds, though few in number at the lowest level, confirm that this was a simple domestic habitation dating to the so-called Dowris Phase of the later Bronze Age. Hundreds, perhaps thousands, of similar sites probably dotted the Irish landscape at this time. Sherds of the normal, coarse, hand-made pottery were found as well as a disc-headed pin, a pair of tweezers, several rings, a possible cauldron fragment – all bronze – and a small penannular gold ring of the type generally referred to as 'ring-money'. Sixteen clay mould fragments

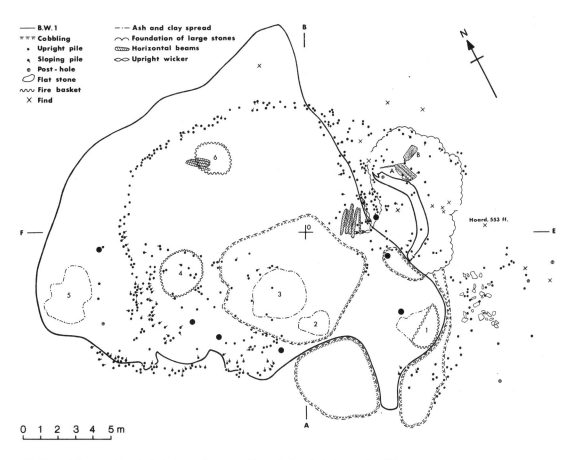

Legend:
- ——— B.W.1
- ⊼⊼⊼ Cobbling
- • Upright pile
- ◄ Sloping pile
- ⊕ Post - hole
- ⌒ Flat stone
- ⌇⌇ Fire basket
- ✕ Find
- —·— Ash and clay spread
- ⌢⌢ Foundation of large stones
- ⊏⊐ Horizontal beams
- ∞ Upright wicker

Hoard, 553 ff.

0 1 2 3 4 5 m

18 Plan of the transitional, Period 2 settlement at Crannóg 61, Rathtinaun, Co. Sligo. B.W. = brushwood.

indicate that bronze-working was carried on at the crannóg and portions of several wooden vessels were also recovered.

When the level of the lake rose the site was abandoned by its inhabitants. A layer of lake sand formed, sealing beneath it the primary levels of prehistoric occupation. But after an interval of no great duration the lake receded and the crannóg was reoccupied. This happened during the autumn as was shown by the presence of ripe hazelnuts. Layers of brushwood were again laid down, this time around an area of central cobbling. The brushwood rods, mostly hazel, had been laid down in bundles, then flattened out. As in the earlier period there were no clearly discernible house structures but there were six large hearths, formerly in fire baskets identical to those in Period 1. In fact, one of the hearths belonging to Period 1 had been reused in Period 2. A typical example was 2.5 m in diameter and had a basal hearthstone. The walls of the basket, made of hazel rods, were 50 cm high and of carefully woven basketry turned inwards at the top. The overhang thus created was supported by hazel uprights and the basket was protected from heat by a layer of yellow clay.

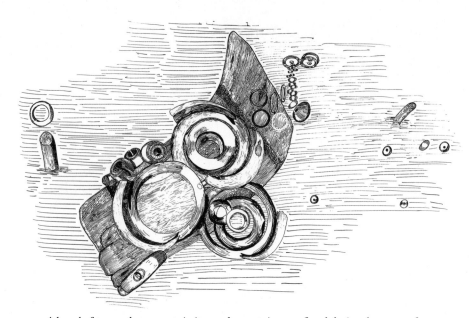

19 *A hoard of personal ornaments in its wooden container, as found during the course of excavations at Rathtinaun. c. 2/5.*

The stratigraphy showed clearly that there was no great chronological discrepancy between the two levels at Rathtinaun, and this is supported by the finds which point to close cultural identity between the two. Most of the artifacts from Period 2 are thus also typical of the Dowris Phase horizon of the Irish Late Bronze Age. The most important of these artifacts are two disc-headed pins, a pair of bronze tweezers similar to that from the lower layer, a bifid razor, a tanged chisel and a circular mount (phalera) of bronze. There were wooden vessel fragments, too, and potsherds of the same types as those from the lower level.

fig. 19   Of particular interest was the discovery of a hoard of objects contained in a wooden box apparently hidden in the floor of the Period 2 crannóg. Inside the box had been placed a necklace of amber beads, rings of bronze, of pure tin and three of lead with gold-foil cover. There was also a pair of tweezers, a bronze pin and six boars' tusks, intended perhaps for use as pendants or amulets. The hoard is clearly the personal fortune of one of the occupants of the Period 2 crannóg, doubtless a female, of some substance. We may wonder if it was rapidly rising lake water or a human threat which caused her hasty departure. At any rate she clearly intended to return, for the position of the box had been carefully marked with slender wooden pegs.

The culture represented at Rathtinaun Period 2 is thus wholly typical of the indigenous Late Bronze Age. It is therefore of great importance that several objects of iron were present at this level. These consisted of a short, straight-shanked pin with bent-back head, a fork-like implement with three curved prongs, a broken bladed implement with split socket (probably a sickle), a
fig. 20   shafthole axehead with the remains of an ash shaft and an amorphous fragment.

Here at Rathtinaun, therefore, we witness a stage in the peaceful transition from a 'Bronze Age' to an 'Iron Age' where the indigenous Bronze Age inhabitants were beginning to add a few iron objects to their repertoire of ornaments and subsistence equipment. Most significant is the axehead. It was forged of three sheets of iron and there can be little doubt that it was locally made. It certainly shows no small degree of technical competence even if the method of manufacture is somewhat awkward and clumsy (see p. 149). This implement is evidence that the art of iron-smelting had been mastered, and shows familiarity with the new form of shafthole as opposed to the older socketed type of axehead. Rathtinaun is thus the clearest evidence of an incipient iron industry as yet recognized in Ireland.

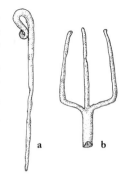

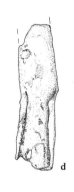

The dating of Rathtinaun, however, presents some problems. On conventional archaeological grounds the Late Bronze Age material should not date much later than the sixth century BC, and the iron pin from Period 2 (reminiscent as it is of Hallstatt C swan's-neck pins) is in broad agreement with such a dating. Thus the presence of iron at the site would overlap with the appearance of Hallstatt C material in the country and might be taken to reflect inspiration from Hallstatt Europe. But the matter is complicated by a series of radiocarbon determinations for the two earliest levels at Rathtinaun. Two calibrated dates for the Period 1 occupation gave a date range between 410 BC and AD 100. Four dates for Period 2, when calibrated, gave a range between 490 BC and AD 140. Even if the earliest extremes are taken, the dates are not wholly compatible with conventional archaeological dating. Thus, while the possibility of the late introduction of iron to an archaic Bronze Age society at Rathtinaun must be considered, it seems more likely that the precision of the 40-year-old radiocarbon dates should be questioned.

The end of the Bronze Age

The archaeological evidence is beginning to suggest, however dimly, that in the years leading up to the middle of the last millennium BC important changes were taking place in Ireland's cultural development. New influences from the Hallstatt world of iron were appearing and the new technology of iron-smelting was being introduced. It is not yet clear how these changes came about, but there is little evidence for any significant alteration in the population structure of the country. Nor is it clear when and in what circumstances the Bronze Age finally came to an end or if the arrival of Hallstatt elements in the country had anything to do with its disappearance. In seeking the end of the Bronze Age, however, our problems are, to a large extent, conceptual ones. The use of terms such as 'Bronze Age' and 'Iron Age' is a reflection more of the methodology of modern archaeology than of the reality of prehistoric events. Such rigid categorization into discrete 'ages' based on a single technological criterion tacitly implies that change from a non-ferrous to a ferrous technology is an inevitable indication of wider cultural change. That this need not be so is shown by the evidence of Rathtinaun. The replacement by iron of bronze was a long-

20 Iron objects from the Period 2 occupation at Rathtinaun. (a) Pin of swan's neck type; (b) flesh-hook; (c) shafthole axehead with a portion of wooden haft surviving; (d) remains of a socketed implement, probably a sickle. Various scales.

drawn-out, uneven and halting process which might, in fact, have gone largely unnoticed by significant sections of contemporary Irish society. Attempts to draw a rigid distinction between a Later Bronze Age and an Early Iron Age in Ireland are, therefore, to a large extent illusory.

Archaeology must, however, base its interpretations on the evidence available at any given time. Thus we are struck by the fact that the two major cultural assemblages of the last pre-Christian millennium – the Dowris Phase material of its earlier part and the La Tène material of its later part – are totally unrelated. There is not the slightest hint of technological, typological or stylistic overlap between these two archaeological horizons. Clearly, radical changes were taking place in the centuries spanning the middle of the millennium which brought about the demise of the Dowris Phase industries. Indeed, in the absence of any evidence for contact between the industries of the Dowris Phase and those of the La Tène phase in Ireland we are compelled to the view that the former were no longer in existence when the latter were making their appearance in the land.

The reasons for the changes are not yet fully understood but appear to have been varied. Climatic deterioration was probably a factor but its influence was not as sudden and dramatic as has often been assumed. It was once thought that a uniform palaeobotanical horizon, known as a recurrence surface or *Grenzhorizont*, could be recognized in the bogs of northern and western Europe indicating a synchronous change to cooler, wetter conditions. It has become evident, however, that this *Grenzhorizont* is not uniform across western Europe and even in individual bogs detailed studies have shown that there is no single, consistent *Grenzhorizont*. Local conditions were thus important in affecting environmental change. In addition, the critical role of human beings as agents of environmental change is only now becoming apparent. Climate was certainly changing, but not suddenly. Pollen analysis suggests that there was a series of climatic fluctuations, beginning in the latter part of the second millennium BC, with a particularly bad phase in the second quarter of the last millennium.

In human terms, it seems that there was a significant increase in land under cultivation during the Later Bronze Age with a corresponding expansion of population. There was also considerable advance in forest clearance. Over-cultivation and soil exhaustion could have led to leaching and increased podsolization (the loss of soil minerals) at a time when natural climatic trends conducive to podsolization were already in train. Grasses could not thrive in such conditions and acid heathlands developed over former agricultural land. Continuous ploughing could also have altered local drainage patterns, further contributing to soil deterioration. During periods of increasing rainfall bogs, too, began to spread, putting further pressure on agricultural land. A drop in temperature, even if it was no more than the single degree Celsius which has been suggested, would have affected the length of the growing season and placed restrictions on the altitudinal limits of agriculture. There are indications, too, that fluctuating sea levels in the last millennium BC would have led to the danger of marine transgressions in coastal areas. The seas themselves were becoming stormy and this might have affected overseas communications.

Clearly, therefore, both natural and human agencies combined to put mounting pressure on land, which became a diminishing and increasingly valued resource. The inevitable results of such pressures must have been a burgeoning of internecine tensions and consequent political instability. We may wonder if such conditions of climatic and political uncertainty led to the custom of depositing metal artifacts, singly or in hoards, in wet places, perhaps by people ever more desperate to appease the forces of nature. With waterlogged and ruined crops, with rivers bursting their banks and weeks of leaden skies and unceasing rain, Ireland's Late Bronze Age farmers – soaked, cold and hungry – could have felt themselves on the brink of Armageddon.

It was during these years of economic decline that iron made its hesitant appearance in the country. Conditions were scarcely ideal for an embryonic iron-working industry to expand significantly. The evidence remains slight but it may well be that early iron-smelting never developed beyond its initial stages. In this regard it is worthy of note that Hallstatt C influences in the country were not followed by those of Hallstatt D (the late Hallstatt phase). Apart from a few bracelets and perhaps a cauldron or two, the latter is wholly absent from the Irish archaeological record. There is also no suggestion that Ireland had any contact with the earliest European La Tène traditions. The fine dagger series which succeeded the Hallstatt C swords in the Thames valley in southeast England has no counterpart in Ireland. We may take it that in England the workshops established under Hallstatt C influences continued, adapting vigorously to new impulses from the Continent. In Ireland on the other hand, as economic stagnation and decline set in, the initial Iron Age impulses withered as the country, for a time, slipped into uncharacteristic insular isolation. These centuries are obscure in archaeological terms and have been rightly described as a Dark Age. We have, in truth, no clear idea of what was happening in the country at this time. It seems, however, that new impulses from abroad were needed for the Iron Age in Ireland to be reborn.

CHAPTER 3

Hillforts

Who knows but he will sit down solitary amid silent ruins, and weep a people inurned and their greatness changed into an empty name?

CONSTANTIN DE VOLNEY (1757–1820)

It is only through the excavation of relevant occupation sites that we can gain a reliable picture of domestic life in Iron Age Ireland and a proper understanding of the changes which were taking place in the last centuries BC when the Bronze Age was in decline and the Iron Age developing. In this regard, the study of hillforts offers the greatest potential for shedding light on the nature of society in late prehistoric Ireland.

But what constitutes a hillfort? Inevitably sites defy rigid classification, but a working definition of a hillfort might be a hilltop enclosure of considerable size and strength, which deliberately exploits the natural properties of the situation for defensive purposes. The size of the enclosure denotes a centre of tribal rather than family significance. Genuine, prehistoric hillforts are not to be confused with the large and heterogeneous body of enclosure types in the country – mainly ringforts – which date to the early historic or medieval periods. (Ringforts, the most common field monument in the Irish country-side, are small circular homesteads averaging about 20 m to 50 m in internal diameter. They are defined by a bank-and-ditch enclosure or, in stony areas, by an enclosure of dry-stone walling. They occur only rarely in overtly defensive situations.)

The precise number of hillforts in Ireland is difficult to ascertain, but present counts give a total between sixty and eighty. Outside Ireland, on the continent and in Britain, hillforts were in use for a lengthy period, but became increasingly common from the earlier part of the last millennium BC until the final destruction of Celtic independence around the birth of Christ. It was during the Iron Age in particular that hillforts achieved their greatest popularity and their most widespread distribution. For this reason, hillforts and the Iron Age are often regarded as synonymous concepts and this view has often been applied to Ireland. But as we will see, the cultural and chronological position of hillforts in Ireland is not so simple.

The typology of hillforts

Most hillforts in Ireland are as yet unexcavated. All discussion of them is therefore based almost entirely on an analysis of superficially and often

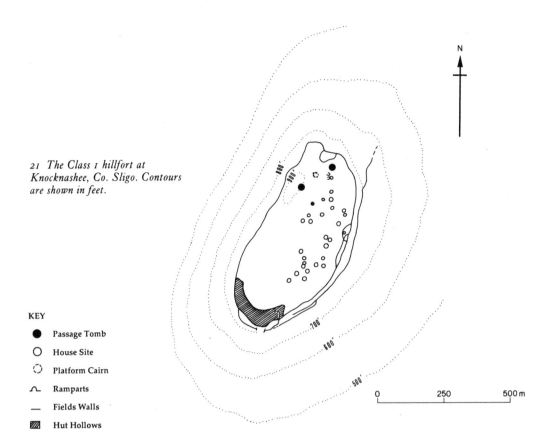

21 The Class 1 hillfort at Knocknashee, Co. Sligo. Contours are shown in feet.

KEY

●   Passage Tomb

○   House Site

◌   Platform Cairn

⌒   Ramparts

—   Fields Walls

▨   Hut Hollows

indistinctly observed surface features. On this preliminary basis three different hillfort types have been isolated.

Class 1 hillforts. The first group of Irish hillforts comprises those with a single line of defence (univallate) of which up to forty possible examples are known. By far the largest, at 22 ha, is the fort at Knocknashee, Co. Sligo, which is included here in the univallate group even though the defences along the east are enhanced by a stretch of outer walling. These forts are otherwise relatively small as all but five are less than 3.5 ha in area. Eight lie at an altitude of less than 200 m above sea level; the highest, the fort on Claragh Mountain, near Millstreet, Co. Cork, is situated at 446 m above sea level.

fig. 21

Ramparts are generally of collapsed rubble, occasionally with external ditches. Entrances, where they can be recognized, are simple gaps in the banks. Details of construction are rarely evident. We do not know to what extent timber-lacing of the ramparts was involved. The presence of vitrified material in the rampart of a small fort at Banagher Glebe in Co. Derry, however, indicates that timber-lacing was known in Ireland but the date of this fort is unknown.

As well as damage due to natural erosion, masonry has often been robbed for the building of field walls, so it is difficult to visualize the defences in their

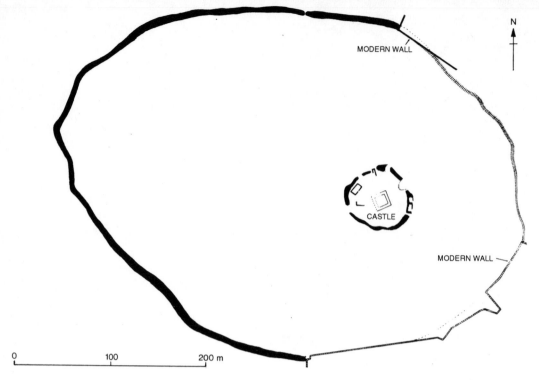

22 *Class 1 hillfort at Caherdrinny, Co. Cork. The inner enclosure is probably medieval.*

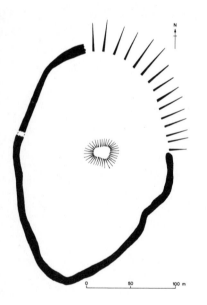

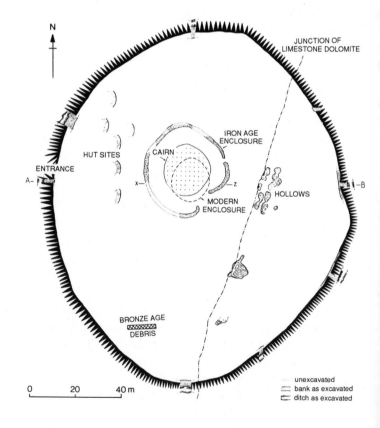

23 *(Above) Class 1 hillfort with central cairn; Carn Tigherna, Co. Cork.*

24 *(Right) Class 1 hillfort with central, Early Bronze Age cairn; Freestone Hill, Co. Kilkenny.*

original state. We can take it, however, that in most cases high, vertically faced walls of carefully laid masonry presented an imposing aspect to the exterior. There might have been internal terraces or timber breastworks. Such constructions, winding around lofty hilltops, would have been clearly visible for many kilometres in all directions. They would have been an ever-present focus of power for the inhabitants of the surrounding regions, dominating the people visually as well as physically. Great enclosures such as Knocknashee or Caherdrinny in Cork must have been immensely impressive sites in their *fig. 22* heyday. Carn Tigherna, near Fermoy in Cork, though little more than 2 ha in *fig. 23* area, is also impressive, not only in its massive stone rampart but also in the way in which it towers over one of the few north–south routeways through the east-west-running sandstone ridges of Munster. The fort might have been built to dominate this routeway.

Without excavation our knowledge of hillfort interiors is limited. The thirty or so circular hut sites observed within the enclosure at Knocknashee, Co. Sligo may be contemporary with the hillfort but this is not proven. The same applies to the hut sites visible at Dun Concobhair on Inis Maan, Aran, Co. Galway. *pl. 8* Where excavation has taken place the picture is scarcely improved. On the summit of Freestone Hill, Co. Kilkenny, an occupation area enclosed by a low, circular wall was found and a number of hut platforms was recognized on the *fig. 24* western slopes within the defences. Some occupation debris, but no huts, were found at Clogher, Co. Tyrone, although the relationship of this material to the primary hillfort is not clear.

At least eleven of the recognized univallate sites have burial mounds, presumably of either Neolithic or Early Bronze Age date, within their enclosures. With only two exceptions, burial mounds are absent in other types of hillforts. Intriguing questions are thus raised as to whether the hillfort-builders deliberately chose particular sites for defence because of the pre-existing burial mounds or whether the juxtaposition of the two types of monument was purely coincidental. If there was some connection, we may then wonder if the presence of an earlier tumulus on the hilltop gave the site a particular status or sanctity which was important to the hillfort-builders, either because they were of indigenous stock and so revered their past or were newcomers who sought to dominate the natives by occupying their sacred places. At Freestone Hill in Co. Kilkenny, however, there was no respect for the Early Bronze Age cairn there, for it was robbed by the later inhabitants to build a wall and a cist was emptied and used as a hearth.

Class 2 hillforts. The second group of Irish hillforts includes some of the finest examples in the country. They are characterized by the possession of two or three concentric lines of defence (multivallate), with a space varying from as little as 10 m to as much as 150 m between the surrounding banks. The majority of these forts have two or three ramparts. There are two, Grianan Aileach, Co. Donegal, and Rathgall, Co. Wicklow, which have four concentric enclosures, *pl. 5* the innermost in each case being a small, ringfort-like structure. In both forts,

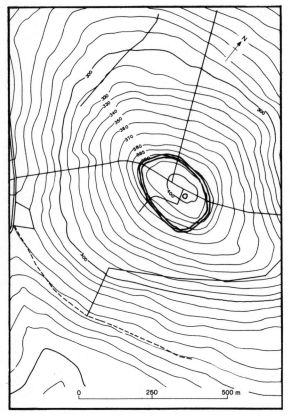

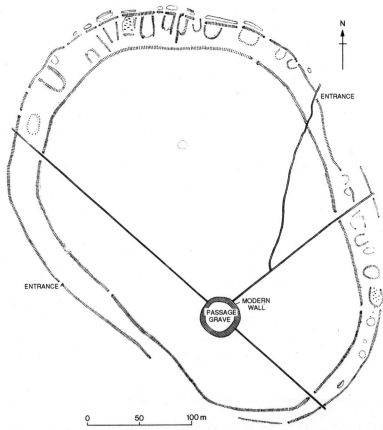

25 (Left) Class 2 hillfort at Knockadigeen, Co. Tipperary.

26 (Below) Class 2 hillfort at Rathcoran, Baltinglass Hill, Co. Wicklow. The hummocks and hollows to the north and east, together with the interruptions in the ramparts at these points, indicate that the hillfort was never finished.

27 (Right) Class 2 hillfort at Mooghaun, Co. Clare. Secondary ringforts built on the walls of the abandoned hillfort can be seen in the south and west.

28 (Far right) Class 2 hillfort at Toormore, Co. Kilkenny.

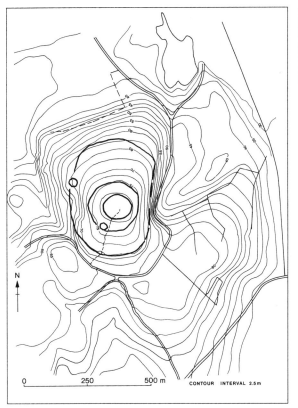

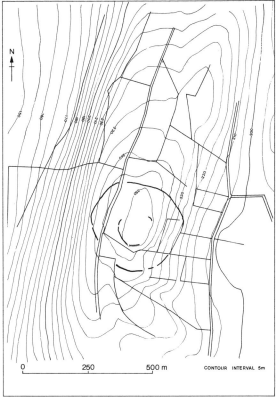

however, the latter is likely to be a late addition which probably had nothing to do with the prehistoric hillfort. Indeed, large-scale excavation is needed to determine whether the Class 2 forts in general are one-period sites, conceived as single defensive units. However, at Haughey's Fort, Co. Armagh (a trivallate construction 8 ha in area), similar radiocarbon dates from the three enclosing ditches show that all three were dug at more or less the same time.

There are at least twenty-five sites which might be considered for inclusion in this group. Classic examples are the great contour forts of the south and west, but a few cliff-top sites with ground plans similar to the contour forts could be related to them. Six Class 2 hillforts cover an area of less than 3 ha, and there are eight examples which exceed 10 ha in area. The largest site is a bivallate enclosure at Ballylin, Co. Limerick, which covers an area of about 20 ha. The banks, however, are narrow and unimpressive so that it is far from certain that this is, indeed, a true hillfort. Classic sites, by any standard, and still imposing today, are Knockadigeen, Co. Tipperary (16 ha), Mooghaun, Co. Clare (12 ha) *figs. 25, 27*: pl. 9 and Rathcoran on Baltinglass Hill, Co. Wicklow (10.5 ha). Toormore, Co. *fig. 26*: pl. 11 Kilkenny (12 ha), though now ruinous, was once a great site and so, too, in all *fig. 28* probability, were the forts of Hughstown Hill, Co. Kildare (14 ha), and Glanbane, Co. Kerry (12 ha). Both are now, unfortunately, completely pl. 12 ploughed out and it is only from the air that their outlines are clearly visible. All but four of the Class 2 hillforts are more than 100 m above sea level. Eight are over 200 m, the highest, at 525 m, being Toormore, Co. Kilkenny.

The most impressive of the Class 2 forts survive as massive rubble ramparts which clearly once represented defensive enclosures of considerable strength. Ditches are occasionally present and in some instances, as for example at Mooghaun, Co. Clare, traces of well-laid masonry are visible. As with hillforts of Class 1, entrances, where recognizable, are simple gaps. At Mooghaun and Rathgall the gaps were lined with slabs.

An indication of the scale of the undertakings involved in the construction of these forts is arrived at by calculating the total lengths of stone ramparts erected on individual sites. At Mooghaun, for example, walls totalling 2225 m in length were constructed. Bearing in mind that hundreds of tonnes of stone for the construction of these great ramparts had to be quarried – perhaps using only antler picks – then lifted and carried to the designated spot where the walls were erected, it is evident that these hillforts represent impressive achievements of communal effort.

fig. 26 Information concerning methods of construction is provided by the apparently unfinished bivallate fort of Rathcoran in Co. Wicklow. In the north and east the defences of this site are discontinuous and here, between the two ramparts, there is a series of small depressions with heather-covered mounds of rubble piled up around their edges. These are probably quarry scoops from which the material for the construction of the ramparts was originally extracted. The stone was initially piled up around the scoops, to be transported the short distance up- and downslope where the banks were being built. It is possible that a final task would have been to join up the quarry holes, thereby deepening the hollow space between the banks and increasing their defensive effectiveness. This was never done, however, and we have no way of knowing why the enormous work of construction, having proceeded so far, was interrupted and abandoned.

Three spectacular stone forts on the Aran Islands in Co. Galway are particularly curious. In terms of morphology they share features with the hillforts of Class 2 but, in some details, they are atypical and it is by no means certain that they belong to the same cultural horizon as the classic Class 2 structures. Inevitably, too, their chronology is uncertain and there are those who would argue a post-Christian dating for them. One recently excavated site (Dun Aengus) has produced Late Bronze Age material, but this is not certainly related to the fortifications there. The three forts have all been reconstructed in modern times thus exaggerating, perhaps, the differences between them and the rest of the Class 2 forts, which are generally in a ruinous state. Enough was preserved before restoration, however, to indicate that in their present form the Aran forts are close to their original appearance.

Two of the forts are on Inishmore, the largest of the Aran Islands. The first of these is Dun Eochla, a bivallate fort of 1 ha situated on the highest point of the island. The innermost enclosure, a small structure of ringfort type, is strongly built and possesses terraces along its inner face. More imposing, however, is the great fort of Dun Aengus, surely one of the most astounding pl. 10 structures of its type in Europe. This is a triple-walled site, its semi-circular, widely spaced defences built up against the vertical sea cliff almost 100 m above the boiling Atlantic. The fort has undergone modification and expansion during its period of use and it now covers a total area of just over 4 ha. The innermost wall is the most massive. It is 4 m thick and rises about 4 m above the exterior. It is made up of three thicknesses and has a pair of terraces around its inner face. A single, lintelled entrance leads to the interior. The outer walls, less massive but still of stout construction, are also internally terraced. Most spectacular of all, however, is the *chevaux de frise* defence which encircles the second wall. This consists of a broad band of densely packed limestone pillars wedged into cracks in the natural limestone. These are up to a metre in height and are either vertically set, or slope slightly to the exterior. A narrow, diagonal passage leads through this limestone forest to the entrance in the second wall. The term *chevaux de frise*, used by archaeologists to describe this defensive technique, comes from the custom – associated particularly with the Fresians in medieval Europe – of surrounding their positions with concentrations of sharpened stakes in order to impede the movement of enemy cavalry.

The third of the great Aran forts, Dun Concobhair on the central of the three pl. 8 islands, Inis Maan, has already been referred to. This fort, 1.4 ha in area, straddles the highest point of the island, physically dominating it. It can be seen on the skyline from far out at sea. It consists of a massive terraced wall forming a small oval enclosure with internal dimensions of 50 m by 27 m. There is a narrow entrance in the east which leads into a large annexed enclosure. This, too, has a single entrance gap, in the northeast. External hornworks, forming a much smaller annexe, protect this entrance. Within the main enclosure there is a series of conjoined hut foundations.

Class 3 hillforts. Inland promontory forts are a third type of upland fortification in Ireland. These are far less numerous (fewer than a dozen) than the contour hillforts and there is considerable variety among them in both size and details of defensive construction. Not all the forts grouped together under this class are necessarily contemporary; in fact, they may not belong to the same cultural horizon as that of the contour hillforts. It may well be that inland promontory forts, or some of them at least, are related to the far more numerous coastal promontory forts.

The finest inland promontory forts in terms of size and defensive complexity are two examples in Antrim, situated on lofty basalt plateaus some 350 m above sea level. These great forts tower over the coastal plain far below and overlook two of the Antrim glens which lead deep into the heart of Ulster. The first of these is Lurigethan which crowns a vertical-sided promontory of some 13 ha. This promontory is defended by a series of ramparts and ditches which extend diagonally from cliff edge to cliff edge for a length of 300 m. The banks and ditches are closely spaced – in contrast to the widely spaced arrangement of the defences on Class 2 hillforts – and the number of banks varies in places from three to six. In the southeast there is a narrow passageway leading through the defences. The second fort on the Antrim basalts is Knockdhu, which covers an *fig. 29* area of about 8 ha. Here, too, the defences are of closely spaced bank and ditch construction. There are three lines of fortification running for a length of about 360 m along the western end of the promontory. A third inland promontory fort in Co. Antrim is that known as MacAirt's fort on Cave Hill. This is situated on a tongue of land, some 3 ha in area, which juts from the vertical cliffs overlooking Belfast. A single curving rampart, with external ditch, defends the area of the fort.

Other examples of inland promontory forts are found far to the southwest of Ireland. There is, for example, a small site on the Limerick/Cork border at Carrighenry in the Darragh hills which could belong to this group. In this instance, two substantial, closely set ramparts of stone cut across the base of a rocky knoll, and, though less than 1 ha in area, the fort is strongly sited and the intent was clearly defensive. It may well date to the late prehistoric period.

It is in Kerry, however, that two of the most extraordinary forts of any type in Ireland are to be found. These are the promontory forts of Caherconree on Slieve Mish and Benagh on Mount Brandon. Hidden in the remote and desolate wastes of the mountains of southwest Ireland they are by far the highest and most inaccessible forts in the country. The fort of Caherconree lies

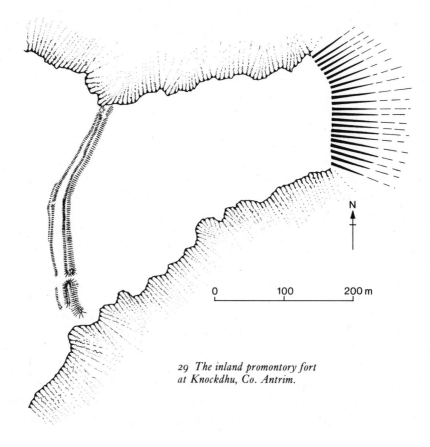

N

0   100   200 m

29 *The inland promontory fort at Knockdhu, Co. Antrim.*

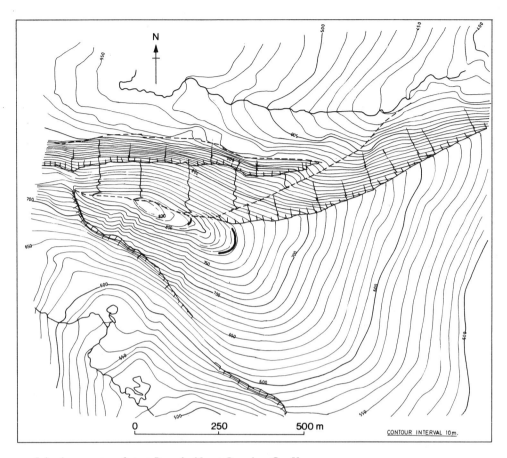

30 Inland promontory fort at Benagh, Mount Brandon, Co. Kerry.

at 615 m above sea level on a rocky crag which projects from a shoulder 150 m below the summit of the mountain. The site is small, less than 1 ha in area, but the fort is otherwise exceptional. Dangerous precipices flank the northern and southern sides of the triangular defended area, while to the east where the ground is more level, a high wall of large and regularly laid sandstone blocks still stands to a height of over 2 m. There are traces of an internal terrace to be seen on the inner face of the wall and there is a single narrow entrance leading to the gradually ascending interior.

pl. 13

Spectacular though the situation of Caherconree is, it is surpassed by the other Kerry fort on Mount Brandon, which occurs at an altitude of no less than 850 m above sea level. This astounding site is situated on a sharp, narrow ridge (an *arrête*) between two glacial corries which fall away sharply on either side for several hundred metres. Two curving stone walls straddle the narrow promontory from one cliff edge to the other. The outer wall is 134 m in length and still stands in places as high as 2.1 m. There is a single narrow entrance gap. Inside this wall the ground rises sharply to the second line of defence, 150 m upslope. Here the promontory is so narrow that a wall a mere 32 m in length was

fig. 30: pl. 14

sufficient to impede further movement along the ridge. This is similar in size and construction to the lower wall and it also has a single narrow entrance. Inside this wall the promontory extends for a distance of about 170 m, rising continuously to a maximum height before falling away again to the west in a narrow tongue.

Coastal promontory forts. The presence of closely spaced multivallation at the inland promontory forts of Lurigethan and Knockdhu, however, clearly sets these two Co. Antrim sites apart from all the other hillforts in the country. Only at Clogher, Co. Tyrone, is there a hint of this type of defensive construction but there it occurs only around part of the defensive circuit. On grounds of siting and of defensive construction, therefore, the two Antrim forts have more in common with coastal promontory forts than with the contour hillforts for, in contrast to the latter, the custom of closely spaced multivallation is a recurring feature on the coastal sites.

About 250 of these coastal forts are known and they are found in most areas where suitable promontory sites are available. Defences vary considerably from single to multiple ramparts. The latter may be closely or widely spaced. Unfortunately, despite the fact that several examples have been subjected to extensive scientific excavation, coastal promontory forts remain the most enigmatic and mysterious of all the fortified enclosure types in Ireland. A first-century AD Gallo-Roman potsherd from disturbed occupation soil at the *fig. 132*: pl. 15   multivallate fort of Drumanagh at Loughshinny, Co. Dublin suggests that some of these sites at least may date to the period around the turn of the millennium and hints at possible influence from abroad (p. 207). Otherwise, apart from the doubtful significance of an early first millennium BC radiocarbon date from a coastal promontory fort at Dunbeg, Co. Kerry, we know nothing of the chronology and origins of these structures. They have on occasion, however, been regarded as evidence of cultural links with either southwest England or northwest France, both areas where coastal promontory forts are common.

Function

Irish hillforts may well have served a variety of different purposes. Defence must, however, have been a paramount consideration in the choice of situation and in the scale and disposition of rampart construction. But once built, how were the defended interiors used? Outside Ireland, hillforts were often occupied on a permanent, or at least a semi-permanent basis, by substantial numbers of people. Towards the end of the La Tène period in certain areas, these forts approached the status of towns. There were also, however, defended hilltop enclosures which appear to have been designed as places of short-term refuge in times of danger for the inhabitants of surrounding regions. It seems likely that some, at least, of the Irish hillforts were similarly places of temporary refuge, especially the more inaccessible sites such as those in Kerry, where

1 Part of a great hoard of bronze artifacts discovered in the 1820s in a bog at Dowris, Co.
Offaly. Probably deposited some time during the first half of the seventh century BC, the
Late Bronze Age cache included a cauldron, trumpets, spearheads, numerous crotals (top
right, associated perhaps with a bull cult because of their resemblance to bulls' testicles),
axeheads and other tools.

Late Bronze Age Ireland

2 (*Left*) A Late Bronze Age bog trackway made of hazel rods; Derryoghil, Co. Longford.

3 (*Below*) A selection of trumpet-ended gold 'fibulae' from Ireland. These are generally described either as bracelets or dress fasteners.

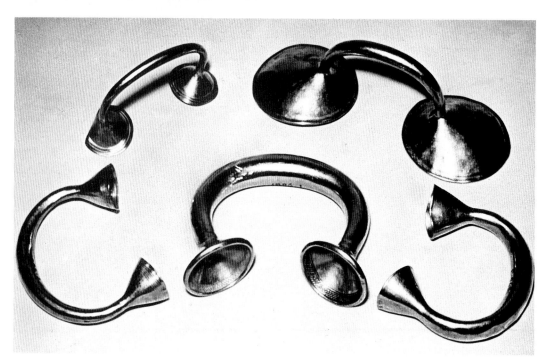

4–6 The settlement at Rathgall, Co. Wicklow. (*Above*) Bedding trench for the wall timbers of a Late Bronze Age hut. In the foreground holes for the doorposts and a groove for a wooden threshold are clearly visible. (*Right*) Aerial view of the multivallate hillfort at Rathgall. In the background, a second, univallate hillfort can be seen. (*Below*) This coarse, hand-made pot from the site is typical of the domestic ware of Late Bronze Age Ireland. Found in a burial, the pot contained a cremation deposit; ht 19.5 cm.

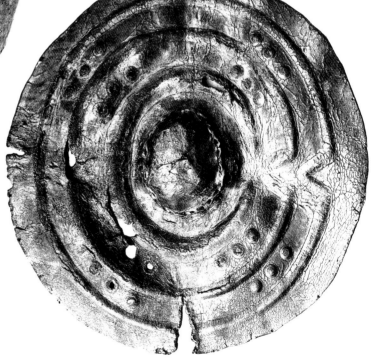

7 (*Right*) A leather shield of Late Bronze Age type, from Clonbrin in Co. Longford. The main part of the shield would have been made by hammering wet leather over a mould, while the central boss was produced separately and stitched on. Diameter 51 cm.

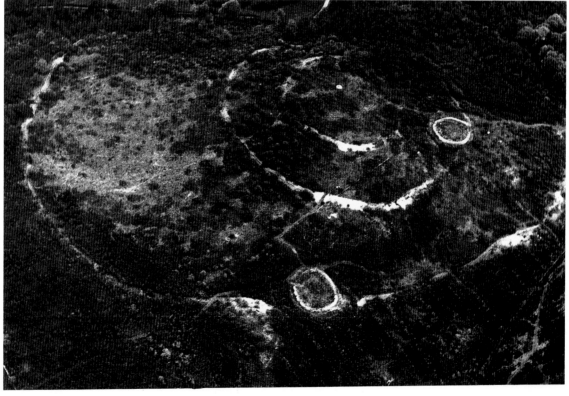

8 (*Above*) The Class 1 fort at Dun Concobhair, on the Aran island of Inis Mean in Co. Galway. Bounded by a single stone wall, the site contains two annexed enclosures; traces of stone houses and internal terracing are also visible.

9 (*Below*) Aerial view of the triple-ramparted, Class 2 hillfort at Mooghaun, Co. Clare. Two later ringforts (built on top of the ruins of the prehistoric fortifications) illustrate well the contrast between the family-based ringfort and the massive, presumably tribal, hillfort.

10 Dun Aengus, Inishmore, Aran Islands, Co. Galway. This great cliff-top fort, with its three stone ramparts (and remains of a fourth), is one of the most impressive prehistoric defended sites in western Europe. The closely packed stones of the *chevaux de frise* can be seen outside the second wall.

11,12 Class 2 hillforts. (*Above*) The bivallate fort at Rathcoran, Baltinglass Hill, Co. Wicklow. Interruptions in the ramparts and hollows between them indicate that this fort was never completed. The circular enclosure on the summit is a modern wall surrounding a Neolithic passage tomb. (*Below*) The remains of this double-ramparted fort at Glanbane, Co. Kerry have been almost completely ploughed away. Indeed, at ground level the fortifications of this once-great site are virtually invisible.

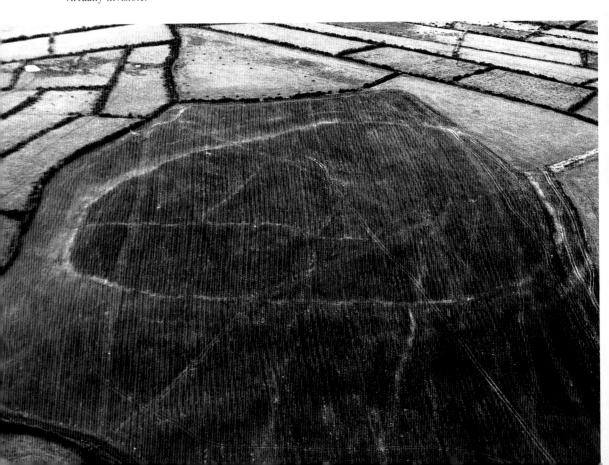

The typology of hillforts

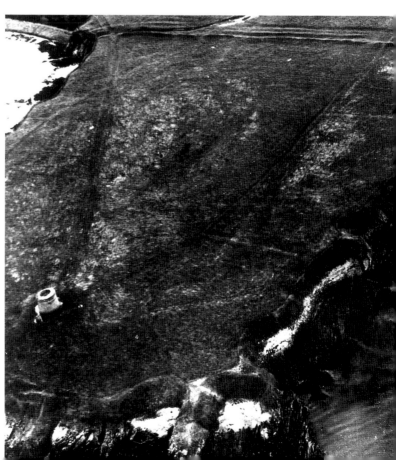

13,14 Inland promontory forts. (*Above left*) Aerial view of Caherconree, Co. Kerry. Sitting atop a rocky crag 615 m above sea level, it commands superb views of the surrounding land. (*Above right*) Looking northwest along the outer wall of Benagh, Co. Kerry. Situated some 850 m above sea level, this is one of the most spectacular forts of its kind in Ireland.

15 (*Right*) Coastal promontory fort at Drumanagh, Loughshinny, Co. Dublin, with closely spaced multivallate defences. A Roman potsherd from the first century AD has been recovered here.

16 Excavations at the central enclosure of Rathgall, Co. Wicklow. The circular wall-slot of the large central house is clearly visible.

permanent settlement in the cold and mist-enshrouded mountains is difficult to envisage. Others, e.g. Rathgall, bear evidence of more long-term occupation.

Could it be, nonetheless, that among the sites we call hillforts there were those which were not in fact fortresses built to be defended? It is possible, for example, that these were focal points within the tribal area, designed for communal gatherings at certain times of the year to conduct the business of the tribe, to engage in commercial activities and, perhaps, to meet delegations from neighbouring tribes? Perhaps in such cases the massive ramparts were raised to enhance the status of the ruling dynasties. Or is it possible that some were constructed for purely ceremonial purposes, places of pilgrimage such as Croagh Patrick in Co. Mayo, today a hilltop Christian festival with roots in the pagan Iron Age? Is there indeed a functional link between the hilltop enclosures and the prehistoric burial mounds which so often occur within them? Limited excavation to date at five sites, however, has uncovered evidence of sedentary, domestic activity. At three of these sites – Freestone Hill, Rathgall, and Haughey's Fort – the scale of occupation revealed suggests that they might have approached the status of small defended villages.

If, however, we take the view that hillforts in Ireland, as in other areas, were indeed built with defence as a primary concern, interesting avenues of enquiry are opened relating to the role of hillforts in action. We may wonder, for example, at the form of attack envisaged by the defenders and the means they would have adopted to conduct their defence. Were hillforts built to withstand sieges or were they merely to protect against hit-and-run assaults? Were hillforts, in fact, ever attacked? Could they even have been places where the non-combatants remained while the fighting men settled their bloody accounts beyond the ramparts? While we have no accounts of battle tactics in late prehistoric Ireland, the writings of Caesar do give us some information about native methods of fighting in Gaul in the last century BC. It seems that many of the tactics adopted by the Gauls at this time were taken from the Romans, but there is one interesting description of the 'normal' methods of indigenous warfare. Caesar writes: 'The Gauls and the Belgae use the same method of attack. They surround the whole circuit of the walls with a large number of men and shower it with stones from all sides, so that the defences are denuded of men. Then they form *testudo*, set fire to the gates and undermine the walls.' (*Testudo* from the Latin for 'tortoise', means that the attackers of the fort held their shields horizontally above their heads, interlocking them, to form a protective screen against defensive fire. This was a widely used Roman battle custom.) We may wonder whether such a scene was ever witnessed at any Irish hillfort.

Differing arrangements of defensive construction presumably imply differing methods of defence. The strategic concepts which underlie a single line of defence are, after all, quite different from those involved with multiple defences. Similarly, there is a fundamental, tactical difference between widely spaced and closely spaced multivallation. The former, assuming that all the ramparts are in contemporary use, allows defenders to fall back on inner defensive lines when hard-pressed. The latter gives defence in depth and has been linked outside Ireland with the use of the sling. Thus, defenders, standing on the highest, innermost bank, could pour a hail of fire on attackers as they appeared exposed on the crests of successive ramparts.

Chronology and culture

As early as Neolithic times, hilltops were occasionally enclosed by rampart-and-ditch defences. This is clearly shown by the excavations at Donegore, Co. Antrim and perhaps also by the enclosure on Lyles Hill in the same county. But the principal period of hillfort construction was in the last millennium BC.

Hilltop occupation during Late Bronze Age times has been demonstrated at Downpatrick, Co. Down, Rathgall, Co. Wicklow and Navan Fort, Co. Armagh. And it is becoming increasingly apparent that hilltop defences were being built at this time. This is most comprehensively shown by J.P. Mallory's investigations at Haughey's Fort, Co. Armagh which yielded a significant quantity of coarse potsherds and a range of occupation debris unequivocally associated with the fort and clearly Late Bronze Age in date. Calibrated radiocarbon determinations indicate principal occupation to have taken place somewhere within the time-span of 1170–770 BC. At Rathgall, so far the most extensively investigated Irish hillfort, a major Late Bronze Age settlement was found within the main ramparts. A large circular structure on the summit of the *fig. 31*: pl. 16 hill, enclosed by a shallow fosse, appears to have been the focus of activity. There was much evidence for domestic habitation and bronze-working was also practised. Among the many artifacts uncovered were objects of bronze, gold, glass, lignite and stone, and there was a large quantity of coarse potsherds, many very similar to those from Haughey's Fort. It is likely, despite the discovery of evidence for sporadic, small-scale occupation in both the early centuries AD and the medieval period, that the hillfort at Rathgall was built in the earlier part of the last pre-Christian millennium. Sherds of coarse, bucket-shaped vessels comparable with those from Rathgall and Haughey's Fort were also recovered during excavations at the small hillfort at Clogher, Co. Tyrone. This suggests the possibility of a Late Bronze Age presence, but there is otherwise no independent dating evidence nor is the coarse pottery positively related to any of the phases of hillfort construction.

The only other excavated Irish hillfort is that at Freestone Hill, Co. *fig. 24* Kilkenny. On the summit there was a stone wall enclosing a circular occupation zone 36.5 m in diameter. No house structures were recognized. On the western slopes, at least six hut platforms were identified and some of these were excavated. Again, however, no house plans were revealed. Among the finds were provincial Roman bronzes and a Roman coin of the fourth century AD and these were used to date the construction of the hillfort. However, a large quantity of coarse pottery was found which is indistinguishable from that discovered in unequivocally Late Bronze Age levels at Rathgall, raising doubts about the dating of the Kilkenny hillfort. It is possible, even likely, that the

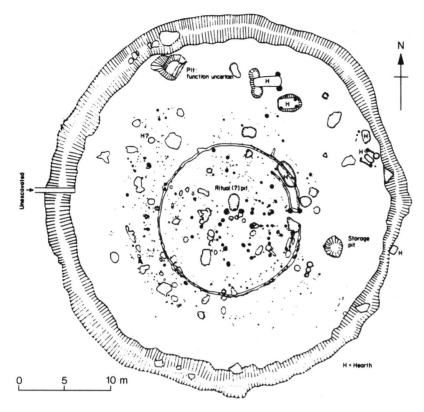

31 Rathgall, Co. Wicklow. Plan of a Late Bronze Age enclosure showing the post-slot for the wall of the central circular structure. Pits, hearths and postholes can also be seen.

potsherds, which were certainly found in association with the Roman items, derive in fact from an earlier, Late Bronze Age level which was undetected in the course of the excavation. Could it be, therefore, that the hillfort at Freestone Hill was built in the Late Bronze Age and was reoccupied, after an interval, in the fourth century AD?

The available evidence shows, therefore, that hilltop occupation undoubtedly occurred in Ireland during the Late Bronze Age and there are strong indications that hillfort building was already well in train during this period. At several sites there is evidence of the occupation or reoccupation of hilltops in the early centuries AD, but it is not clear if this involved the construction of any new hillfort defences. None of the excavated hillforts, with the possible exception of Haughey's Fort, Co. Armagh (which yielded two radiocarbon dates in the last centuries BC; see Appendix 1, p. 229), has produced evidence of settlement which could be dated to the long period between the Late Bronze Age and the early centuries after Christ.

The absence of La Tène material at these sites is noteworthy. The only instance of a possible La Tène presence on any Irish fort is at Dun Aengus on

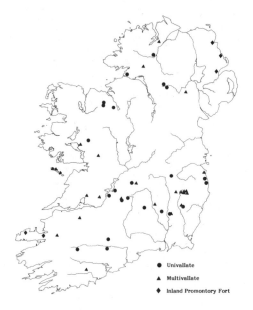

32 *Preliminary distribution map of Irish hillforts.*

● Univallate
▲ Multivallate
◆ Inland Promontory Fort

Aran where a bronze fibula is said to have been found in the earlier part of the nineteenth century. The circumstances of the object's discovery are unclear, however, and its relationship to the building of the fortifications is unknown. The evidence of excavation is given added significance when it is viewed against the distribution pattern of Irish hillforts. The most up-to-date map, with all newly discovered sites included, indicates that there is a marked and *fig. 32* unmistakable concentration of hillforts in southern and southwestern areas of the country. This contrasts sharply with the paucity of hillforts, especially contour hillforts, in more northerly regions. Many of the greatest Irish hillforts, in particular those of Class 2, are found in the very areas of the country where the La Tène archaeological horizon is all but absent. This suggests that the southern Irish hillfort horizon is unrelated to the horizon represented elsewhere in the country by the La Tène material. But who, then, built the southern Irish hillforts and what, if anything, is their relevance to discussions on the Irish Iron Age? The evidence so far implies that the forts were constructed by indigenous Late Bronze Age peoples, perhaps during a period of internecine tension. There is nothing in the available evidence to indicate the presence of intruders among the occupants of Irish hillforts.

There have in the past, however, been a number of attempts to identify foreign influences in constructional details of some Irish hillforts.[8] None is entirely convincing. Sites with a single line of defence, for example, are too simple and too basic to provide any clue as to their origins. Such structures outside Ireland are widely distributed both geographically and in time. Forts with widely spaced, multiple ramparts are superficially reminiscent of those with similar ground-plans in various parts of Britain and in central and northwestern Iberia. Again, however, the comparisons are not compelling, and the possibility that many of the sites in question may be multi-period constructions diminishes greatly the relevance of this type of defensive arrangement as an index of cultural interaction.

An Iberian element in the genesis of southern Irish hillforts has, however, been suggested more specifically on the basis of the *chevaux de frise* defence at Dun Aengus on the Aran Islands in Co. Galway. Apart from a few examples in northern and western Britain, this type of defence in stone occurs principally in *fig. 33* north-central Iberia. In Ireland, as well as at the cliff-top site of Dun Aengus, *chevaux de frise* is found at two coastal promontory forts, Dun Dubhcathair on Aran and Doonamo in northwest Mayo, and at the impressively built circular cashel at Ballykinvarga, Co. Clare. All three types of fort are known from Iron Age contexts in Iberia, and it may be significant that among the Spanish sites with *chevaux de frise* there are at least three built up against cliff edges in exactly the manner of Dun Aengus. Moreover, the extraordinary discovery of the skull

33 Distribution map of European chevaux de frise *sites. Most of these are of stone construction (closed circle), but some earlier wooden* chevaux de frise *have been encountered in Germany and France (open circle).*

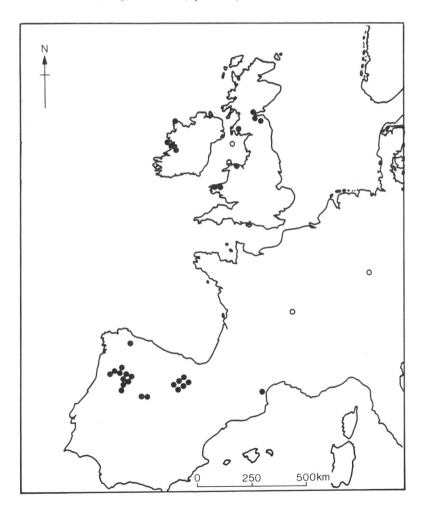

fig. 45

of a north African Barbary ape at Navan Fort, Co. Armagh (see p. 79) clearly shows that the Atlantic seaways between Ireland and Iberia were open in late prehistoric times. While direct influence from Iberia is, therefore, possible, an alternative hypothesis has been put forward by Peter Harbison.[9] This envisages the stone *chevaux de frise* as no more than the survival in stone of the custom of fortifying settlements with sharpened wooden stakes which Harbison suggests might have been widespread in late prehistoric Europe. If this hypothesis is correct then we do not need to explain our Irish *chevaux de frise* forts in terms of Iberian influence.

Hillforts in southern Ireland thus remain enigmatic. It could be that they had nothing to do with outside developments, representing rather an entrenched Late Bronze Age population which was hostile to innovating La Tène influences. The hillfort builders were perhaps of entirely native stock who acquired iron gradually but never absorbed the cultural traditions of La Tène regions further north. This, however, raises further problems in view of the clearly Celtic nature of southern Irish society in the early historic period for this hypothesis implies that the origins of the Irish language are at least as old, if not older, than the early first millennium BC. Modern philologists would reject this view; but this is a problem for philologists rather than archaeologists.

The Spinans Hill complex

On either side of the Slaney Valley, focused on the village of Baltinglass in Co. Wicklow, a concentration of multivallate hillforts forms a striking feature of the prehistoric landscape. At the centre of this cluster, on Baltinglass Hill, are two sites, Rathcoran which crowns the summit and Rathnagree situated at the end of a ridge downslope, some 500 m north of Rathcoran. West of the river, in Co. Kildare, Hughstown Hill and Tinoran Hill are crowned by two greatly denuded hillforts which must once have been massive and impressive monuments. But most extraordinary of all is the series of stone enclosures

fig. 34 which occurs on Spinans Hill, 3 km northeast of Baltinglass Hill.

The hill extends in a northwest-southeast direction, rising to peaks of 405 m and 400 m with a broad hollow between. In the southeast a 5 ha univallate hillfort referred to as Brusselstown Ring has long been known to archaeologists, and in the early 1970s traces of a second stone-built fort were recognized on the northwest summit by Patrick Healy. Recent work by the archaeologist Tom Condit, following a detailed examination of aerial photographs, has revealed the existence of a series of hitherto unrecognized ramparts which totally transform our picture of the features on Spinans Hill. In the first place Condit has shown that Brusselstown Ring is not univallate but bivallate. Far downslope from it a second substantial enclosing wall can be traced around the northern, eastern and southern sections of the hill, forming an enclosure in excess of 17 ha. An even more dramatic discovery, however, is that of a continuous stone-built rampart, doubled for much of its length, extending from Brusselstown Ring just above the 1000-foot (300-m) contour in a

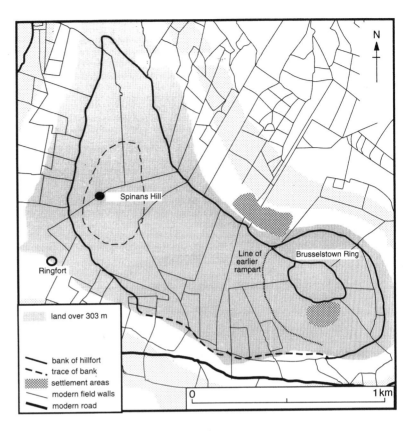

34 *Plan of the enclosure complex on Spinans Hill, Co. Wicklow.*

land over 303 m

- —— bank of hillfort
- — · — trace of bank
- ▨ settlement areas
- modern field walls
- modern road

0   1 km

northwesterly direction to enclose almost the entire hill. The maximum width of the double rampart is 15 m and it could be traced on the ground for a distance of at least 4 km. The enclosure thus formed is no less than 132 ha in area!

This remarkable and dramatic discovery prompts more questions than answers regarding its date and purpose. Recent media speculation has at times been grossly intemperate, and headlines in some of the Irish daily newspapers referring to the discovery of a lost Iron Age city in Wicklow are seriously misleading. Its date is as yet unknown – although a prehistoric date, probably late prehistoric, is likely – and it seems impossible to consider this vast enclosure as ever having constituted a single defended settlement. Could it have been to delimit a major area of tribal assembly or should we view it as in some way comparable to the Dorsey 'enclosure' (p. 85), perhaps representing a series of cross-dykes rather than an enclosure proper? We might also wonder what is its relationship to Brusselstown Ring and the other ringworks on the hill. It is clear, however, that the building of the stone ramparts on Spinans Hill represent a huge and concentrated effort by significant numbers of people, and we must assume that at the time of the construction of the ramparts, whatever their purpose, Spinans Hill was a place of exceptional importance. Tom Condit's discoveries at this amazing Wicklow site have added a new dimension to our perceptions of the nature of late prehistoric Ireland and have opened avenues of enquiry which have to date been completely unsuspected.

CHAPTER 4

King and Tribe

The great settlement of Tara has died with the loss of its princes;
great Armagh lives on with its choirs of scholars . . .
The fortress of Cruachain has vanished with Ailill, victory's
child; a fair dignity greater than kingdoms is the city of
Clonmacnoise . . .
The proud settlement of Ailenn has died with its boasting hosts;
great is victorious Brigit and lovely her thronged sanctuary.
The fort of Emain Macha has melted away, all but its stones;
thronged Glendalough is the sanctuary of the western world . . .
Old cities of the pagans to which length of occupation has been
refused are deserts without worship like Lugaid's place . . .
Paganism has been destroyed though it was splendid and far flung
. . . The great hills of evil have been cut down with spearpoints . . .

OENGUS THE CULDEE (*c*.AD 800)

Royal sites

Thus wrote the scholar monk Oengus in his lengthy martyrology. He exults at
the triumph of Christianity over paganism and contrasts the populous centres
of Christianity with the ruined and abandoned sites which were once the focal
points of pagan worship. Clearly, the memory of a heathen past is still fresh in
his mind and he is familiar with the centres which were important in the
centuries immediately preceding the coming of Christianity to Ireland. He
mentions four of them – Tara, Cruachain, Dún Ailinne and Emain Macha –
and these are the four great sites of early Celtic tradition. For Oengus, they
were the embodiment of paganism.

Oengus would probably have known the locations of these sites, and in his
day – just a few short centuries after their final desertion – they must have
retained in their appearance at least some of their ancient glory. Today, almost
twelve centuries after Oengus, they survive as impressive and dominant
monuments on the Irish landscape. Steeped in tradition and folklore they
retain, in the popular memory, their essentially pagan ethos. They figure
prominently in the early Irish literature, and with them archaeology and the
written sources begin to coalesce. Much that is written about them is, of course,
a gallimaufry of spurious fantasy but there is a factual core which is gradually
emerging through archaeological investigation. We can be confident that they
were, indeed, royal centres of the Celtic Iron Age and there can now be little
doubt that they were, as Oengus believed, centres of pagan ceremonial.

It is unclear, however, despite the early writings, to what extent these were also populated centres. Excavation has not been sufficiently extensive to determine this. But the presence at three of the four sites (the exception is Cruachain) of a hilltop enclosure defined by a sizeable earthen rampart with *internal* ditch seems clearly to preclude defensive intent. Thus, it is erroneous to describe these sites as hillforts (as is so frequently done), despite their hilltop situations and imposing dimensions. Their primary purpose was, in all probability, ritual.

Archaeological excavation in recent years has shed considerable light on the character of these royal sites, and they have increasingly assumed a critical role in contributing to a greater understanding of the Irish Iron Age as a whole. For it seems that these sites represent an important element in changes which were taking place in the Irish archaeological record from the third century BC onwards. This is the period when La Tène cultural traditions first appear in the land, mainly in the form of scattered items of fine metalwork. In technology and art these objects show a dramatic change from all that has gone before. Indeed, the La Tène artifacts are, in very large measure, high-quality, prestige items – clearly the trappings of an aristocratic élite. It remains a matter for debate, however, to what extent the élite is an intrusive element at the time in the Irish population structure. But it seems likely that this warrior aristocracy, represented by the fine metalwork, is also responsible for the great royal sites. It may be that at this time there was large-scale tribal reorganization and territorial expansion as powerful ruling dynasties emerged to harness and control the energies of the growing population. It is possible that this was the period when the tribal divisions evident in the earliest literature began to crystallize. Monumental centres were built, prominently situated within the tribal areas, to serve as triumphant symbols of power and wealth and to provide an expression of communal cohesion and tribal belief.

The period also saw the construction of other great works, such as the extensive linear dykes which may have been grandiose attempts to proclaim the limits of tribal hegemony. At this time, too, massive timber roadways were built across the bogs, on a scale of construction far beyond anything hitherto attempted (and indeed unmatched during any subsequent period until the modern era).

Most important from the point of view of modern archaeological studies is the fact that through a combination of radiocarbon dating and tree-ring analysis, we are beginning to achieve a chronological precision for these events which is otherwise unprecedented in the Irish Iron Age.

Tara

Tara is, perhaps, the best known of the early Irish royal sites. By the historic period it had attained an eminence in contemporary cultural consciousness which it has retained almost to the present day. Its importance appears to have been largely symbolic, but in our earliest sources it is clearly identified as the focus or 'capital' of the kingdom of *Brega*, a region largely coterminous with the modern county of Meath. In later times, aspirants to the notional High Kingship of Ireland laid claim of necessity to the kingship of Tara, thus emphasizing the extraordinary, enduring status of the site even after it had been abandoned and reduced to little more than a series of grass-grown mounds.

fig. 35: pl. 17   Tara today is a complex of earthworks scattered along a commanding northwest/southeast oriented ridge. Though reaching a maximum height of little more than 152 m above sea level, the site is well chosen, for it commanded extensive panoramic views in all directions.

The monuments are spread over a length of some 900 m along the ridge. Some survive well but a significant number has been ploughed out and these are only discernible through aerial photography and by detailed geographical survey. An early eleventh-century scholar, in compiling a book known as the *Dindshenchas* on the lore of places, visited the hill and composed a lengthy poetic description of the site in which each monument is named and a legend associated with it recounted. While almost entirely fanciful, these tales demonstrate again the continuing high status of Tara in medieval times. In the earlier part of the nineteenth century the noted antiquarian, George Petrie, attempted a detailed correlation between the sites referred to in the eleventh-century manuscript and the actual surviving monuments on the hill. The names used today for the various earthworks at Tara were given to them by Petrie from his reading of the *Dindshenchas*. The names, of course, have no significance apart from their antiquarian interest.

Following a recent geophysical survey of the ridge, the number of recognizable sites at Tara has now been increased to almost forty. These include a variety of enclosures and tumuli of varying size and type, a pair of linear earthworks and traces of possible routeways which may be ancient. Dominating the ridge is the large enclosure known as *Rath na Ríogh* (the Fort of the Kings), said to have been built by King Cormac, within which is situated a series of prominent earthworks. The enclosure is oval in shape and 5.9 ha in area. It is defined by a single bank with internal ditch which straddles the narrow ridge. The bank, best preserved in the northwest and west, was once a massive construction which in places still rises more than 1 m above the silted-up ditch. The latter, excavated in the 1950s, was revealed as a deep, V-sectioned fosse which had been dug to a depth of 3 m into solid bedrock. The excavations also uncovered traces of a deep, vertical-sided trench at the inner lip of the ditch which had once supported the timbers of a stout palisade. The stratigraphical relationship of this feature to the large earthwork enclosure itself is not, however, clear.

Immediately inside the enclosure in the north stands the flat-topped mound known as the Mound of the Hostages because, according to the *Dindshenchas*, hostages collected by Cormac were buried here. A second, smaller barrow formerly existed a short distance to the west of this. Excavation has shown that the Mound of the Hostages was a passage tomb of the late Neolithic period (dating to about 2000 BC) which was reused as a burial place in the Early and

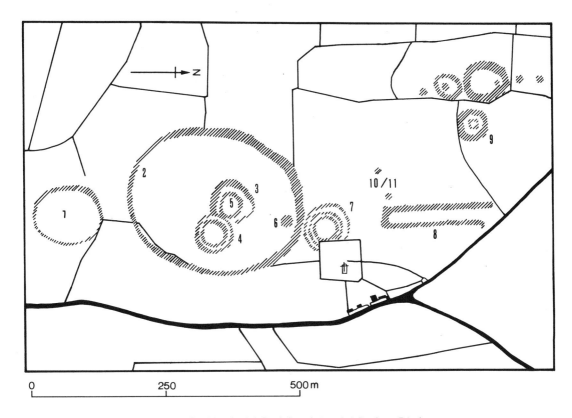

35 *Generalized site plan of Tara in Co. Meath. (1) Rath Laoghaire. (2) Rath na Ríogh.*
(3) Teach Cormaic. (4) Forradh. (5) Lia Fáil. (6) Mound of the Hostages. (7) Rath of the
Synods. (8) Banqueting Hall. (9) Rath Gráinne and Sloping Trenches. (10/11) Traces of
burial mounds.

Middle Bronze Ages. Towards the middle of the enclosure are two conjoined, irregularly circular earthworks each with a raised, flattened centre and each surrounded by a pair of banks with deep ditches between. These are known respectively as *Teach Cormaic* (Cormac's House) and the *Forradh* (Royal Seat). They could be platform ringforts of early historic date, or they could be substantially older burial monuments. This can only be decided by excavation. The outer bank of Cormac's House encloses an earlier burial mound and on the flat, raised surface within its embankments stands the *Lia Fáil* or Stone of Destiny. This is a carved, round-topped monolith which has been moved in pl. 18 modern times from its presumed original position on the summit of the Mound of the Hostages. The *Dindshenchas* tells us that the stone accepted the inauguration of a legitimate king by uttering a cry; if he was rejected the stone remained silent.

To the immediate south of *Rath na Ríogh*, traces of a sizeable, internally ditched, circular enclosure known as *Rath Laoghaire* (named after the king who was confronted by St Patrick) are discernible. Directly adjacent to *Rath na Ríogh* in the north are the greatly disturbed remains of what may have been a

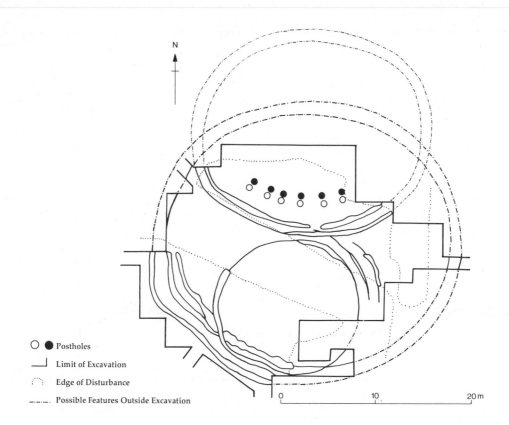

O ● Postholes

—⌐ Limit of Excavation

⌐⌐ Edge of Disturbance

–·–·– Possible Features Outside Excavation

0   10   20 m

36 Plan of the excavations at the Rath of the Synods, Tara. Extensive modern disturbance has obscured the details. The remains of circular post-slots and an arc of postholes can be recognized.

triple-banked ringfort. This is the Rath of the Synods where, in three successive centuries three synods were allegedly held by Saints Patrick, Rúadán and Adamnán. Incorporated into one of the banks is an earlier tumulus. The site was seriously damaged between 1899 and 1902 by a group of British Israelites who dug into it in a (fruitless!) quest for the Ark of the Covenant. Later, in the 1950s, the intact lower levels were excavated by the late S.P. Ó Ríordáin. The full excavation report is pending but preliminary information indicates that this was a multi-period construction, used both for sepulchral (see p. 194) and habitational purposes. Initially a burial mound stood on the site, followed by a series of timber-built enclosures comparable *fig. 36* with those uncovered at Dún Ailinne and at Emain Macha. These were succeeded, after an interval, by a small cemetery of inhumation and cremation burials. In its final phase the ringfort was built. Finds of Roman pottery, glass and other contemporary items came from occupation debris associated with the latter. These belong to the early centuries AD. The burials and the wooden enclosures which preceded the ringfort are not clearly dated but are likely to belong to the later phases of the Iron Age i.e. to the centuries spanning the birth of Christ.

Some 75 m north of the Rath of the Synods is the so-called *Teach Míodhchuarta* or 'Banqueting Hall'. This comprises a pair of straight, parallel banks, 30 m apart, extending gently downslope to the north for a distance of about 180 m. The area between the banks appears to be sunken. A detailed medieval drawing, purporting to be a plan of the 'hall', shows the complex seating arrangement of the different social classes around the great banqueting table. This is, however, a work of imagination. It is out of the question that the site was ever roofed. It could have been a ceremonial avenue leading to the Rath of the Synods or to the Mound of the Hostages, or perhaps it was an Irish version of the rectangular Celtic ritual enclosures which are widely dispersed across the European mainland.

West of the Banqueting Hall, hugging the edge of the ridge at a point where the slope to the west is particularly steep, is a small cluster of three earthworks named the *Claoin-Fhearta* (Sloping Trenches) and *Rath Gráinne*. Not all the details of these monuments are clear because of disturbance, but each consists of a circular bank, apparently with an internal ditch, and they may have had raised centres. They are probably burial mounds. Legend has it that at the southern *Claoin-Fhearta* thirty princesses with their three hundred attendants were massacred when taken unawares by Dunlaing, king of Leinster. The name comes from the northern *Claoin-Fhearta* where – following the exposure (by the youthful Cormac) of an oppressive king, Lugaid Mac Con, for false judgments – 'half his house slipped down the slope' remaining there as a witness to the truth of the tale. Gráinne was the wife of the hero Finn Mac Cumhaill who eloped on her wedding day with Diarmait.

The final sites, scattered between the Rath of the Synods and *Rath Gráinne*, are virtually invisible at ground level. All are likely to have been small barrows which have been removed long since in the course of agricultural activity. Aerial photography also suggests the presence of an early system of routeways which corresponds, to a large extent, with the modern system of roads. We cannot, however, establish the age of these early tracks.

Tara is thus a site of considerable antiquity. It was an important burial place in the Neolithic and earlier Bronze Ages, and two magnificent gold torcs from

37 Tara, Co. Meath. Digital terrain model of Rath Gráinne and Sloping Trenches.

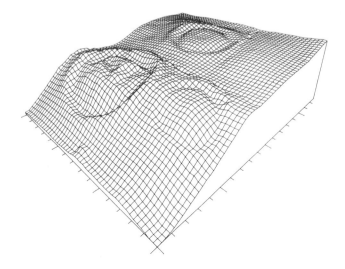

the hill now in the National Museum – dating to the end of the second millennium BC – demonstrate the continued significance of Tara into the later Bronze Age. It may very well be, however, that a majority of the earthworks on the ridge belong to the Iron Age. The preponderance of mounds and barrows, the internally ditched enclosure of *Rath na Ríogh*, the parallel banks and the *Lía Fáil*, seem all to emphasize the overwhelmingly non-secular character of the site. We do not know to what extent the hill was a place of domestic occupation, but there appears to be evidence of habitation for at least one phase of occupation at the Rath of the Synods. The available archaeological evidence, however, supports the traditional view that the primary importance of the Hill of Tara was as a place of long-lived ceremonial significance.

Cruachain

West of the Shannon was ancient Connacht and from there, we are told in the *Táin*, the armies of Medb and Ailill marched on their great hosting against Ulster. Their seat of power was at Cruachain. The early literature is vague about the precise character of Cruachain but it emerges from the writings as a royal palace, as a place of inauguration and ritual and as a major cemetery. It was also a place of entry to the Otherworld.

The site of Celtic Cruachain has been identified with a complex of earthworks and cairns spread over an extensive area of country a short distance to the northwest of the village of Tulsk in Co. Roscommon. Even though there is no townland enshrining the name of Cruachain, the name has survived in folk memory as Rathcroghan (*Rath Chrúachain*), the name of the largest and most prominent mound in the complex. While we can be reasonably confident that the site of Cruachain has been properly located, we do not know if the name referred originally to the region or to a specific group of monuments. The exact limits of ancient Cruachain are thus impossible to establish, especially since many of the surviving monuments are probably of post-Iron Age date.

Some forty-nine monuments have been numbered in the Cruachain complex. These are generally in elevated situations in the rolling limestone countryside. Unlike at Tara, there is no great enclosure forming an obvious centre but the large mound of Rathcroghan seems to be the focus around which the other earthworks were grouped. This is a flat-topped tumulus, 88 m in diameter at its base and up to 4 m in height. Earthen banks may once have surrounded it and on its summit are the possible remains of a small barrow.

pls. 19, 20

Around this are clustered the various enclosures and tumuli. There is a noticeable preponderance of ringbarrows. One of the larger earthworks known as Daithi's mound is crowned by an unhewn monolith standing to a height of 1.8 m. Other ancient features in the area are five linear earthworks, arranged in parallel pairs, some to form avenues of a type reminiscent of the 'Banqueting Hall' at Tara. All apparently oriented towards the main concentrations of tumuli, the longest, at Glenballythomas, runs for 640 m from east to west leading directly to Rathcroghan and its outliers. Best preserved, but considerably shorter, are the northern and southern 'Mucklaghs', the banks of which still stand to a height of 2.4 m. Ancient field boundaries detectable under the modern field pattern are not necessarily prehistoric, and there are also several miscellaneous enclosures and a large number of ringforts which are likely to be of post-Iron Age date. The souterrain and cave known as *Oweynagat*, the legendary entrance to the Underworld, could be similarly late.

On the assumption that the Cruachain of pagan Celtic tradition is, indeed, located in the area near Tulsk, we may assume that within the complex of surviving monuments are those which date to the Early Iron Age. The small and unspectacular ringbarrows may well belong to this period, but without excavation caution is necessary in ascribing earthworks of this type to any specific period. The only modern investigations to have been conducted at Cruachain were undertaken by the archaeologist John Waddell at Daithi's mound in 1981. Though these were generally inconclusive about the nature of the mound, two charcoal samples obtained from under and low in the ringbarrow bank gave a calibrated date range between 350 BC and AD 230, in keeping with the presumed Iron Age context for such monuments at Cruachain.

Dún Ailinne

The other two important royal centres, Dún Ailinne, Co. Kildare, and Emain Macha (Navan Fort), Co. Armagh, differ in significant details from the two centres described above for they are individual enclosures lacking the associated complex of barrows and other earthworks which distinguish Tara and Cruachain. Their relationship with Tara is clear, however, for in both instances the enclosing earthen bank has a deep internal ditch as at Tara's *Rath na Ríogh*. In addition, recent large-scale excavations at Dún Ailinne and at Emain Macha have produced strong archaeological support for the belief that the royal sites of the early literature are, indeed, sites of ceremonial activity.

Dún Ailinne is situated on a great, domed hill rising to 180 m above sea level. In keeping with its royal status the situation, like that at Tara and Emain Macha, is commanding and impressive. Thirteen hectares are enclosed by the *fig. 38* bank and ditch. The bank, in places as much as 4 m above the interior, is among the largest pre-Norman earthworks in the country. The ditch, too, is deep and wide and was described in the early part of this century as broad enough to drive a coach-and-four along it. There is an entrance gap in the east with a corresponding causeway across the rock-cut ditch. Within the enclosure there are no discernible traces of ancient structures.

The site was convincingly identified by John O'Donovan in 1837 as the 'Aillinn' of the written sources. In protohistoric times it was the 'capital' of the kingdom of Leinster but, as with the other royal sites, there were good grounds, even before excavation began, for believing that its roots lay back in the prehistoric period.

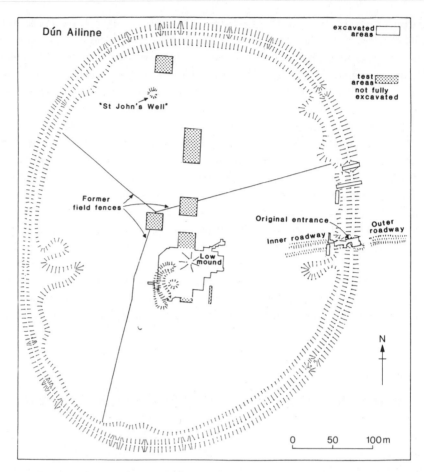

38 Site plan of Dún Ailinne, Co. Kildare showing the excavated areas.

Excavations conducted by the archaeologist Bernard Wailes on the summit of Dún Ailinne between 1968 and 1975 uncovered a stratigraphically complicated sequence of Iron Age activities. Three successive phases of timber-built structures have been isolated. These were revealed in the excavation as overlapping circular trenches which had once held the upright *fig. 39* timbers of substantial palisades. The first phase consisted of a single palisade which enclosed an area 22 m in diameter. In Phase 2 there were three closely set, concentric palisades, enclosing an area with a diameter of 28.5 m. The palisades were carefully graded from the smallest inner to the largest outer. From a gap in the northeast two linear trenches extended downslope in the direction of the entrance through the main bank-and-ditch enclosure. There was also a small gap through the triple palisade in the south which led into a smaller annexed enclosure originally formed by a pair of concentric palisades. In Phase 3, a pair of concentric palisades formed an enclosure 37 m in internal diameter. There was an entrance in the northeast.

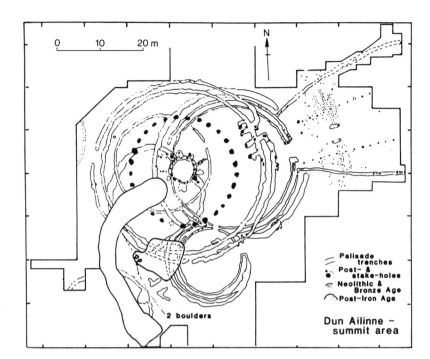

39 Remains of circular, timber-built structures at Dún Ailinne as revealed by excavation. The great post-ring of Phase 3 and the central hut associated with it are clearly recognizable.

Centrally placed within this enclosure a circle of large, free-standing posts (about 25 m in internal diameter) had once stood. The original thickness of the posts could be estimated at around 50 cm. At the geometrical centre of this ring stood a small, circular hut about 5 m across. There was no occupation debris inside the hut and there was no hearth. On the floor, however, there was evidence of intense and extensive burning and there was a curious arrangement of pits set radially around the outer wall. These features suggest that this served no ordinary domestic purpose. After further intensive burning near several of the free-standing posts, the latter were physically removed and the other structures dismantled. There then followed the final phases of activity on the hilltop which seem to have consisted of periodic, open-air feasting. This was

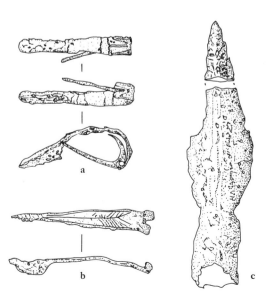

40 A selection of metal artifacts from Dún Ailinne. (a,b) Bronze fibulae of Roman character. (c) Iron spearhead. Various scales.

suggested by layers of charcoal, burnt stones and animal bones, interspersed with thin layers of humic material which probably indicate vegetation growth during the temporary abandonment of the site between the intervals of open-air activity.

All the phases of activity outlined above belong unequivocally to the Iron Age. There is no evidence of later occupation on the hilltop and earlier settlement was small-scale and sporadic. Calibrated radiocarbon age determinations for the sequence (apart from one late date) range between 390 BC and AD 320. Finds from the excavation are scarce and few are closely datable. Among the more important, however, is a short iron sword of Middle La Tène form *fig. 82* which came from the fill of one of the Phase 3 trenches. Two bronze fibulae of Roman type, dating to the early centuries of the Christian era, were also *fig. 40* recovered. Other finds, including an iron spearhead, beads and bracelets of glass and various miscellaneous items, are not accurately datable. The general scarcity of occupation debris is important, however, for it supports the clear impression that all the phases of activity uncovered in the course of the excavation represent specialized practices of a ritual or a ceremonial character. Indeed, Wailes went so far as to suggest that the triple palisade of Phase 2 supported a two-tier viewing platform for spectators rather akin to the terracing at a modern sports ground. More recently, however, archaeologist Chris Lynn has cast doubt on this reconstruction, questioning the contemporaneity of the concentric palisade trenches on the basis of the evidence from Navan Fort (see below). In his view the double and triple palisades represented nothing more than phases of palisade replacement.

The great circle of posts of Phase 3 must, however, have been an imposing structure in its heyday. The timbers, larger than modern telegraph poles, could have stood to a height of 3 or 4 m, and it is not inconceivable that they were joined at their tops by timber lintels, thus creating a sort of wooden Stonehenge. The excavator wondered if the little hut at the centre was the ritual focus of the whole construction, the holy of holies. The latest phases of activity, entirely devoid of any structural evidence, suggest that over a number of years the hilltop was periodically visited by substantial groups of people, and that large-scale banqueting was carried on, perhaps on important feast days during the annual cycle.

Emain Macha

Emain Macha was the capital of the ancient province of Ulster and we can reasonably accept that the great earthwork, generally referred to today as Navan Fort, is the Emain Macha of history and tradition. Situated some 5 km west of Armagh city, the site is on a hilltop in rolling drumlin country, and is commandingly positioned despite being no more than 60 m above sea level. *pl. 21* The enclosure, defined by a rampart with internal ditch, is 4.9 ha in area. Two structures were visible on the summit before excavations commenced in 1963. The first of these (Site A) appeared as a ploughed-out ringwork which survived as a wide, shallow ditch with an external bank about 50 m in external diameter. The second monument, near the summit of the hilltop (Site B), was a large earthen mound 50 m in diameter and 6 m high.

Limited excavations at Site A failed to clarify important matters of function and dating. Two phases could, however, be clearly recognized. The first, *figs. 41, 42* comprising a series of concentric trenches representing the successive rebuilding of a circular timber structure 20.3 m in greatest diameter, was cut by the ditch of the ringwork and thus clearly predates it. These trenches may belong to the later Bronze Age phases of activity on the site. Two concentric trenches (indicating the former existence of a wooden hut, 16.3 m in maximum diameter) overlay the three primary trenches and this structure may be contemporary with the ringwork which was visible before excavation. It might, therefore, be a ringfort of early historic date. This possibility gains support from the presence of two inhumation burials near the house entrance, for one of these was originally in a nailed coffin. The burials were not, however, in unequivocal association with either the Phase 2 house or the ringwork so that either or both of those features might be of prehistoric, even Iron Age, date. Scattered finds belonging both to the Iron Age and the early historic period were found but none came from contexts which help in the dating of the differing structures.

Site B was excavated by the archaeologist Dudley Waterman between 1965 and 1972, during which the mound was removed (and later replaced) and two-thirds of the area underneath investigated. The excavation was carried out with great skill, and a complex sequence of prehistoric activity was revealed. The site was occupied initially, on a small scale, during the Neolithic period, after which followed a phase of cultivation. Phase 3 was represented by a long, and it seems unbroken, period of occupation from perhaps the eighth century BC onwards, during which the site moved culturally from the later Bronze Age into the Iron Age. During these centuries there was a small palisaded enclosure on the hilltop. Within this stood a series of circular wooden huts with annexed enclosures which were frequently replaced. Though this may have been no *figs. 6, 7* more than a simple farming settlement the presence of a Hallstatt C chape on the site may indicate a more exalted status for the occupants.

While the majority of the circular structures brought to light under the mound belong, in all probability, to the later Bronze Age cultural horizon at Navan, it is likely that the latest of them may be assigned to the Iron Age. These overlay all the other post-trenches uncovered and it was evident from the stratigraphy that they preceded immediately the spectacular Phase 4 construction which represents the undoubted climax of Iron Age activity on the hilltop. It is, in fact, possible that the latest buildings of Phase 3 were dismantled to make way for the Phase 4 building.

At any rate, during the last phase the character of the site changed completely and a single large and elaborate circular structure was erected. This *fig. 43* was 37.3 m in diameter. It had an outer wall of horizontal planking within which were four concentric rings of regularly placed upright posts. At the

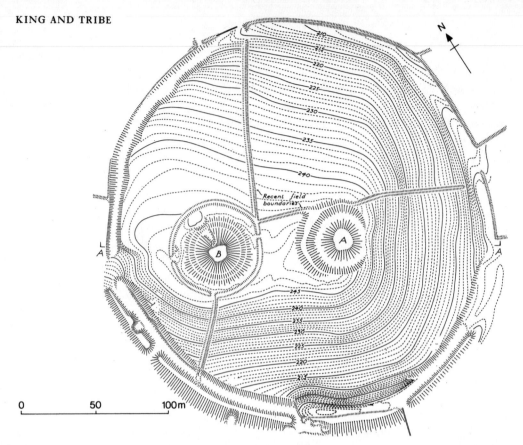

41 *Site plan of Navan Fort in Co. Armagh before excavation. Contours are shown in feet.*

42 *Navan's Site A: the remains of circular, timber-built structures.*

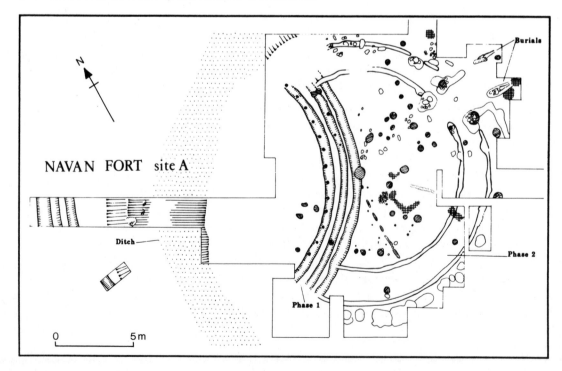

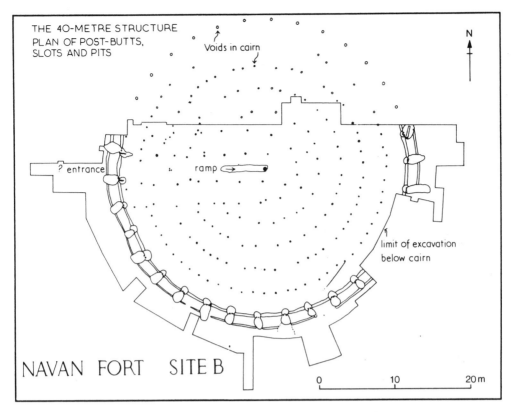

THE 40-METRE STRUCTURE
PLAN OF POST-BUTTS,
SLOTS AND PITS

Voids in cairn

N

? entrance

ramp

limit of excavation
below cairn

NAVAN FORT SITE B

0   10   20 m

43,44 (*Above*) *Site B at Navan: the great circular structure of Phase 4 may have been a temple. (Below)
Reconstruction of this building.*

centre stood a large oak post. The internal post-ring system was interrupted in the west by four roughly parallel rows of posts which appear to have formed an approach to the central post. The latter had been set in a posthole 2.8 m in depth and in this a sizeable portion of the stump was preserved. It was 55 cm in diameter and its original height could have been as much as 13 m. Two mortices had been chopped through its end no doubt to facilitate dragging the massive timber into place. It was, in fact, so big that a sloping ramp 6 m long had to be cut into the edge of the posthole by the Iron Age builders so that they could manoeuvre the post at an angle into the pit before raising it to an upright position.

We cannot say for certain if this construction was ever roofed but there are no architectural reasons why this could not have been the case. The careful arrangement of the post-rings is also consistent with this possibility. Within the Phase 4 structure there were no hearths and not the slightest trace of domestic habitation. The soil cast up from the postholes was directly overlain by stones of the final covering mound, and where this soil was absent the mound material rested on the undisturbed debris of Phase 3. All this, in addition to the unique and extraordinary character of the multi-ring construction and its very presence on a site of known ceremonial importance, strongly supports the view that the Phase 4 building served a purpose which was primarily ritual. The distinct possibility that the huge central post was a non-structural, free-standing timber, reinforces this view. It could have been a totem pole, the focus of cult activities which might well have been carved or painted. We are here reminded of the remark of Maximus of Tyre who wrote, in the first century AD, that 'the Celts devote a cult to Zeus, but the Celtic image of Zeus is a great oak'.

The preservation of the central post-stump and other timbers of the multi-ring structure has important implications, not only for the chronology of Emain Macha, but for the chronology of the Irish Iron Age as a whole. While radiocarbon age determinations gave a broad chronological span for the Bronze Age/Iron Age activity at Navan, this has now been more precisely refined for the final phase on the basis of tree-ring analysis of the surviving timbers. We now know, thanks to dendrochronology, that the felling year for timbers used in the Phase 4 building was 95/94 BC.

This was the final period of Iron Age activity at Site B, as there was clearly no significant interval between the building of the circular structure and its sealing with a monumental cairn. Almost as soon as the multi-ringed structure was erected its interior was carefully and systematically filled with limestone blocks. These were tightly packed into the building while the posts were still standing and the outer wall of wood served as a revetment for the cairn material. When Waterman came to excavate the cairn the voids left by the decomposed upright posts were clearly recognizable. The cairn was heaped to a height of 2.8 m, after which the outer, retaining wall was burnt, it seems deliberately, by piling brushwood against its base. This caused stones from the cairn to spill outwards in places. Then the cairn was covered by a mound of sods which increased its height by 2.5 m.

45 *The skull and jawbones of a Barbary ape were discovered at Navan. The hatched area of the map indicates the approximate distribution of the ape in antiquity.*

Because of the stratigraphical uncertainties at Navan it is generally difficult to relate finds to specific constructional phases. There are few which are unequivocally related to the Phase 4 construction. Most important, however, is the discovery of the skull and jawbones of a Barbary ape, in a context which relates it to the end of Phase 3 or the beginning of Phase 4. The stratigraphical evidence is supported by a recent radiocarbon dating for the skull which, when calibrated, gives a date range between 390 and 20 BC. This creature, a native of *fig. 45* north Africa, can only have come to Navan by ship. Was it a gift, a curiosity, presented by a Mediterranean voyager to an Irish king? Perhaps it was a Phoenician, following in the wake of the sixth century BC seafarer Himilco, who brought the ape to Ireland. The Navan ape, at any rate, underlines the major importance of this Ulster royal site at the end of the last pre-Christian millennium.

Function and significance

These then are the four pre-eminent sites of Celtic Ireland, sites whose ancient importance has been preserved for us largely because of their intimate association with the dominant dynasties of early historic times. But Ireland had many kings and nobles, of varying rank and status, and there must have been other royal centres which failed to gain foothold in the earliest sources and are thus not readily identifiable. Were some of the enclosures we call hillforts royal sites, especially, perhaps, the forts with associated burial mounds?

There is a number of large hilltop enclosures, as yet unexcavated, which may belong in the same grouping of ceremonial sites as Tara, Dún Ailinne and Emain Macha. This suggestion is based on the fact that they are defined by ramparts with internally dug ditches. There is one at Carrowmably, Co. Sligo, spectacularly situated with wide views over the Atlantic. Another, at Knockbrack, Co. Dublin, covers an area of no less than 21.8 ha and has on its summit a prehistoric burial mound. A third, sometimes wrongly described as a hillfort, is Cornashee, near Lisnaskea in Co. Fermanagh. This is on a low but prominent rise, its centre crowned by a large and dominating mound. Unfortunately, we know nothing about the dating of these sites and in one instance at least (Carrowmably), it is not even certain that the enclosure is prehistoric. Both Knockbrack and Cornashee could well date to the Iron Age and the presence of what may be burial mounds of presumably earlier date within the enclosures is consistent with this possibility, for there is a recurring and intimate association between prehistoric burial mounds and sites of ancient Celtic importance. The documented use of Cornashee as an inauguration site in the medieval period could also reflect traditions stretching back to pagan times.

Recent excavations at Raffin, Co. Meath suggest that here too there may have been a monument comparable in function with the great royal centres. The site consists of an enclosure 65 m in diameter formed by an earthen bank with internal fosse. Centrally placed within this was a circular house, 9 m in diameter, which was surrounded, at a distance of 6 m, by a ring of freestanding posts regularly spaced and some 10 m apart. A pit within the enclosure, near its northern edge, contained a human skull, probably of an adult male, and some animal bones. The pit was marked by a squat, naturally rounded boulder. A calibrated radiocarbon date of 100 BC–AD 130 for the skull is in keeping with other dates from the site and is supported by the discovery of a bronze fibula of the early centuries AD. There was no occupation debris and all the indications are that Raffin, like the other internally ditched sites, was a centre of non-secular significance.

The exceptional importance of the named royal sites is, at any rate, clearly evident from the historical sources. The same sources, however, are generally vague and ambiguous in describing their functions and there is much embellishment which may be regarded as poetic fiction. In attempting to interpret the character of these sites, therefore, it is of the utmost importance to use the written sources with the greatest caution. For with these royal centres we enter a convoluted world of myth and legend, a world where the distinctions between fact, fantasy and fabrication are usually blurred and often unrecognizable. But if we can succeed in stripping away the inventions of the early Irish synthetic historians we can discern a sacral kingship with a quasi-divine king, hemmed in by awesome religious taboos and onerous social obligations. He is the personification of his tribe and upon him rests the well-being of his people. Thus he must marry the earth in an elaborate inauguration ceremony to ensure the fertility of the crops and the animals. The enactment of this ceremony, in effect a fertility cult, was in all probability a primary activity carried out at these

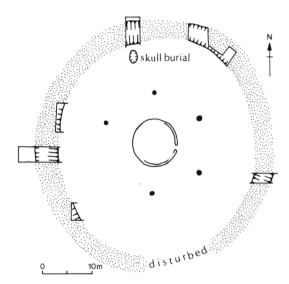

skull burial

disturbed

46 Raffin, Co. Meath: an
Iron Age hilltop enclosure of
suggested ritual character.

0   10m

royal sites – which thus became the ritual and symbolic embodiment of tribal consciousness. Such was the critical role of these ceremonies that in Christian times, shorn of their pagan significance, the royal sites still retained their ancient prestige.

The problems associated with reconciling the evidence of prehistoric archaeology with that of the literary sources are particularly acute when considering sites, other than the named royal centres, which were certainly places of assembly and inauguration. For such is the persistence of native Irish tradition that ancient rites, even ones with deeply pagan undertones, continued into the Middle Ages. We need only remember the extraordinary twelfth-century description of a Donegal inauguration which so shocked Giraldus Cambrensis. He described how a white mare was embraced by the king-to-be, then sacrificed and its meat boiled in water. The king bathed in this water, surrounded by his people; then all ate the meat while the king also drank of the water in his bath. Even though the account is hearsay and is rehearsed for undoubtedly political purposes, it can hardly be pure invention and must surely have a kernel of truth. In the absence of extensive excavation it is thus impossible to tell which of the known medieval inauguration and assembly sites in Ireland are, in fact, sites with pagan Iron Age beginnings.

Places of assembly

Our earliest historical documents clearly show that assemblies or *óenachs* were commonly held throughout Ireland. In fact, a law tract of the eighth century stipulates that it was the duty of every king to convene an *óenach* at regular intervals. The more important the king, the more important was his *óenach*. Feasting, games and horse-racing were laid on and the legal and other business of the tribe transacted. Important festivals in the rural calendar could also be celebrated (see below). The sources imply that such gatherings were held on ancient burial grounds and some modern scholars feel that there may be something in the claims of the poems and tales that the *óenach* originated in the funeral games held for kings and heroes.

A number of important *óenachs* are referred to in the literature and two are described in lengthy and fanciful detail. From the point of view of archaeology we can say little about their origins and we can only guess that some of them, perhaps most, have roots in the pre-Christian Iron Age. An *óenach* was held at, or near, Emain Macha and there was also one at Cruachain. There, the many ancient burial mounds provide a classic setting for such an assembly. Another major *óenach* was at a place called Carman, the location of which has not as yet been identified positively. Some scholars believe that it took place on a plain in Kildare known as the Curragh, others suggest that Carman was on the River Barrow in south county Kildare. It was the principal fair of Leinster and the fact that it was a Lughnasa festival (one of the major Celtic festivals, celebrated at the beginning of August) suggests pagan beginnings. The fame of Carman, however, derives from a long poem in the eleventh-century *Dindshenchas*, which describes in detail the events of the *óenach*.

Another important assembly was held at Tlaghta in Co. Meath. The site today is known as the Hill of Ward and lies close to the village of Athboy. Here, crowning a low eminence, are four closely spaced concentric ramparts of pl. 22 imposing dimensions with an external diameter of 149 m. A disturbed mound at the centre may be of artificial construction or the scarped summit of the hill. The *óenach* was held at *Samhain*, a significant festival in the pre-Christian calendar celebrated at the end of October, and this may again imply origins in the Iron Age. As late as 1168, however, the High King Rory O'Connor presided there over a national synod of kings and prelates.

Most important of the ancient Irish fairs was without doubt that held at Tailtiu (*Óenach Tailten*). This was because it was the gathering convened and presided over by the monarchs of Tara, as Tara itself had no *óenach*. Like Carman, the fair of Tailtiu was held on the festival of *Lughnasa*. The site has been identified near the River Blackwater in Co. Meath, not far from its confluence with the River Boyne. The townland of Teltown preserves the ancient name, and a tradition of the old assemblies there was still alive in the early nineteenth century.

The visible remains are not impressive and provide few independent clues as to their date. Several monuments of ringfort type are present but one of these, *Rath Dubh*, could conceivably be a prehistoric burial mound with external banks. A number of allegedly artificial ponds in the area were referred to in the nineteenth century but the precise nature of these, and indeed their date, are vague. Most interesting, however, is a pair of parallel linear earthworks which extend in an east–west direction for about 100 m. These earthworks, known as the Knockans, clearly call to mind the Mucklaghs at Cruachain and the 'Banqueting Hall' at Tara where there is a strong possibility of an Iron Age date.

Like the assembly sites, the earliest dating of the inauguration sites documented in our early written sources is, as yet, impossible to determine. In many cases, however, Iron Age roots may be suspected. Important in medieval times were sites such as Magh Adhair in Clare where the inauguration of the kings of Thomond took place; Carnfree, south of Cruachain in Roscommon, where as late as 1310 a king of the O'Connors was inaugurated; and Cornashee, Co. Fermanagh, the inauguration place of the Maguires. Another possible inauguration site, associated with the Northern Uí Néill dynasties, is Glasbolie in south Donegal where a small hilltop enclosure encircles a prominent earthen mound.   pl. 23

Another feature of early Irish inauguration sites is the *bile* or inauguration tree. Such trees, it seems, were associated with at least four inauguration sites in the medieval texts, notably Magh Adhair, Co. Clare and Tullaghoge, Co. Tyrone, and at these sites the tree was clearly a focal point. In fact, the sacred tree notionally stood at the centre of the tribal territory symbolizing its integrity and cohesion. The felling of such a tree by enemy forces was the greatest insult which could be shown to those in whose territory it stood. A sacred ash tree also stood at Uisneach, Co. Westmeath, an important assembly place where the festival of *Beltaine* (one of the great feasts, held at the beginning of May) was annually celebrated. The *bile* leaves no trace in the archaeological record but we can assume that this custom is of pagan Celtic origin for there are clear indications that it existed in Gaul in the pre-Roman Iron Age.

Linear earthworks

Linear earthworks are discontinuous lines of bank-and-ditch construction which are most significantly concentrated in southern areas of Ulster and the north midlands. The principal surviving stretches are found in south Down, south Armagh, Monaghan, Cavan, Fermanagh, Longford, Leitrim and   fig. 47 Roscommon. Comparable earthworks also occur occasionally in the south of the country. In the past, these have been a source of wonder and speculation and they have been the subject of an extensive folklore. This has given rise to the curious names by which the various stretches are known in different parts of the country, commonest of which are the Black Pig's Dyke (or Race of the Black Pig) and the Worm Ditch. In Down and Armagh the linear earthworks are known as the Danes' Cast and a section north of Granard in Co. Longford is known as *Dunclaidh*. John O'Donovan, the greatest Irish antiquarian, was moved by the scale of the Black Pig's Dyke to write in 1835 that 'it must have been a tremendous Ollpheist (Huge Worm) that ran across the country when she formed so deep a track but her coils, voluminous and vast, cannot have been more terrible than the tusks of the huge boar that rooted the Valley of the Black Pig'.[10]

Today the earthworks are rarely preserved on the scale which so impressed O'Donovan, and are often barely distinguishable from existing field boundaries. There are stretches, too, long removed by agricultural activity, which can

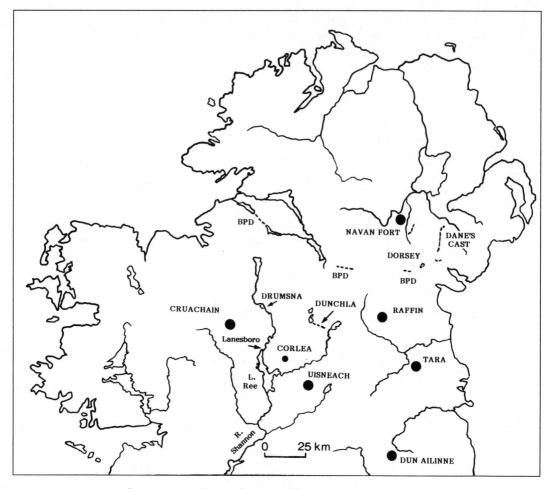

47 *Location map indicating the principal linear earthworks and major royal inauguration and assembly sites in Ireland. BPD = Black Pig's Dyke.*

only be detected from the air. In some places, nevertheless, sections as long as 10 km of more or less continuous dyke can be traced, such as the portion running south from Scarva, Co. Down, or the length extending east-west across Monaghan. Superficial observation of surviving stretches of linear earthworks indicates some variety in constructional details. In south Down, for example, the Danes' Cast in its northern section is composed of a pair of banks with a ditch between, the total width being about 15 m. Further south it is composed of a single bank and ditch. Towards the west the earthworks of the Black Pig's Dyke manifest themselves either as a pair of closely set banks and ditches up to 24 m in total width (and where best preserved 1.4 m high), or as a bank flanked by a ditch on either side, sometimes with lesser banks outside these again. Occasionally only a single bank, usually set downslope from its ditch, can be observed. In hilly drumlin country the earthwork is always on the

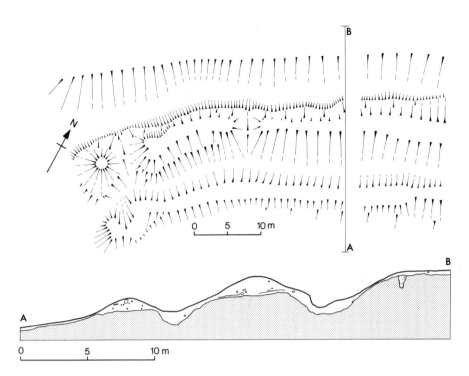

48 Black Pig's Dyke, Co. Monaghan. Plan of the closely spaced ramparts at Aghareagh West near Scotshouse, with an excavated cross-section.

south-facing slopes of the hillocks and the ditches are always upslope from the banks. It has been noted, too, particularly in Monaghan where double bank-and-ditch construction is typical, that the larger banks tend to be those on the *fig. 48* upper slope. Excavations on the Black Pig's Dyke in Co. Monaghan have also revealed that a substantial timber palisade once stood on the inner edge of the inner ditch, and such structures doubtless existed elsewhere. Indeed, older investigations on other sections of dyke indicate the probability that timber palisading was a significant element in their construction.

In two areas of the country linear earthworks combine with natural features to create what appear to be huge enclosures. The first of these is the so-called Dorsey, in south Armagh. This is an irregularly shaped, elongated, east-west running enclosure, low and boggy at the centre, which rises in the east and west to straddle the ends of two low ridges. From end to end the enclosure measures *fig. 49* 4 km and its total area is about 125 ha. For much of its circuit the earthworks are still visible or are traceable from the air. In the main these consist of a rampart, with ditches on either side, which in places still towers to a height of as much as 6 m above the modern land surface. In several sections where the rampart runs into boggy land wooden posts have been found which continue the line of the bank. These posts could be the remains of former palisading. A gap through the rampart in the southeast with a corresponding causeway across the ditches appears to be an original entrance.

85

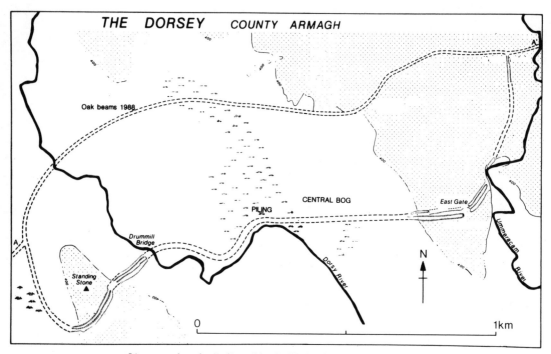

49 Linear earthworks (indicated by double hatched line) known as the Dorsey in Co. Armagh.

The other large enclosure formed by the travelling earthworks is called the Dun of Drumsna which is situated on the Roscommon side of the River Shannon, opposite the Leitrim village of Drumsna. Here a great loop of the Shannon has been cut off by an east-west running earthwork, 1.6 km in length. The area thus enclosed is about 100 ha in extent. The principal element in the earthworks is a massive rampart 30 m wide at its base and in places as much as 6 m high where it is best preserved. There is a double bank and ditch running along the northern edge of this bank and some 30–40 m south of the main rampart the remains of a low bank can be seen; this seems in places to be doubled with a ditch between the two banks. To the west the defences narrow and continue upstream along the right bank of the river for a further 1.6 km. There are two original gaps in the main earthwork, one near the centre, the other nearer the eastern end. In each instance the rampart ends turn sharply southwards forming funnel-shaped entrance passages which vary in width from 16 m to 23 m.

These extraordinary linear earthworks, and especially the great 'enclosures' of Dorsey and Drumsna, are among the most enigmatic monuments of the Irish prehistoric landscape. There are many question-marks concerning their purpose and the identity of the people who built them. One deeply entrenched belief is that they served as the frontier defences of ancient Celtic kingdoms. A generalized correspondence between the east–west line of the Black Pig's Dyke and the ancient boundary of Ulster does indeed lend support to this hypothesis

fig. 50

and it is perhaps worth bearing in mind, in this context, that one of the leaders of the Tuatha Dé, the *Daghdha*, is described in the early sources as possessing a magical club which, when he dragged it behind him, 'left a track as deep as the boundary ditch between two provinces'. It has also been suggested that the southward-running Danes' Cast in Co. Down could represent the western defences of a reduced Ulster after its dismemberment by the expansion of the Uí Néill dynastic family in the fifth century AD.

The matter is, however, more complex than it at first appears. The earthworks are not continuous and, in spite of the views of some early commentators, there is no evidence that they ever were. Undoubtedly, there are places where they run between bogs or lakes which would, in ancient times, have formed natural obstacles to military or marauding movement. This is particularly evident in the case of the Danes' Cast in Co. Down. But elsewhere there are wide areas of dry land where the dykes are absent. Suggestions that these gaps would have been barred by forests are less than satisfactory. It should also be borne in mind that we do not know if all the extant stretches across the country were part of a common phase of construction or even belong to the same cultural horizon. This may well be so but it remains to be demonstrated.

50 The Dun of Drumsna ('the Doon') in Co. Roscommon.

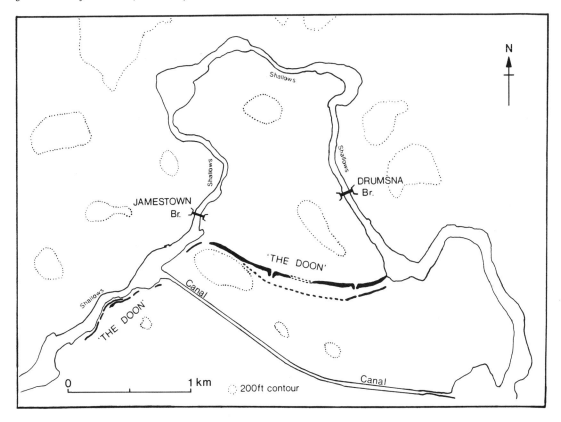

Even more difficult to explain are the Dorsey and the Dun of Drumsna. Such enormous enclosures could not have been for settlement, nor is the suggestion that they were huge cattle kraals plausible in view of the extensive areas of bogland enclosed in each instance. Were these linear earthworks in fact truly defensive in the military sense? Clearly, they could not have been manned or policed on such a scale as to provide permanent and effective border security in the manner of a modern frontier. We may wonder, indeed, if such earthworks were ever the scenes of military confrontation. Suggestions that they were intended to hinder and obstruct large-scale cattle raiding might, perhaps, be nearer the truth. It is equally possible that some of them might also have served as cross-dykes built to control and regulate movement along major routeways. The Dorsey has been seen in this light (and the derivation of the name from the Irish *doras*, a door or gate, is interesting in this regard) and the section of Danes' Cast south of Emain Macha could have barred access to the Ulster capital. The Dunclaidh, too, stretching between Lough Kinale and Lough Gowna in Longford, might have been intended to hinder movement northwards into Cavan. The Dun of Drumsna, most clearly, seems to be related to the need to control movement across numerous fording places in the loop of the Shannon north of the earthworks. It was thus not an enclosure but a defensive earthwork constructed with protection against the north in mind. By contrast, the Black Pigs' Dyke was built by northerners to impede approaches from the south. It is not clear, however, if the Co. Down Danes' Cast faces to the east or the west. Both possibilities have been suggested and we must be cautious in relating this earthwork to any historical event.

But what of the date of these earthworks? Until recently it was tacitly assumed that they were local imitations of the Roman walls of north Britain which were built in the second century AD. A number of important recent investigations have shown, however, that they belong in fact to the pagan Iron Age and have nothing whatever to do with the Roman concept. The first of these excavations was carried out by the archaeologist Aidan Walsh in 1982 on a
fig. 48 well-preserved stretch of the Black Pig's Dyke near Scotshouse in Co. Monaghan. As noted above, traces of a timber palisade were discovered; this had been burnt, leaving extensive charcoal deposits. This charcoal gave two calibrated radiocarbon dates which ranged between 390 BC and 70 BC. A third date from charcoal found in the body of the northernmost bank of the dyke gave a radiocarbon date of 490–90 BC. On the basis of this evidence a likely destruction date for the palisade of the Co. Monaghan Black Pig's Dyke is some time in the last centuries BC. Such dating is broadly consistent with a calibrated radiocarbon determination of 350–30 BC for charcoal from the main rampart of the Dun of Drumsna, and fits well with a series of dates from the Dorsey in south Armagh.

Excavations at the Dorsey were carried out by Chris Lynn in 1977. Although the investigations were on a small scale the results were of major importance for Irish Iron Age studies. Immediately under the main northern rampart the remains of burnt boards or posts of oak were found. Their date cannot be far

17 Aerial view looking north over the royal site of Tara in Co. Meath. The large oval enclosure dominating the picture is *Rath na Ríogh* or Fort of the Kings; inside, the two conjoining earthworks known as the *Forradh* (Royal Seat) and *Teach Cormaic* (Cormac's House) appear in the foreground, with the Mound of the Hostages behind. The Rath of the Synods is immediately north of the Mound of the Hostages, and behind this the parallel banks of the Banqueting Hall can be seen.

Inauguration and
assembly

THIS PAGE

18 (*Left*) The *Lia Fáil* or Stone of Destiny, at Tara. According to legend, the stone was used during inauguration ceremonies.

19,20 Cruachain, Co. Roscommon – the royal centre of ancient Connacht. (*Below*) A ringbarrow at the site, known as Rathbeg. (*Bottom*) The great central mound at Cruachain: Rathcroghan.

FACING PAGE

21 (*Above*) Emain Macha (Navan Fort), Co. Armagh, the ancient capital of Ulster. Within the hilltop enclosure can be seen Site A, left, and Site B, right.

22 (*Centre*) The assembly site at Tlaghta, Hill of Ward, Co. Meath. The great festival of *Samhain* was held here at the end of October.

23 (*Below*) The hilltop enclosure of Glasbolie in Co. Donegal might have been the inauguration site of the northern Uí Néill.

**Inauguration and
assembly**

24 (*Above*) The construction of the 2-km roadway across the Corlea bog in Co. Longford required considerable technical expertise, as well as a sizeable workforce and vast quantities of timber. This photograph shows excavators at work at the site.

FACING PAGE

25–28 (*Above*) Iron Age labourers laid the foundations of the road by placing long birch runners end to end in two parallel rows. On top of these they arranged transverse oak sleepers, some of which they secured in place with wooden pegs. The sleepers were split off from great oak tree trunks using heavy wooden mallets (*centre*, 71 cm long), and some were adzed to achieve a smooth surface (*below left*). At one stretch of the road, excavators found the runners and sleepers in a jumbled heap (*below right*): either the road here was never finished, or perhaps it was deliberately dismantled.

An ancient Irish roadway

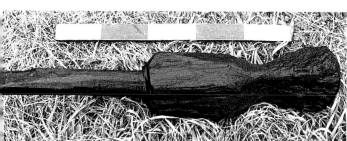

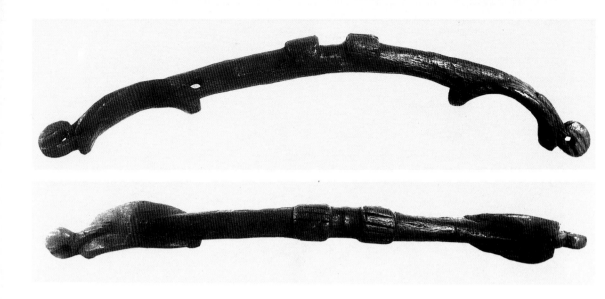

29,30 The Corlea road was probably built for wheeled carts or chariots. Indirect evidence for the use of such vehicles in Ireland comes from the horse-trappings and numerous horse-bits found. (*Above*) Side and top view of a wooden yoke found in Co. Tyrone; the yoke has shoulder pads for two horses and holes at either end for the reins; length 124 cm. (*Below*) A pair of hollow bronze horns which may have been mounted on the ends of a wooden yoke; from Lough Gur, Co. Limerick. Ht 16.4 cm.

31–33 Decorated bronze horse-bits. (*Above left*) Detail of an unprovenanced horse-bit. The cutaway areas were once filled with red enamel using a technique known as *champlevé*; max. width 1.8 cm. (*Above right*) The outline of a stylized human face is visible on this unprovenanced horse-bit; max. width 2 cm. (*Below*) A bronze horse-bit of later type, found in a hoard with other horse-trappings at Attymon, Co. Galway; length 31.2 cm.

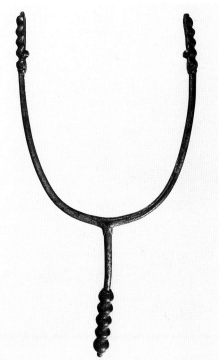

34 (*Above*) Horse-bit and *repoussé* disc of bronze from Annlore, Killeevan, in Co. Monaghan. The disc or *phalera* was probably used to adorn the forehead of the horse; diameter 11.6 cm.

35 (*Left*) One of the many curious Y-shaped artifacts found in Ireland, thought to be part of a horse harness; from Kishawanny, Co. Kildare; length 31.2 cm. Although the exact purpose of such objects has never been conclusively demonstrated, they may have served as pendants or leading pieces.

removed from that of the rampart, since the stumps were still standing when incorporated within the body of the earthwork. Three radiocarbon dates for charcoal from these timbers yielded calibrated radiocarbon dates between 400 BC and AD 80. In the southwest, the line of the enclosure was continued by a ditch with a palisade running 7 m inside it. This palisade was made of roughly squared oak posts. These had been hammered into a V-sectioned trench and were held in position by adzed oak boards wedged lengthways into the trench on either side of the uprights. The timbers were well preserved and 30 were taken away for dendrochronological analysis. The results were spectacular for they produced a felling date of 95 BC ± 9 – the same year as that in which the central post at Emain Macha had been felled.

The demonstration of broad contemporaneity between the great circular building at Emain Macha and the Dorsey earthwork is not, of itself, proof that they were built by the same people. It would, however, be an extraordinary coincidence if they were unrelated. By linking the royal centre of ancient Ulster with its probable periphery, therefore, dendrochronology provides us for the first time – through these monumental constructions – with a physical manifestation of king and tribe in Iron Age Ireland.

CHAPTER 5

The Road to God Knows Where

No person had ever walked out on the bog but after that Eochaid commanded his steward to watch the effort they put forth in making the causeway. The steward went into the bog. It seemed to him as though all the men in the world from sunrise to sunset had come into the bog. They all made one mound of their clothes and Midir went up on that mound. Into the bottom of the causeway they kept pouring a forest with its trunks and its roots, Midir standing and urging on the host on every side. One would think that below him all the men of the world were raising a tumult . . .

In 148 BC Corlea bog in Co. Longford was doubtless the scene of such activity. For in that year an enormous roadway of split oak planks was laid there across the waterlogged marsh. The passage above, taken from the Wooing of Étáin, one of the early Irish tales, tells how the hero Midir of Bri Leith, having lost a game of chess to Eochaid, king of Tara, is obliged to carry out four great tasks, one of which is the building of a road across a previously impassable bog. It was clearly seen as an undertaking of daunting magnitude. The vast and impressive scale of the Iron Age roadway uncovered at Corlea lends reality to the epic description. Building a road such as that at Corlea was truly a hero's task.

Corlea bog is situated near the village of Kenagh, 13 km south of Longford town. It lies near the southern extremity of the raised bog zone which covers extensive areas of central Ireland. Most of this bogland is now in State ownership and is undergoing large-scale industrial exploitation. Dissected and desiccated by long straight drains the bogs are shrinking year after year, planed away inexorably by the giant machines of Bord na Móna, the Irish Turf Board. Unending supplies of peat are required to stoke the fires of the electricity generators and to provide domestic fuel for thousands of Irish homes. Today the Irish midlands are dominated by immense brown deserts of flat peatland.

But the boglands were different in prehistoric times. Then they were dangerous, menacing worlds of reeds and rushes with stagnant pools and quaking mosses lying in wait to engulf the unwary traveller. The Irish bogs were vast wet areas, impassable obstacles to travel for much of the year. In winter especially, they must have been grim and foreboding places and the lights from combusting bog-gasses were probably a subject of superstitious awe and dread to the inhabitants of the surrounding regions. It may well be that many of the artifacts so often found in bogs were deliberately placed there to placate the malign and shadowy beings who were believed to inhabit these soggy wastes.

In Iron Age times the land around the bog was well wooded. This emerges clearly from the pollen studies carried out at Corlea. Birch, willow, hazel scrub and some alder grew around the perimeter, oak and ash were concentrated on the higher ground. But about the middle of the second century BC a phase of increased dampness ensued. It was decided to lay a timber roadway across the bog. Soon, however, the roadway was swallowed by the rapidly growing bog, which embalmed the timbers in a covering of living peat. In the anaerobic conditions thus created the prehistoric wood survived in a state of almost total preservation until revealed again to human eyes after an interval of some twenty-one centuries.

Excavation commenced at Corlea in 1985. Before that, timbers from the roadway had been exposed by the harvesting machines and sent off to Belfast for dendrochronological analysis. All the samples taken pointed consistently to a tree-felling date of 148 BC. It thus seemed evident that the road had been constructed in a single phase. This was the first time that a trackway in Ireland had been dated to the Iron Age.

The Corlea roadway ran in a north-west/south-east direction across the bog for an original length of about 1 km. In the west it terminated at a small island of dry land beyond which there was a further expanse of bog in the townland of Derraghan More. A trackway similar to Corlea in size and construction details, which extended westwards to dry land for a further kilometre, was investigated there in 1957. A recent tree-ring date of 156 ± 9 BC for surviving timbers from this track leaves little room to doubt that it and Corlea are part of the same communication system. The total length of the Iron Age roadway was thus some 2 km.

The construction of such a road involved sophisticated planning and organization, and a massive quantity of timber. A rough calculation based on the excavation results suggests that a minimum of between 200 and 300 large oak trees of good quality was needed to supply the wood for the road surface, and at least as many birches for the substructure were required. The number of pegs which had to be prepared to help stabilize the timbers may well have been in excess of 5000. A sizeable labour force was also required, and many thousands of man-hours were expended. The builders were resourceful and ingenious and as the work progressed constructional details of the road varied in response to differing local conditions encountered in the bog.

We must imagine the scene in early 148 BC as the work parties began their assault on the forests around Corlea. Oaks and birches were the principal trees selected for use but alders, elms, hazel and an occasional yew tree were also felled. Birches with long, straight stems were specially chosen for the substructure and these were brought untrimmed to the bog where the branches were lopped-off and thrown onto the wet surface to help support the weight of the upper timbers. The trimmed birch logs, some more than 10 m in length, were then laid down end to end on the bog in parallel pairs 1.2–1.4 m apart. These were necessary to prevent differential subsidence of the upper timbers which would rapidly have made the road unusable.

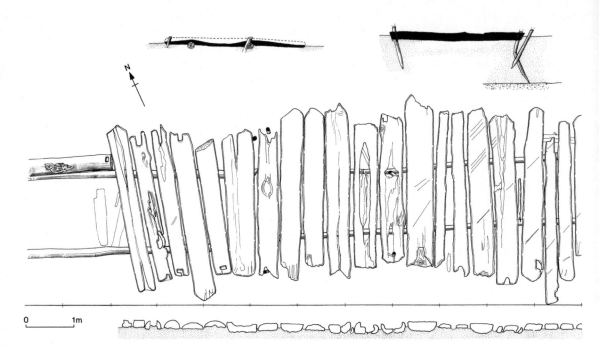

51 Plan of the Iron Age timber trackway at Corlea, Co. Longford.

fig. 51: pl. 25

pl. 26

pl. 27

On top of the birch runners, transverse oak sleepers were placed edge to edge to provide a broad and level walking surface. These were for the most part planks split radially from massive, centuries-old trees, using narrow-bladed wedges of oak hammered into the wood with heavy wooden mallets. In the course of the excavation a discarded mallet with a worn head was found and a single oak wedge was also uncovered. All the planks were chopped at the ends; there is no evidence that the saw was used. They were 3–4 m in length, up to 65 cm wide, and as much as 20 cm thick. In some cases the plank was carefully adzed along its entire length to ensure a smooth, flat surface. During the modern excavation, some timbers required six men to lift and carry them a few metres. Transporting and manoeuvring thousands of such timbers for several kilometres during the original construction of the road, by whatever means, was a considerable achievement.

In some places, perhaps where the bog was dryer than elsewhere, the transverse oaks lay unsecured on the longitudinal runners, their weight alone sufficient to keep them in place. In wetter, softer areas, however, the sleepers were secured in position by pegs, and where pools or little rivulets lay in the path of the road the number of runners was increased. In one spot there were no fewer than eight runners tightly packed together to form what was virtually a pontoon bridge across a particularly troublesome area of wetness.

Where pegs were used they were placed generally at each end of the individual sleeper, hammered through rectangular mortices which had been skilfully adzed into the oak planks. Some of the larger sleepers were double-pegged at one end, each peg in a separate mortice. In a surprising number of cases sleepers were encountered with mortices which were empty and which clearly had never been pegged. More often than not the empty mortice was the only one cut into the timber. Is this a clue to the means of transport? Were the mortices cut in such instances to facilitate the dragging of the timbers to the bog as was surely the case with the great central oak at Navan Fort? In some instances where transverse mortices occur, this can be the only explanation. In other examples, however, it is possible that the mortices were prepared by separate work parties away from the area of road building and that pegs were inserted only where local conditions warranted it.

A few of the pegs were of oak but the majority were of straight birch branches measuring 5–8 cm in thickness. The longest was as much as 1.8 m in length. Most had been adzed all round at their ends to give long, tapering points or were chopped diagonally from one side to give a more blunted tip. They were hammered deep into the bog, probably by means of a wooden mallet. In several instances the pegs were so long and hammered with such force against the hard limestone bedrock below that they buckled and broke. At the level of the roadway the tops of the pegs, before modern damage, projected 5–10 cm above the walking surface.

The associated wooden artifacts

The outstanding importance of peatland archaeology is the anaerobic, waterlogged nature of the environment which enables the most delicate of organic materials to survive in near perfect condition. Once exposed to the air, of course, immediate steps must be taken to counteract the processes of disintegration which commence instantly, but with the right treatment objects of wood, reeds, leather, textiles, and even human remains can be retained in their original state. At Corlea the preservative qualities of the bog are excellent. Many hundreds of the timbers found displayed toolmarks of exceptional clarity, but no axes or other metal objects were brought to light. A range of interesting and important artifacts of wood was, however, recovered and these have provided hitherto unsuspected insights into the nature of carpentry in Iron Age Ireland. Almost all were discovered under the sleepers of the road where they had been discarded when broken and useless. The most numerous items were fragments of wooden vessels but the finds also included an ard-head, a wooden mallet, notched pegs and a possible knife handle. One of the runners forming the substructure of the road, with one end carved into a strange knobbed shape, was also of considerable interest (p. 186).

In one part of the Corlea bog a group of fragmentary wooden artifacts was found concentrated together below the timbers of the road at a point where they had been thrown into a small pool, along with brushwood, shavings and random branches to help support the superstructure of the road. The collection included bits of worked planks and a number of straight lengths of rectangular

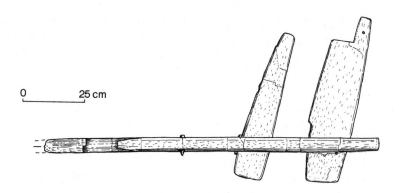

0   25 cm

52 Fragmentary, composite object of carved oak from Corlea, which may once have formed part of the frame of a cart.

fig. 52 section, all of which displayed the remains of transverse slots. Especially interesting, however, was a large composite piece which lay in close proximity to the other, smaller fragments. It consisted of three principal units. The main element was a straight, square-sectioned length of oak, 145 cm long, broken at one end and pierced by three thin transverse slots, two of which contained short planks.

This object was clearly part of a larger unit, but it is not certain what this might have been. The most likely possibility is, however, that this and the other pieces found nearby came from a broken cart or wagon. The large composite fragment could have been part of the frame or chassis, or perhaps it formed part of a side-element of a type still to be seen in parts of southern and western Ireland. Another fragment, round-sectioned and perforated at its end, could be the tip of the draught-pole which ran between the two traction animals.

Directly under the large, composite piece lay two thin boards of ash: one simple, the other a carving of considerable complexity with mortice-and-tenon

53 Finely carved board of ash from Corlea. The object was evidently part of a larger unit, but its function remains enigmatic.

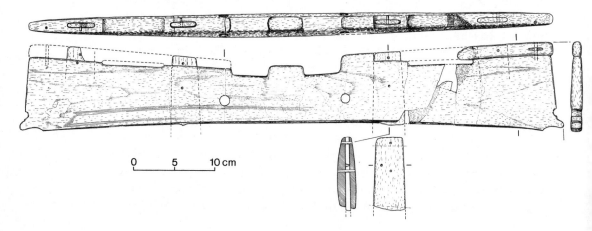

0   5   10 cm

joints and fine, transverse dowelling (see p. 117). The fact that it was found *fig. 53* directly below the putative wagon parts described above might suggest that it, too, belongs to such a vehicle. But the rough and robust treatment to which a farm cart would undoubtedly have been subjected in Iron Age times is difficult to reconcile with the fine and delicate craftsmanship of this piece.

Cultural significance

The road at Corlea was no ordinary road. It was something quite different from the brushwood trackways of earlier times, which generally served as little more than footpaths across the bogs for the local farming communities. The construction of the Corlea road was a gigantic undertaking comparable to the effort involved in the erection of the linear earthworks or in the building of the great royal centres. Corlea is, in fact, among the largest of its kind in prehistoric Europe. It is only in northern Europe, notably in the bogs of lower Saxony, that contemporary roads of similar construction are found. There, particularly in a large area of former peatland at Dümmer, south of Oldenburg, trackways dating to the last centuries BC occur which are startlingly similar in all details of construction to that at Corlea. Whether this is indicative of cultural interaction between the two areas or derives simply from a common response to common problems of roadway construction is unclear. Lacking other evidence of culture contact, the latter interpretation seems to be more likely.

The Corlea road is, however, more massive than any of those in Germany. It was more than simply a means of crossing the bog, for it has a grandiose, monumental character indicative of power, prestige and authority. But what precisely was its purpose? It seems reasonable to suggest, from its size alone, that it was built for the passage of wheeled vehicles, as has been demonstrated for the comparable north German tracks. This theory would be further supported if the wooden fragments from underneath the road are indeed the remnants of a cart. But strangely, there were no wheel ruts noticeable on any of the upper timbers and nowhere was there evidence of wear. There are, however, indications that the road was in use for only a very short time before its abandonment. Indeed, it is possible (however unlikely it may seem), that for some unknown reason the road was never completed, for near the centre of Corlea bog there was a short stretch – about 7 m in length – where the timbers lay in loose and irregular piles in such a way as to suggest that they had never *pl. 28* been formally laid. Some of the timbers were, however, burnt so that it is also possible that the roadway there had been deliberately and systematically dismantled and an attempt made to destroy it.

Significant numbers of people must have been involved in the construction of the Corlea road. Presumably they lived in the surrounding regions in small, dispersed habitations. Such occupation sites, however, have left no recognizable traces on the visible landscape. The distribution map of scattered archaeological material in the country which might be considered likely to be contemporary with the Corlea roadway reveals a startling scarcity of artifacts in the area around Corlea. In fact, apart from a pair of bridle-bits of La Tène type found at Abbeyshrule, 12 km east of Corlea, there is nothing.

The Corlea roadway thus poses many questions. For instance, was it constructed to serve the immediately local needs of the inhabitants of the area, or was it part of a larger regional, even national, network of communications? Was its significance economic, military or ritual, or was it built to enhance the status of a local ruling dynasty? If we choose to think of the Corlea roadway in wider, regional terms as a significant artery of communication, intriguing avenues of enquiry are opened as to the destinations of those travelling along the road. Corlea lies 12 km southwest of the modern village of Lanesborough, a village which is situated at an ancient crossing of the Shannon where it begins to narrow at the northern tip of Lough Ree. About 25 km further to the northwest is Cruachain, the royal centre of Connacht. Some 25 km southeast of Corlea, in Co. Westmeath, is Uisneach, an early cult centre dedicated to the festival of *Beltaine* and reputed by legend to have been the navel of Ireland. While it cannot be stated positively that either of these last two sites was already important in the second century BC, it seems highly likely that Cruachain was a place of ritual significance at this time, and whereas none of the remains visible today at Uisneach need be Iron Age in date, we can accept a deep-seated pagan origin for the site which could well reach back to the time when Corlea was built. It is thus interesting to note that anyone journeying between Cruachain and Uisneach would have made straight for the Shannon-crossing at Lanesborough and from there might well have proceeded along the line of the Corlea roadway. In such a context we might be tempted to view Corlea as part of a pilgrims' highway linking two great ceremonial centres. We might even see it as a toll road across the bog, built by the local population to derive material benefit from the flow of traffic across their territory. The possibilities are thus tantalizing, but the truth as yet eludes us.

Chariotry and horses

It is likely that the Corlea road was built to accommodate wheeled vehicles. As we have seen, however, there is little physical evidence for such vehicles in Iron Age Ireland apart from the wooden fragments found at Corlea which were tentatively identified as portions of a cart or wagon. Unfortunately, no wheel fragments were found at Corlea. In fact, the only wheels of prehistoric date from Ireland are the block-wheels earlier referred to from Doogarymore, Co. Roscommon (p. 21) and the portions of a similar specimen from Timahoe *fig. 54* East, Co. Kildare. Radiocarbon age determinations for the Roscommon wheels indicate that they are several centuries older than the Corlea road, but it is likely that similar wheels continued in use into the Iron Age. They can hardly, however, have been from chariots such as are known from Iron Age contexts abroad and described in the Classical and the early Irish heroic tales.

Outside Ireland, in the earlier phases of the La Tène culture, the chariot was a significant element of the panoply of the ruling classes. Greek and Roman

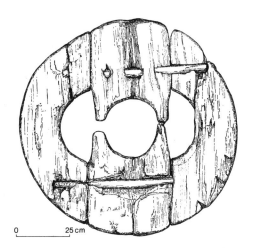

54 The better-preserved of a pair of block-wheels found together in a bog at Doogarymore in Co. Roscommon. Dating to the fourth or third century BC, this is the oldest wheel yet discovered in Ireland.

0 _____ 25 cm

commentators tell us that they were employed with great skill on the field of battle but state that they were also used for purposes of secular travel. In later La Tène times the chariot became obsolete in Europe, surviving only occasionally into the Late La Tène period. In Britain, chariot-burials are known from Yorkshire where they date at least as early as the third century BC, but in that country the chariot evidently survived for some time, for Caesar, to his surprise, encountered them on his southern English campaigns in the first century BC. Fragments of a chariot of second or first century BC date were found in a presumed votive deposit at Anglesey in Wales and, in fact, chariots were still being used by the Caledonians and the Maeatae of Scotland as late as the third century AD.

The evidence of archaeology combined with contemporary representations on coins and stone carvings shows us that the Celtic chariot in Europe was an expertly made, two-wheeled vehicle which was light, speedy and manoeuverable. The wheels, each with a felloe of innovative single-piece construction, were spoked and had shrunken-on iron tyres (which required considerable metalworking skill). Iron linch-pins, sometimes with decorative heads of cast bronze, were inserted into the axle-ends to keep the wheels in place. The rectangular wooden frame had openwork, arcaded sides (possibly made of basketry) and was open at the back. A long pole, to which a pair of horses was yoked, was fixed at the front. A range of mounts and other metal fittings was attached to different parts of the chariot. In many instances, small loops or terrets, through which the reins passed, were fitted to the yoke.

Did chariots of similar type exist in Iron Age Ireland? This is uncertain for we have little to go on apart from the sometimes fanciful descriptions in the earliest literary sources. An attempt by the philologist David Greene to reconstruct from the early accounts the original appearance of an Irish Iron Age chariot yielded an image of a simple, two-wheeled vehicle possessing a pair of spoked wheels, iron tyres, a rectangular frame with low, solid sides and two seats inside which accommodated the charioteer sitting in front and a warrior

fig. 55

fig. 56

fig. 57

pl. 30

pl. 29

behind. Two shafts projected at the back of the chariot and there was a pole at the front to which the horses were yoked.

A vehicle of this type, almost entirely made of wood and apparently with few metal fittings, would have little or no chance of survival except in wetland sites. Its virtual absence from the Irish archaeological record is not, therefore, an indication that it never existed. Indeed, the wooden fragments from Corlea described above serve as a reminder of what might once have been, and it is likely that the straight bar of yew (99 cm long and perforated at the ends), found not far from the wheels in Doogarymore bog, is also part of a wheeled vehicle.

In metal we can, however, point to a few bronze objects which might be chariot components. A pair of hollow, cast-bronze, horn-like objects, found at Lough Gur, Co. Limerick, could have been mounted on the ends of a chariot-yoke, and a linch-pin is said to have been found at Dunmore East, Co. Galway. A single bronze terret from Co. Antrim, a British import of the first or second century AD, is probably also from a chariot. This object is unique in Ireland, however, for in this country the reins appear to have been controlled by the simpler (and cheaper) expedient of passing them through holes drilled into the yoke. This is best illustrated on a specimen from Co. Tyrone. About 1.24 m long, it is a light, finely carved piece with expanded pads at either end to fit on to the horses' necks. Transverse perforations pierce the wood on either side of each pad. It has rounded ends and is ribbed at the centre. In most details it resembles two wooden yokes from La Tène in Switzerland which probably date to the second century BC.

55 Reconstruction of an Irish chariot, based on early literary references.

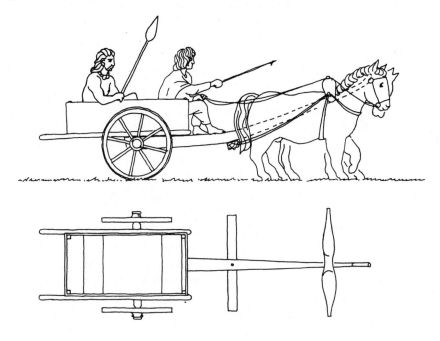

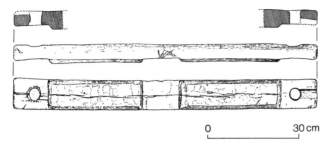

56 (Left) A wooden artifact from Doogarymore, probably part of the chassis of a cart.

57 (Below) Bronze chariot fittings. (a) One of a pair of cast-bronze horns which may have decorated the ends of a yoke; from Lough Gur, Co. Limerick. (b) Terret from Co. Antrim. (c) Linch pin from Dunmore East, Co. Galway.

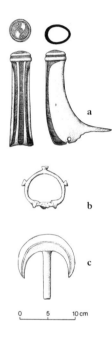

Indirect indications of the use of wheeled transport in Iron Age Ireland are provided by the evidence of the horse bridle-bits. These are occasionally found in matching pairs, and there are also a few examples which bear ornament on one side only of the mouthpiece, or which are asymmetrically worn, thereby suggesting that they too were used in paired draught. A pair of horse-bits, found with a matching pair of horse 'pendants' in a bog at Attymon, Co. Galway in the last century, is interesting in this context because of new evidence which has recently come to light. Following local enquiries with relatives of the finder by the archaeologist Etienne Rynne it appears that two curved and perforated knob-headed bars of metal (possibly bronze) were also present in the hoard at the time of discovery. These lost objects may well have been linch-pins. If this were indeed the case, the Attymon hoard would be the clearest indication to date of the former existence of chariotry in Iron Age Ireland.

The great majority of Irish bridle-bits are, however, single finds and this might suggest that horse-riding was widespread in Iron Age Ireland. But this contrasts with the evidence of the earliest epic literature where horse-riding is only rarely implied as a feature of contemporary life. Thus again is raised the question of whether the epic tales are a true reflection of pre-Christian Iron Age society in Ireland.

Horse-bits, at any rate, represent the single most numerous metal artifact type from Iron Age Ireland. This emphasizes the contemporary importance of the horse in all areas of La Tène Ireland – whether it was ridden or used as a draught animal. The number of known examples is now about 140, and almost all of these are of bronze. There is one two-link specimen. Otherwise the bits have a mouthpiece of three links and a pair of cheek-rings to which the reins were attached. On each of the rings there is generally a pair of stop-knobs which are either separately made, pegged-in units or are cast with the ring. These flank the side-links of the mouthpiece, thereby preventing the rings from rotating freely within the link-ends. A feature typical of most Irish horse-bits is the presence of a raised V-moulding on the inner end of each side-link.

On the basis of the form of the side-links, five groups of horse-bits have been isolated, and there are good reasons for believing that in this grouping a typological progression may be recognized. While we are uncertain of the absolute dates for these specimens, we can assume that they were in use in the centuries spanning the birth of Christ.

figs. 58, 59   The presumed earliest bits have side-links which are generally hollow-cast and which frequently retain their clay casting-cores. They are circular or oval in section and usually have rounded ends. Decoration is rare and, when it occurs, is usually simple. There is one fragmentary example, however, which stands apart from all the other Irish bits, for on the end of its one surviving side-

pl. 32   link is a cast, stylized human face of great character and expressiveness. At the inner link-ends of the same specimen the cast mouldings skilfully combine to evoke the shapes of crested birds' heads. Palmette forms can also be identified in the complex casting. Another interesting horse-bit has curious animal-head forms cast on the ends of the side-links and on the stop-knobs.

figs. 58, 59: pl. 33   The links of later horse-bits are more angular, solid castings with mouthpieces which are often sharply bowed along their length. The side-links usually have one surface which is pronouncedly gabled with a dividing,

pl. 31   longitudinal spine. On these bits the side-links are often elaborately decorated with cast, engraved or *champlevé* (enamelled) ornament. Only two bridle-bits have ornament on the rings and these are unique in the whole of the Irish series.

The fact that the decoration on the side-links would have been largely obscured when the bits were in use seems not to have been a consideration of any significance. These objects thus appear to have been intrinsically important in their own right and were probably prized and valuable possessions among the well-to-do classes. Indeed, they might have served as status symbols, as marks of rank and privilege and were repeatedly, at times almost obsessively, repaired (see p. 159).

The actual functional portion of the mouthpiece on the Irish horse-bits is small, being generally 14 cm or less in length; in some cases it is less than 12 cm long. This indicates that the horses in those days were far smaller than their modern counterparts, and is in keeping with the estimated average size of 10 to 14 hands for horses in the western European Iron Age. This is also supported by the single complete horse metatarsus found in the excavations at Dún Ailinne, Co. Kildare, which represented an animal with a withers' height estimate of 123.7 cm or just over 12 hands. Today this is roughly the equivalent of a Shetland pony.

We can assume that the animals were not shod and, if they were indeed ridden, that they were ridden bareback or with a saddle-cloth. We know nothing about the arrangement of the harness but it is likely that on occasion the trappings were embellished with mounts of bronze or iron. One such mount

pl. 34   was found with a horse-bit in a bog at Killeevan, Co. Monaghan. It is a circular bronze disc of so-called *phalera* type with hammered, curvilinear ornament. It may have been mounted on the horse's forehead.

Apart from the Killeevan find the only other items discovered in association with horse-bits in Ireland are curious, Y-shaped artifacts which, with a single

fig. 61: pl. 35   iron exception, are always made of bronze. They have an average total length of between 28 and 32 cm. The distance between the prongs of the Y is generally between 12 and 16 cm. In a few instances the fork is narrower, one in particular having the prongs as little as 7.8 cm apart. An attachment facility always occurs

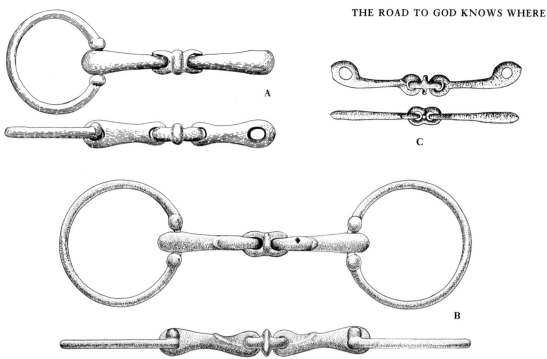

58 Irish horse-bits of types A–C: (A) Llyn Cerrig Bach, Anglesey, Wales; (B,C) No provenance. c. *1/3.*

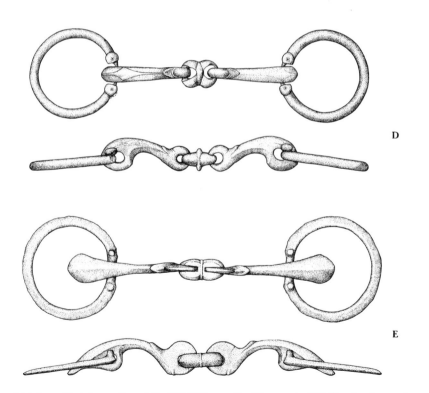

59 Irish horse-bits of types D and E: (D) Killucan, Co. Westmeath; (E) Co. Antrim. c. *1/3.*

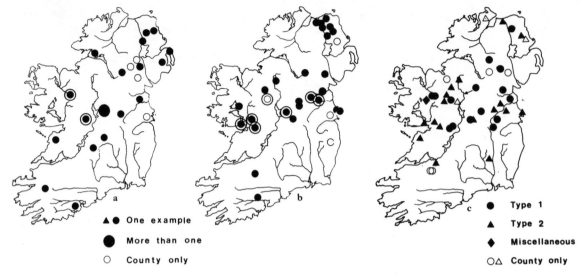

ONE example: ▲ ● One example
● More than one
○ County only

● Type 1
▲ Type 2
◆ Miscellaneous
○△ County only

60 *Distribution maps of (a) earlier forms of Iron Age horse-bits; (b) later forms of Iron Age horse-bits; (c) Y-shaped 'pendants'.*

at the ends of the prongs. This is in the form either of tiny, inward-projecting loops or, more simply, of perforations through the prong-ends. There is considerable variety in the shape and decoration of the stem- and prong-terminals and these are often separately cast units.

Almost one hundred of these Y-shaped objects have been found in Ireland. The type is unknown outside the country. As with the horse-bits, the majority are stray finds. There are, however, a few exceptions. A single Y-shaped object has been found with a single horse-bit on seven occasions. In four instances a pair of such objects has been found, twice unaccompanied, once associated with a single horse-bit and once in association with a matching pair of horse-bits. Finally, there were three instances in which Y-shaped objects occurred in hoards with other items.

These objects seem to have been an intrinsic element of the horse harness, but their precise function is unknown. For well over a century, antiquarians and archaeologists have pondered on the mystery of these enigmatic artifacts and a variety of often imaginative proposals concerning their possible use has been put forward. Thus they have been regarded as plume-holders, curbs, yoke-saddles, leading-pieces, stirrups, spurs and pendants. In the archaeological literature they are most often referred to as 'pendants'. For the moment the least unlikely hypothesis is that they were suspended under the horses' mouth and used as leading pieces in processions or other ceremonial occasions.

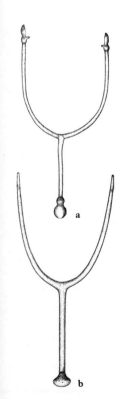

Travel and transport

In conclusion, it seems evident that during the centuries of the Iron Age in Ireland there were important advances in the nature of travel and transport. The road at Corlea is a dramatic development in the means of crossing the

61 *The two main forms of Irish Y-shaped 'pendants': (a) no provenance; (b) Drumanone, Co. Roscommon. c. 1/6.*

marshy wastes and this might have been intended as a major highway in second-century BC Ireland. It could well have been part of a wider communications network. Such roads imply the existence of wheeled vehicles. The widespread use of the horse during Iron Age times was also a significant development, for the horse, whether ridden or used in draught, increased appreciably the speed and comfort of human land transport. Horse transport is, in fact, as much as ten times faster than transport by oxen (which existed in Ireland from the early Neolithic). The horse must thus have acquired an increasingly high status in society, and the mounted warrior would have enjoyed an exalted position in the contemporary social hierarchy.

It is not unreasonable to assume that rivers were also important arteries of communication and that dugout canoes, already known at least from the later Bronze Age, continued to be a common mode of travel. Thus far, only in a single instance has a date within the Iron Age for such vessels been suggested. This is an example of a dugout canoe from Gortgill, Co. Antrim for which a calibrated radiocarbon date of 350 BC–AD 70 has been established. Skin-covered coracles were probably also in use at this time (see p. 204) but these are perishable and would have little chance of survival in the archaeological record. Movement around the coasts is likely to have been in larger vessels, and the fine gold model of a ship with oars and mast, found with other gold objects at Broighter in Co. Derry, gives us an insight into the nature of deep-sea travel *fig. 62: pl. 36* around Ireland in the last century BC. With a mast and sail, eighteen oarsmen, and a substantial carrying capacity, it was a vessel eminently suitable for traversing the waters between Ireland and the Celtic world outside. Despite some assertions to the contrary, the model does not indicate whether the original upon which it was based was made of hides or was clinker- or carvel-built. Boats of carvel construction, a Mediterranean technique, do seem to have been known in Ireland around the turn of the millennium to judge by recent radiocarbon dates for a vessel found on the bed of Lough Lene, Co. Westmeath. An early Roman context for this vessel seems, however, to be the most appropriate (p. 208).

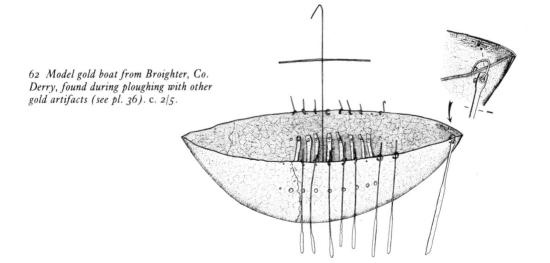

62 *Model gold boat from Broighter, Co. Derry, found during ploughing with other gold artifacts (see pl. 36). c. 2/5.*

CHAPTER 6

The Invisible People

O world invisible, we view thee,
O world intangible, we touch thee,
O world unknowable, we know thee.
FRANCIS THOMPSON (1859–1907)

The great Corlea road encapsulates one of the baffling conundrums of Irish Iron Age archaeology. Its construction was clearly a substantial undertaking which involved the time and energies of many people, perhaps the energies of an entire tribe. But of these people, apart from the road itself silently stretching across the Co. Longford peatland, there is no trace. We must assume that the remains of the homes and settlements of the builders exist under the soil of the surrounding regions, but these have yet to be found.

The Corlea roadway thus tellingly illustrates the deficiencies of the contemporary archaeological record, deficiencies which have hampered our ability to reconstruct the character of everyday life in Iron Age Ireland. The secular habitations of the ordinary people are almost totally unknown, so a whole cultural stratum of Iron Age life is denied us. Archaeology is therefore at an acute disadvantage. For, in seeking to present a picture of Iron Age society at all its levels in Ireland we must lean heavily on the scattered artifacts now in our museum collections which are generally devoid of context and, more often than not, even of provenance. The majority are arguably high-status items, clearly the trappings of an élite stratum of society. Many of these are of considerable technical and artistic quality and thus, in the past, have come to dominate discussions of the Irish Iron Age. We may well question, however, the extent to which such splendid objects are relevant to an understanding of Iron Age society as a whole.

Of course, the ornate scabbards and the superbly fabricated trumpets tell us much about the artistry and the technical sophistication of the bronzesmiths and of the cultural climate within which they were working. Such artifacts also demonstrate the existence in the land of a powerful upper class under whose patronage this material was produced. This class was certainly a significant, possibly even dominant, element in contemporary society, but all the indications are that this group was numerically small. In the archaeological record the majority population of Iron Age Ireland is largely underrepresented. These people existed but we cannot see them. Thus we may truly describe them as the invisible people.

Hearth and home

Iron Age houses of demonstrably domestic character are extremely elusive in Ireland. Indeed, the remains of a small, oval, timber-built hut at the Rath of the Synods, Tara, though belonging to a late phase, are as yet the only example archaeologists can point to with confidence (p. 212). At Feerwore in Co. Galway occupation debris dating to the centuries around the birth of Christ occurred but the excavations there revealed no traces of hut-sites. In sandhills at Whiterocks, Co. Antrim a hearth was found with an apparently associated bronze fibula fragment but again, there were no other structures. Similarly, a bronze fibula found during the excavations at Lough Gur, Co. Limerick indicates an Iron Age presence of some sort there but none of the house structures found at the site could be associated with this phase of activity. The use of the Lough Crew, Co. Meath passage tomb chamber by Iron Age groups was probably for specialized purposes and is unlikely to be an indication of normal habitational use (see below, p. 120).

The small, round, timber-built hut at the centre of the Phase 3 structure found at Dún Ailinne, Co. Kildare was probably related to the ceremonial activities taking place there. A circular, timber-built hut 9 m in diameter, the remains of which have recently been uncovered within a small, ditched enclosure at the hilltop site of Raffin, Co. Meath, may have served a non-secular purpose. The large round building of Phase 4 at Navan Fort is also scarcely to be considered as a normal building, but it, along with those at Dún Ailinne and Raffin, probably serve as pointers to the nature of contemporary dwellings. These are likely to have been circular and of timber but considerably smaller than the Navan structure. The outer wall of horizontal planking identified at Navan indicates that wattle constructions need not have been the only method of wall-building at this time, and the absence of any evidence for the use of nails at Navan indicates that a system of pegs or dowels, or some more elaborate carpentry technique, may have been employed to construct the wall. In addition, we may wonder if houses had carved and painted jambs or lintels, or carefully hewn roof-beams or internal supports. The walls, too, might have been brightly painted or hung with woven, multicoloured tapestries. Iron Age houses in Ireland were not necessarily always dark and squalid hovels.

The possibility that tents once existed is raised by the discovery, in association with the Iron Age road at Corlea, of two wooden pegs, one complete, one fragmentary (see *fig. 63*). The intact example in particular has been carved with great care to produce a rectangular section and flattened top, and has a deep triangular notch at one end and a pronounced barb at the other. In every detail the object is virtually indistinguishable in form from a modern tent-peg. Tents, flimsy and impermanent and made entirely of perishable materials, would normally leave no trace in the archaeological record. So perhaps at Corlea we have a rare pointer to the former existence of tents. It is necessary to bear in mind, however, that there is no Irish word for a tent: in the early literature the Irish *pupall* (tent) was borrowed from Latin (*papilio*).

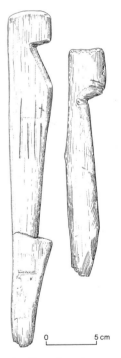

63 Carved wooden pegs found under timbers of the Iron Age road at Corlea. c. 1/2.

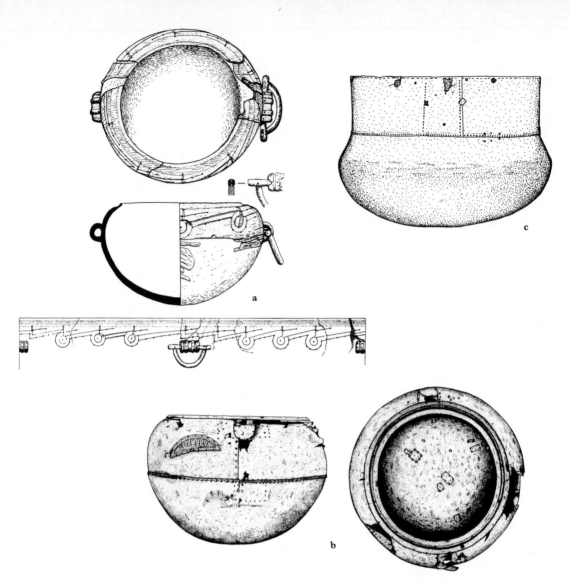

64 *Irish Iron Age cauldrons. (a) This example from Altartate Glebe, Co. Monaghan, is carved in poplar and has a band of incised decoration around the shoulder. (b) Ballyedmond, Co. Galway. The cauldron is of sheet-bronze and has been frequently patched in antiquity. (c) Ballymoney, Co. Antrim. This sheet-bronze example is of the so-called projecting-bellied form. Various scales.*

Our knowledge of the domestic accoutrements in general everyday use is based on a number of finds of varying date from different parts of the country. The cauldron, often seen as the focus of domestic activity within the home, is represented by a small number of examples of varied type, which probably differ widely from one another in date. Less than a dozen examples are known, which is only about one quarter of the total dating to the later Bronze Age. Perhaps wooden cauldrons were more common during the Iron Age.

A globular specimen of riveted, sheet-iron plates from Drumlane, Co. Cavan is unique and, as noted in Chapter 2, may well be the earliest Iron Age cauldron, for it seems to reflect Bronze Age traditions of manufacture. Quite different is another globular vessel, carved from a single block of poplar, which was found in a bog at Altartate Glebe, Co. Monaghan. This example, perhaps dating a few centuries before Christ, bears simple incised ornament around the shoulder and has ingeniously made, two-piece suspension rings of wood. A third globular cauldron, this time of sheet-bronze, also came from a bog, at Ballyedmond, Co. Galway. This example probably dates around the birth of Christ though an earlier dating has been argued. More clearly dating to the turn of the millennium is a handful of so-called projecting-bellied cauldrons. These are all of sheet-bronze and are composed of a hemispherical lower portion to which a more or less cylindrical upper portion is attached. These had a significant capacity and must have been heavy when full. Their rims would have been strengthened by iron hoops, which are known abroad, but have never survived on any Irish specimen. If used in cooking, perhaps in the preparation of meat stews, they had to be suspended over the fire on a tripod or on some form of rope or chain suspension mechanism, perhaps hanging from a rafter. In Celtic areas outside Ireland elaborate wrought-iron suspension chains are well known but none has ever been found in Ireland.

fig. 64

fig. 64: pls. 37, 38

fig. 64: pls. 37, 38

Cauldrons may have been used in the preparation of communal meals, but the deep-seated magico-ritual importance of the cauldron in Celtic mythology as a source of healing, rebirth and resurrection should not be forgotten. In Iron Age Europe the frequent discovery of cauldrons in watery contexts – suggesting some association with a water cult – is also interesting, for every provenanced Irish cauldron has come from a wet site (see p. 184).

Utensils used in the actual consumption of the food and drink and in the preparation and storage of the foodstuffs are poorly represented in the

65 (a,c) Bronze bowls from Keshcarrigan, Co. Leitrim and Co. Roscommon respectively (c. 2/5); (b) bird's head handle of a cup or bowl from Somerset, Co. Galway (c. 2/3).

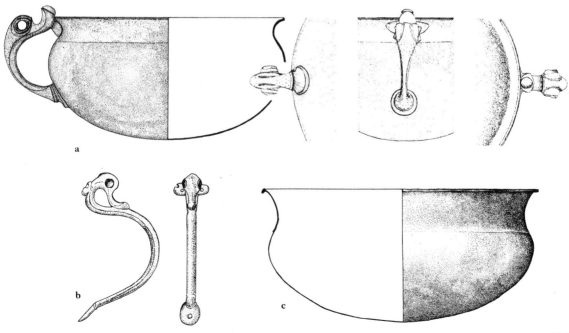

fig. 65

pl. 39

pl. 40

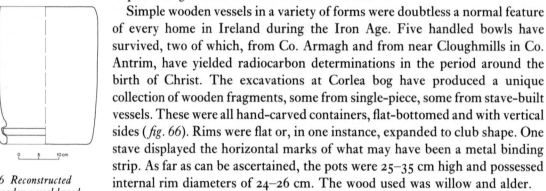

66 Reconstructed wooden vessel based on fragments found under the Iron Age road at Corlea.

archaeological record. A few bronze bowls and handled cups survive which could have been used in the home, though several – especially the two with exquisitely cast bird-head handles (from Keshcarrigan, Co. Leitrim and Somerset, Co. Galway) – could have served a function more lofty than that of simple domestic food consumption. The stave-built, bronze-bound tankard from Carrickfergus, Co. Antrim is more clearly a drinking vessel, perhaps intended for the consumption of an alcoholic beverage such as beer. It is unique in the country and is an imported piece of the first Christian century, perhaps acquired to grace the table of a local aristocrat.

Simple wooden vessels in a variety of forms were doubtless a normal feature of every home in Ireland during the Iron Age. Five handled bowls have survived, two of which, from Co. Armagh and from near Cloughmills in Co. Antrim, have yielded radiocarbon determinations in the period around the birth of Christ. The excavations at Corlea bog have produced a unique collection of wooden fragments, some from single-piece, some from stave-built vessels. These were all hand-carved containers, flat-bottomed and with vertical sides (*fig. 66*). Rims were flat or, in one instance, expanded to club shape. One stave displayed the horizontal marks of what may have been a metal binding strip. As far as can be ascertained, the pots were 25–35 cm high and possessed internal rim diameters of 24–26 cm. The wood used was willow and alder.

Corlea has also yielded two incomplete wooden platters and the lug or handle portions of two large containers which might have been churns. A large, trough-like object of carved oak, 90 cm long with one of its long sides open, is an enigmatic piece. The suggestion that it could have served as a dough board offers the intriguing possibility that here we have evidence for bread-making during the Iron Age.

In considering the home in Iron Age Ireland, the most glaring discrepancy is the absence of domestic pottery. This is quite inexplicable. It may be that pottery will one day be found when the normal settlements are discovered and excavated. We should, however, remember that neither Feerwore nor Dún Ailinne produced a single scrap of Iron Age pottery, and that the ringforts of the early historic period are similarly devoid of this material. It is not until late in the millennium that native wares again appear, in ringforts. There is no demonstrably Iron Age pottery from Navan Fort and the coarse wares from Freestone Hill, Co. Kilkenny cannot any more be certainly linked to the later occupation on the site. All the indications are that for some unknown reason the custom of pottery-making was abandoned in Ireland at the end of the Bronze Age and was not revived until late in the first Christian millennium.

This is all the more surprising when one considers that the varied properties of clay must have been known: clay moulds were undoubtedly used for casting bronzes, and pottery crucibles were probably employed in other metal-working processes too. The decision to cease making domestic pots of clay must thus have been a conscious one, and we can only assume that containers of metal, wood and leather were thought adequately to serve all the needs of contemporary society.

Domestic crafts

Most households would have been largely self-sufficient in their day-to-day economy, and all members must have had their specific duties and skills. Wood-working was probably among the more widespread activities, since wood was readily available for an extensive range of domestic purposes. While the perishable nature of timber has meant that few wooden artifacts have survived in the material record, we can assume that the inhabitants of Iron Age Ireland were intimately acquainted with the varying properties of the different tree species.

Oak, of course, would have been widely used for its strength and its load-bearing qualities, and also for the ease with which it could be split into long, straight planks. This timber was also important because of the tannin in its bark (which was used in the tanning of leather), and would have been a major source of charcoal in the iron-working industry. Alder was popular for a variety of uses because it is tough, yet light and easily workable. In addition, different parts of the tree produce red, yellow, green and pinky-fawn dyes. Alder was ideal for the manufacture of shields, as the example from Clonoura shows, but on this object the vital grip is of the harder oak. The lightness of alderwood, allied with its strength, may also have played a part in its choice for the manufacture of the Doogarymore and Timahoe East wheels. Its suitability for use in waterlogged conditions could also have been important: alder's durability when regularly wetted made it particularly suitable for the manufacture of liquid containers. The wheels illustrate well the selective use of differing wood types. The dowels which held the three alder units of the wheels together were of yew, chosen because of its compact hardness even when used in small pieces, while the cylindrical sleeves within which the axle articulated are of ash – a tough, elastic and easily workable wood.

The expertise of the Iron Age artisans is again evident from an examination of the enigmatic, skilfully worked board from Corlea. This was made primarily *fig. 53* of ash, since it is straight-grained and particularly suitable for fine joinery (it would also have had many other uses, especially as spearshafts). The tiny dowels used to secure the various elements of the Corlea board, however, are of maple, chosen because of its light, fine-grained hardness which made it an appropriate material for the manufacture of structurally important pins and dowels. The versatility of birch would also have been well known to the occupants of Iron Age Ireland. Birch-bark, for example, could be sewn into containers and could also have been used for the manufacture of roofing-shingles. Birch-charcoal, too, has excellent iron-smelting properties, and if the pitch is extracted and prepared it makes a useful glue. Hazel and willow were probably popular for their springy and pliable rods, which must have been used for making baskets, sieves and fish-traps as well as hurdles, fences and wattle-walling. Willow bark also contains tannin and its roots make a deep red dye. The medicinal qualities of the bark as a remedy for headaches and rheumatism may already have been known in the Iron Age. Poplar appears not to have been

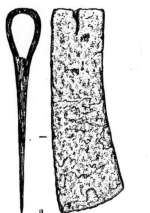

67 Iron Age axeheads from
(a) Kilbeg, Co. Westmeath, 1/4; and
(b) Feerwore, Co. Galway, 1/2.

particularly prized in antiquity because of the coarseness and softness of the wood. It may be, however, that the latter quality was the reason for its selection in the manufacture of the cauldron from Altartate, Co. Monaghan.

The investigations on the Corlea trackway tell us most about Iron Age woodworking techniques, and here we witness not merely the competence of the woodworkers in dealing with heavy timbers but also, in some of the artifacts, the exceptional delicacy of the master joiner. This is best demonstrated by the carefully shaped and polished ash-board described above. Skill of a different sort was used in the manufacture of the Altartate cauldron. The object was hollowed out from a single block, perhaps by initially burning the centre and then by fine tooling. The shaping of the ribbed handle lugs was competently achieved and the production of the two-piece handles displayed both skill and ingenuity. Dugout canoes would presumably have been hollowed out in the same manner as the cauldron. The construction of the Doogarymore wheels also required a considerable measure of technical competence, especially in drilling the transverse dowel-holes through the three elements which made up each wheel.

The occurrence of such carved wooden artifacts obviously implies the existence of a wide range of specialist woodworking tools. Few, however, have survived. A handful of iron axeheads is known, including the presumed early looped-and-socketed specimens from Co. Antrim; the unlooped, socketed axehead from Feerwore, dating to the turn of the millennium; and the shafthole axeheads from Kilbeg, Co. Westmeath, which belong early in the first Christian millennium. A small number of adzes, possibly of sub-Roman origin, is also known, and a round-sectioned rod from Dún Ailinne may have been associated with wood-working.

fig. 67

The Corlea excavations, though yielding no metal finds, nonetheless shed considerable light on the nature of the wood-working implements used. Axe facets were numerous. Where best preserved, the cutting edges seemed to average 5 cm in width with gently convex blades. The implements were sharp-edged and efficient and could, at a single stroke, bite deeply into the hardest oak. Evidence for the use of adzes was also clearly recognizable on the flat surfaces of some of the planks which had been dressed to provide a suitable walking surface. One plank had the marks of the wedges used in its splitting and, in fact, a wedge of oak was recovered in the course of the excavations. It is worth noting again that despite the examination of thousands of worked timbers at the site, there was no evidence that a woodsman's saw had been used.

pl. 27

On the smaller objects found at Corlea, indications of the use of other tools could be seen. Knives, chisels and gouges were used in the manufacture of the wooden vessels, and some sort of fine drill must have been used to bore the longitudinal perforation through the knife-handle and to make the tiny dowel holes and the thin mortices of the mysterious composite object of ash referred to above. The smooth and polished surface of this object could imply the use of a plane or spoke-shave. It is possible, too, that a fine saw was used to shape this piece, though there was no specific evidence of this. The existence of the saw about this time is, however, indicated by the marks on a bone object from Dún Ailinne, Co. Kildare.

Spinning and weaving are likely to have been widely practised and, as a consequence, dying – using the materials of nature – must have been a standard activity. Only in three instances, however, have tiny fragments of textile of probable Iron Age date been recognized adhering to objects of bronze. Two are from burials, at Carrowbeg North, Co. Galway and Betaghstown (Bettystown), Co. Meath; the third is on a mount from Navan Fort, Co. Armagh. The textiles are probably linen and they are technically described as tabby weaves. An exception is one of the fragments from Betaghstown which is part of a very fine gauze or net, probably of horsehair, woven in tabby.

The absence of loom weights suggests that only the horizontal loom was in operation, as in the later Bronze Age. A few spindle whorls survive and there are two so-called weaving combs. Their function as combs has, however, been disputed, and it is possible that they were used for carding the wool.

fig. 68

There can be little doubt that leather was another substance used for many purposes in every Iron Age home in the country. Leather was used to make capes and head gear, shoes, belts and horse-harnesses, as well as a wide range of

68 Iron Age weaving combs of bone (a) and horn (b), from Navan Fort (Site A), Co. Armagh and Glassamucky Brakes, Co. Dublin respectively.

a

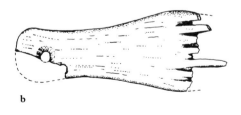

b

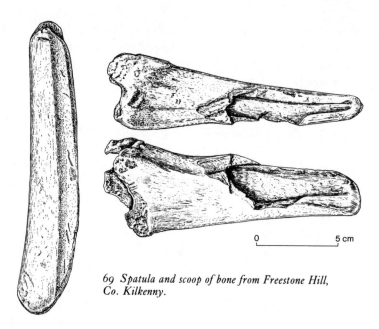

0   5 cm

69 Spatula and scoop of bone from Freestone Hill,
Co. Kilkenny.

containers such as pouches, satchels, bags and knapsacks. Leather containers
might also have been used to boil water and to provide storage containers
within the home. Slings, if they existed, would have been of leather, and Iron
Age warriors probably also possessed leather scabbards and sheaths.

fig. 97 For all of this there is only scanty surviving evidence. The three bronze
horns from Cork, presumably the remains of a ceremonial headpiece, are said to
have had fragments of leather adhering to them when found. A bronze strap-
tag from Rathgall, Co. Wicklow undoubtedly once adorned the end of a leather
belt. Most striking evidence of the use of leather is, however, provided by the
fig. 89 leather-covered wooden shield from Clonoura, Co. Tipperary. This object,
made of an alder plank, is covered on each face by a sheet of leather drawn
tightly across the surface and secured by narrow binding strips stitched in place
by means of thin leather thongs.

It is possible that the spatulae made of polished animal ribs with rounded
ends from the fourth-century hilltop site of Freestone Hill, Co. Kilkenny may
fig. 69 have been used in the process of tanning hides and the two large, heavy iron
needles from the same site could also have been used for stitching leather. A
needle of pig bone from Dún Ailinne, Co. Kildare could have been similarly
used.

The working of bone must have been another virtually ubiquitous domestic
craft which has left few traces in the material record. The hilt-fittings of
swords, as far as we can tell, were generally of bone or antler, and most of the
smaller domestic cutting implements and other tools, few of which have
survived, probably also had handles made of the same materials. Pins, needles
and weaving implements of bone have been found, and the site at Freestone
fig. 69 Hill also produced a range of scoops made of cattle bones. But the largest
collection of Iron Age bone artifacts comes from the passage tomb chamber at

Lough Crew, Co. Meath. There, almost 5000 fragments of carefully made, highly polished rib-bones were found, some bearing engraved compass ornament. Their purpose is unknown (see below) but they display great delicacy of workmanship which, along with the ornament on them, underlines their special character. The remains of twelve finely made bone combs were also recovered from Lough Crew. These are smaller and finer than the so-called weaving combs, and are likely to have been for personal use.

Bone was also used for items generally regarded as gaming pieces. These include dice, small rectangular plaques and the remains of a pegged board game found in a grave at Knowth, Co. Meath. The dice are not cubical like Roman (and modern) examples. They belong to a class referred to as parallelopiped and are, on average, twice as long as they are broad. The ends were plain and the four faces usually had values 3, 4, 5 and 6. Thus they can never have been intended for use in the manner of the cubical dice. Two plaques, one from a *pl. 41* burial at Cush, Co. Limerick, the other, devoid of context, from Mentrim Lough, Co. Westmeath, bear finely engraved ornament on each flat face and on *fig. 70* both of these, and on the two narrow edges, the same values as those on the dice (i.e. 3, 4, 5 and 6) are present. Here, even more than in the case of the dice, it is evident that these objects were not intended to be thrown. It may be that they were used in some sort of guessing game.

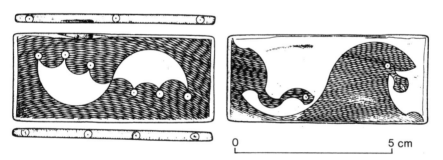

70 Two faces of a decorated bone gaming piece found at Mentrim Lough, Co. Meath.

The production of food

Food production, inevitably, was the principal preoccupation of the mass of the people and, as in all pre-industrial societies, took up much of their waking day. The main Celtic festivals were related to critical phases of the annual agricultural cycle. Lughnasa, the greatest feast, was a celebration of the successful harvest.

The evidence for agricultural activity during the centuries of the pagan Iron Age is rather surprising. For in several parts of the country, pollen studies in raised bogs strongly suggest that an actual decline in agricultural activity may have taken place during this period. Investigations in Red Bog, Co. Louth and Littleton Bog, Co. Tipperary are particularly informative, and the results have

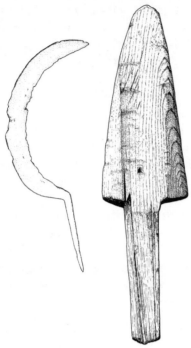

71 *(Far left)* *Iron sickle from Lisnacrogher, Co. Antrim. c. 2/5.*

72 *(Left)* *Wooden ard-head found under timbers of the Corlea road. c. 1/5.*

been repeated elsewhere. The picture that emerges seems to suggest that after a period of forest clearance and agriculture in the later Bronze Age, the evidence of agriculture gradually fades away. Weeds traditionally associated with cultivation disappear, then cereals and bracken. At the same time grass and plantain fall in value. Simultaneously, hazel values begin to rise, followed by increases in the pollens of ash, elm and oak. The low value of herbaceous pollen suggests that there must have been a considerable expansion of secondary woodland, leaving only restricted areas of the countryside still open. It was not until about the third century AD that this situation was again reversed with what seems to have been a dramatic expansion of agriculture. At Corlea, too, the botanical evidence indicates a significant increase in hazel scrub shortly before the construction of the Iron Age road in 148 BC, which continued unabated for several centuries. This implies again that the clearings were being filled with secondary forest growth, hinting once more at a decline in agriculture. Lesser rises in elm and ash at this time may be further evidence of such a decline. The decrease in oak pollen evident at Corlea could well reflect the extent of oak clearance necessary for the construction of the road.

Agriculture may have declined during the centuries of the Iron Age but it would be quite wrong to imagine that it ceased altogether. Moreover, we should not forget that the picture emerging from a small number of individual bogs is not necessarily representative of all areas of the country. However, there are some archaeological indications which may lend support to this theory. The excavations at Dún Ailinne for example produced no more than thirteen identifiable barley grains, a tiny amount despite the very large area excavated,

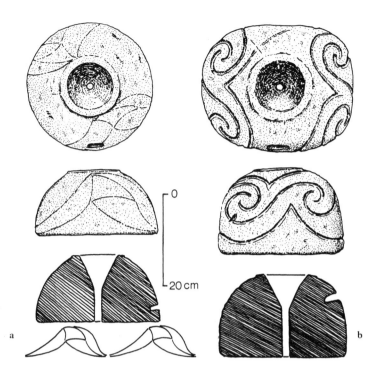

73 *Upper stones of beehive rotary querns from (a) Clonmacnoise in Co. Offaly and (b) Ticooly-O'Kelly in Co. Galway.*

a

b

and in sharp contrast with the 19,000 animal bones recovered from the site. This may simply reflect the ceremonial character of the hilltop enclosure, but it could equally be seen as a symptom of a decline in agricultural activity during the Iron Age.

As well as the thirteen seeds of barley, Dún Ailinne also yielded a sizeable quantity of hazelnut shells. This is a useful plant food as it is storable and rich in protein, fat and carbohydrates. Some wild plant seeds were also found – some of which are probably weeds associated with cultivation but others, such as pale persicara (*Polygonum persicaria*) and goosefoot (*Chenopodium album*), may have been deliberately collected to supplement the diet. Grains of barley, rye and oats, dating perhaps to a Bronze Age/Iron Age transitional phase were recovered from a pit at Carrowmore, Co. Sligo.

We can thus reconstruct something of the pattern of agriculture in Iron Age Ireland, but what of agricultural techniques? A single iron sickle has been recovered from the Co. Antrim bog deposit of Lisnacrogher. The only example *fig. 77* of its type yet discovered in the country, it could have been used for reaping cereals. A wooden ardhead, dated to the middle of the second century BC by its association with the Corlea roadway, demonstrates the type of ploughing implement in use in Ireland at this time. Closely similar, unassociated bog finds *fig. 72:* pl. 42 of ards from Gortygeeheen, Co. Clare and possibly Attavally, Co. Mayo pl. 43 (though one commentator has suggested that the latter could, in fact, be a spade) are likely to be of similar date. An example from Gortnacartglebe, Co. Donegal has been radiocarbon dated to the fourth–third centuries BC. These objects, all of oak, had a long shaft and a sub-triangular head which was flattened on one side, gently convex on the other. They were mounted in a curved wooden frame (the beam) which was drawn by oxen and may have had a narrow oak blade (the foreshare) attached. Experiments have shown that such implements were surprisingly efficient and could plough to a depth of 20 cm.

The only other evidence in the archaeological record for agricultural pursuits is provided by the extensive range of rotary quernstones from the *fig. 73*: pl. 44 country. Such items, developed in Europe during the Iron Age, represent a major advance on the long-established method of grinding the grain manually on a saddle quern. There is some discussion as to when the rotary quern was introduced to Ireland, whether it was in the centuries before or after the birth of Christ. There is also discussion as to which of the two main types, the disc quern (the upper stone of which is a flattened disc shape) or the beehive quern (with taller, beehive-shaped upper stone) is the earlier. Outside the country it was generally the disc quern, lighter and easier to use, which replaced the more cumbersome beehive. It seems therefore reasonable to suggest that in Ireland, too, the beehive quern was the older.

Over 200 of these objects are now known, spread across the northern two-thirds of the country. They are unknown in the south, which has given rise to interesting speculation concerning their cultural significance (see below). The number of extant specimens is indicative of a degree of agricultural intensity not hinted at in the available pollen evidence. There are, however, reasons to believe that the introduction of the beehive quern could date some time after the birth of Christ. Its appearance in Ireland might, therefore, reflect the suggested period of agricultural resurgence in the second or third century AD.

The beehive querns are composed of a lower, flattened disc, generally between 28 cm and 36 cm in diameter, upon which rotates a heavier, vertically-perforated bun or beehive-shaped stone from which comes their distinctive name. The upper stone has a cylindrical boring, which is either vertical or horizontal, into which a wooden handle was inserted. The latter was used to facilitate the rotation of the upper stone on a metal spindle. The corn was fed through the perforation at the top and ground with relative ease to a fine meal.

Objects of this type were probably a standard item in the dwelling places of prosperous farmers and, like the microwave oven of today, must have been a revolutionary time- and labour-saving device in the home. No single example, however, has come from a settlement context: the quernstones are almost exclusively from bogs. Furthermore, many appear to be scarcely worn, begging the inevitable questions as to how and why they came to be deposited in the first place. Is there a ritual element in their deposition, or is the explanation for their abandonment to be sought in their rapid replacement by the lighter, more easily used disc querns, the introduction of which would speedily have made the beehive variant obsolete? The obvious association of the quernstone with food production and the harvest, and the frequency with which these are found in wet places, with no apparent occupational association, strongly suggests that many could have been laid down in the context of votive activities.

The practice of agriculture by a community presupposes the existence of field enclosures of some type to protect the crops from wandering farm-stock and from the depredations of deer. Such are known as early as the Neolithic period in western areas of Ireland, and extensive systems of fields of Iron Age date have been recognized in Britain and elsewhere. Although an Iron Age date has been proposed for a number of early field systems in Ireland, notably those at Cush, Co. Limerick, in no case has such a date been fully proven.

Animal husbandry was probably the dominant food producing activity during much of the pre-Christian Iron Age. Certainly, in the early literature there is a heavy emphasis on the importance of cattle in contemporary society. Cattle were a major element in determining the status of an individual, and cattle were in effect a unit of currency. Cattle raiding was undoubtedly endemic and, as is well known, the greatest of the Irish epic sagas – the Ulster Cycle – has a bull hunt as its central theme, whatever its deeper, mythological undertones.

The most recent and most detailed examination of Iron Age faunal remains in Ireland has been carried out by P.J. Crabtree on the animal bones from Dún Ailinne, Co. Kildare. Here, the great majority of the 19,000 identified bones belonged to cattle and pigs, while sheep and horse were poorly represented. Of the identified fragments, 53.9% were those of cattle, 36.3% were pig; sheep/goat bones comprised only 7.3% and those of horse as little as 2.5%. Only three bones were certainly those of dog, and the same number of bones belonged to red deer. Since all the skeletal parts of the main domesticated species were present, we can surmise that the animals had been driven up to the hilltop and slaughtered on the spot.

The cattle at Dún Ailinne had withers' heights ranging from 1.07 to 1.15 m, measurements in keeping with the size of Iron Age cattle outside the country. A sheep wither's height of 59 cm is also typical of animals of this period. The small size of the horses represented at the site has already been noted.

Butchery marks were noted on 126 of the Dún Ailinne animal bones. These consisted of fine knife cuts, heavy chop marks and axial splitting of the long bones and first phalanges, probably for marrow extraction. Almost all such marks occurred on the bones of cattle. Of the head, the mandible was the most commonly butchered cranial element. Forelimbs and hind limbs were also butchered and on the feet, the disarticulation of the hock joint is marked by transverse knife cuts by which the marrow was extracted.

There is some discussion about the function of the cattle herds. Crabtree's analysis of the bones from Dún Ailinne led her to conclude that cattle were kept in ancient Ireland primarily for dairying rather than for meat. She based this assertion on the age/sex ratio of the animals represented. Although the sample for study was small, she pointed to an apparent preponderance on the one hand of animals of six months and less (71.2%), and on the other of elderly adults which were mostly females. She saw this as consistent with dairy production where, she argued, a high proportion of calves are killed early in life and the elderly, adult females are killed when they can no longer give milk. Crabtree felt that if meat production were intended then there should have been a greater number of adolescent and young adult cattle present.

More recently, however, Crabtree's conclusions have been flatly contradicted by Finbar McCormick who argued that cattle will not give milk unless calves are present. Thus, he suggested, the presence of so many calf remains in the Dún Aillinne faunal assemblage pointed to the rearing of drystock cattle for meat. It may be, therefore, that it was not until the beginning of the early historic period that dairying became widespread in the country.

Another recently excavated site with a significant Iron Age presence is Navan Fort, Co. Armagh. It is not, however, possible clearly to differentiate between Bronze Age and Iron Age levels there. The overwhelming dominance of pig remains is nonetheless of interest in view of the presumed ritual character at least of the later phases of activity there and of the known importance of the pig in Celtic mythology and cult. The only other relevant, excavated sites are Feerwore and Freestone Hill. Unfortunately, the early faunal analysis done at these sites was unsatisfactory. Thus we can only say that cattle, pigs, sheep/ goat, horses and dogs were present. As regards the last, the remains suggest that at Feerwore dogs of Alsatian type were represented while at Freestone Hill the dogs were smaller than an Alsatian and larger than a greyhound.

Other faunal evidence for domestic animals is slight. Cattle ribs were used at Freestone Hill and at Lough Crew to fashion polished artifacts and, in one instance, the grip of a sword from Lough Gur, Co. Limerick has been identified as a carved sheep's metatarsal. Three dice of horse bone were found in one of the inhumations outside the Knowth, Co. Meath passage tomb, and horse hair was used in the manufacture of the supposed hair-net found in one of the burials at Betaghstown, Co. Meath. Obviously, too, the very frequency of horse trappings in the country may be taken as confirmation of the widespread use of the horse in Iron Age Ireland; the scarcity of horse bones at excavated sites is not surprising for these valuable animals would rarely have been eaten other than in exceptional circumstances.

The bones of wild animals are of minimal significance in the surviving faunal assemblages. Red deer was present in small quantities at Freestone Hill, Feerwore and Dún Ailinne. Remains of a single hare were found at Freestone Hill, and at Feerwore archaeologists identified the remains of hare, as well as the fox, badger and probably wolf. None of these sites appear to have yielded bird remains, and in no instance were the bones of fish detected. The bones of the Barbary ape from Navan Fort are, of course, unique.

While there is no direct evidence that the honey from wild bees was gathered in Iron Age Ireland (as was clearly the case in the early historic period), it is highly likely that it *was* – not merely for consumption of the honey itself, but perhaps for the manufacture of alcoholic beverages such as mead, traces of which were discovered in the great cauldron in the early fifth-century BC burial at Hochdorf in Germany. Bees would also have been important in providing the beeswax needed to make the models in *cire perdue* casting (see below p. 152).

Another commodity which must have been used in Ireland is salt. In Britain and on mainland Europe, extensive evidence for salt production during the

Iron Age is provided by containers and troughs and other fragmentary items of clay, as well as varied assemblages of industrial waste. While such evidence continues to elude us in Ireland, salt must have been vitally important here, especially for the preservation of meat for winter.

Personal adornment

The considerable vanity of the Celtic peoples and their delight in gaudy ostentation is often referred to in the Classical writings. In this the Irish epic tales are in full agreement, and across the European mainland, in hundreds of inhumation graves, this picture is comprehensively confirmed. Neck ornaments of varying types, especially the so-called buffer torcs, were commonly worn, by both men and women (though more often by the latter, it seems), and these became symbols of status worn by gods as well as mortals. An extensive range of safety-pin brooches (fibulae), generally of bronze or iron, are also encountered in the burials and these are often castings of the highest quality. They were used, for the most part, to fasten a garment on the shoulder. Armlets, wristlets and anklets were also widely worn and beads of glass, amber and other substances have been recovered in their thousands. The Iron Age Celts wore elaborate and ornate belt fittings too and sometimes earrings – though the latter are less common.

The wealth and variety of personal ornament encountered on the Continent, and also in Britain, is not matched by the Irish evidence. Only a small number of such items is known from the country, some from graves, a few from habitation deposits, the majority, however, devoid of archaeological context.

The use of mirrors in the country is indicated by the discovery of two examples. The first, of iron, is from Lambay Island, Co. Dublin and is probably an import (p. 201). The other, from Ballymoney, Co. Antrim is an ornate bronze casting (see pl. 46). The fine bone combs from Lough Crew are likely to have been for personal use and an iron shears from a burial at Carbury Hill, Co. Kildare might have served to cut the hair of humans rather than the wool of sheep (see *fig. 74*). The Celts, of course, paid special attention to their hair and often dyed it. Strabo, for example, tells us that 'their hair is not only naturally blond, but they also use artificial means to increase this natural quality of colour. For they continually wash their hair with lime-wash and draw it back from the forehead to the crown and to the nape of the neck' and it became so thickened that 'it differs in no way from a horse's mane'. The Irish hero Cú Chulainn, too, had hair which was stiff and of three shades: dark at the roots, brown near the middle and fair at the ends, doubtless also as a result of lime-washing. Women also used personal make-up and the Roman poet Propertius, writing in the last decades of the last century BC, castigates his mistress Cynthia for making up in the manner of the Celts.

We can say little about contemporary clothing apart from the certainty that textiles were worn. Outside Ireland the evidence clearly indicates that brightly dyed garments were commonplace, the men wearing a shirt or tunic with

74 Iron shears found in a burial deposit at Carbury Hill, Co. Kildare. 1/2.

trousers, the women long dresses. Heavy cloaks of sheeps' wool would have been carried. The type was highly prized on the Continent and these were, in fact, exported from Gaul to the Mediterranean. A bog body from Castleblakeney, Co. Galway, shows that capes of deerskin were worn (p. 188). Of shoes there is no trace. A bronze strap tag from Rathgall, Co. Wicklow and pairs of rings from cremation burials at Carrowjames, Co. Mayo and Carbury Hill are probably belt-fittings. Several of the bronze rings from Lisnacrogher are also likely to have been part of a belt. As earlier noted, one of the bodies interred at Betaghstown appears to have worn a hair-net.

Without doubt the neck ornaments, notably those of gold, stand out as the most spectacular objects of personal adornment from the country. The majority, however, appear to be of foreign manufacture. The gold buffer torc from Knock, Co. Roscommon (the 'Clonmacnoise' torc) is a superb example pl. 45 of early La Tène Continental craftsmanship. The bar torcs and the gold-pl. 36 wire necklaces from the Broighter hoard are also non-native. The latter are likely to be of early Roman manufacture and probably derive ultimately from the Mediterranean area. The bar torcs could be from eastern England but their origin is not certain. The bronze beaded torc from Lambay is certainly fig. 127 English.

Of likely native construction is the splendid gold buffer torc found at fig. 75 Broighter, and the ribbon torc discovered with the Knock object may also be a fig. 76 local product. A similar specimen, a few centuries later in date, was found in a fig. 76 hoard of metalwork at Somerset, Co. Galway and some of the many other unassociated ribbon torcs from the country could also belong to the Iron Age. Their dating as a group is a matter for some discussion, however, as they appear to originate in the Middle Bronze Age, to disappear in the Late Bronze Age and to reappear in the Iron Age. We do not yet know if the latest examples represent the reactivation of older, indigenous traditions or if the type was stimulated anew by external influences. There is also uncertainty as to whether the gold buffer torcs were made for personal use or were, from the beginning, objects of votive significance. Their final deposition in wet places is, at any rate, likely to have been carried out for ritual purposes.

These fine neck ornaments are clearly exceptional pieces in the Irish Iron Age. More widespread, though still not numerous, are the dress-fasteners of various forms. These include the safety-pin fibula, perhaps the most characteristic item of La Tène Europe, the related fibula of so-called Navan type and the ring-headed pin. The conventional three-fold typological division long established for La Tène fibulae on the Continent has little direct relevance for the Irish series since in Ireland almost all surviving examples are of manifestly local fabrication. Influences from outside are, of course, evident, probably emanating from southern England and possibly even from the European mainland. Both archaism and innovation are features of the Irish fibulae so that close dating is generally difficult. Most, however, are of essentially late La Tène character dating to around, or shortly after, the birth of Christ.

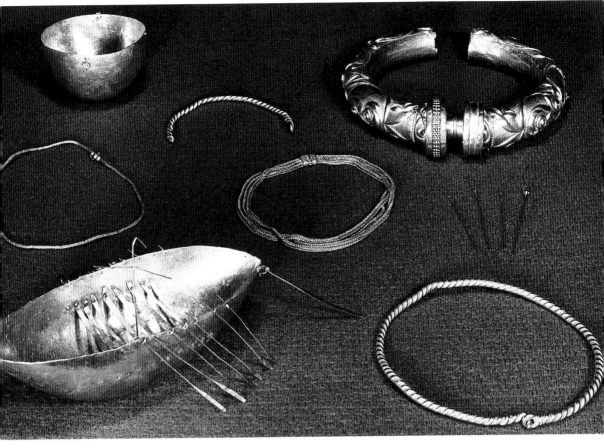

36 This famous hoard of gold objects was unearthed in a field at Broighter, Co. Derry during ploughing in 1896. Particularly splendid are the torc or neck-ring, and the exquisite model boat complete with oars, seats and mast (incidentally the earliest evidence of the use of the sail by Irish seafarers). Length of boat 19.6 cm.

FACING PAGE

40 (*Above*) An unusual bronze-bound wooden tankard found at Carrickfergus in Co. Antrim, probably imported during the first century AD by a local noble. Ht 13.4 cm.

41 (*Below*) Like wood, bone is a perishable material, so this bone gaming piece is quite a rare find. It was discovered at Cush in Co. Limerick, in a burial deposit beneath a tumulus. Length 2.8 cm.

THIS PAGE

37,38 Cauldrons had both practical and ritual use in Iron Age Ireland. (*Top*) Sheet-bronze cauldron of so-called projecting-bellied form, from Ballymoney, Co. Antrim; ht 49.5 cm. (*Above*) Sheet-bronze cauldron of globular form, from Ballyedmond, Co. Galway; ht 43.2 cm.

39 (*Right*) A bronze cup-handle with splendid bird's-head casting, from Somerset in Co. Galway. Max. length 6.1 cm.

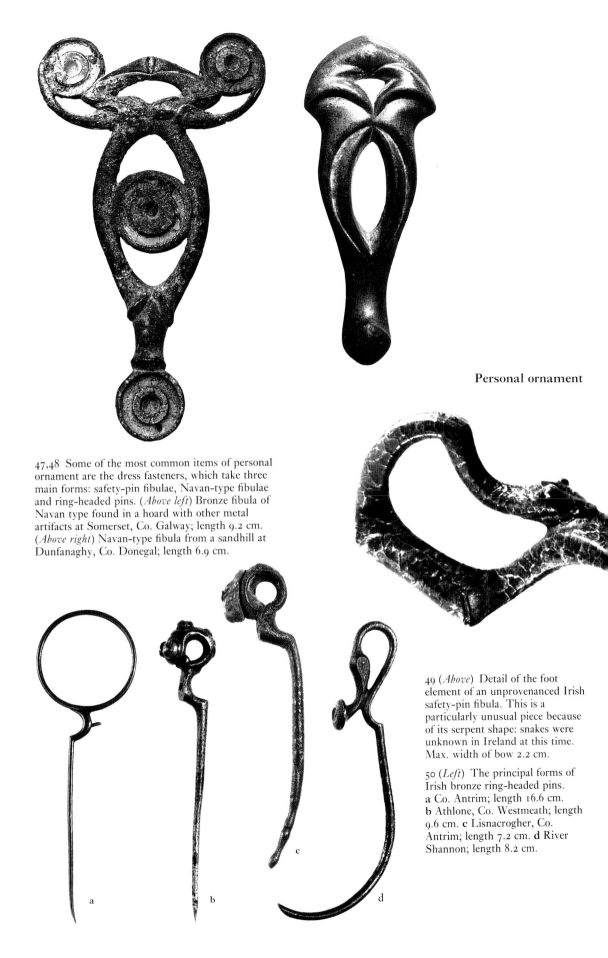

Personal ornament

47,48 Some of the most common items of personal ornament are the dress fasteners, which take three main forms: safety-pin fibulae, Navan-type fibulae and ring-headed pins. (*Above left*) Bronze fibula of Navan type found in a hoard with other metal artifacts at Somerset, Co. Galway; length 9.2 cm. (*Above right*) Navan-type fibula from a sandhill at Dunfanaghy, Co. Donegal; length 6.9 cm.

49 (*Above*) Detail of the foot element of an unprovenanced Irish safety-pin fibula. This is a particularly unusual piece because of its serpent shape: snakes were unknown in Ireland at this time. Max. width of bow 2.2 cm.

50 (*Left*) The principal forms of Irish bronze ring-headed pins. a Co. Antrim; length 16.6 cm. b Athlone, Co. Westmeath; length 9.6 cm. c Lisnacrogher, Co. Antrim; length 7.2 cm. d River Shannon; length 8.2 cm.

Objects of vanity

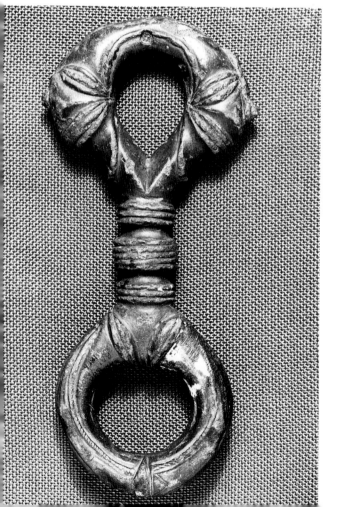

45 (*Above*) Golf buffer torc, found with
another gold ribbon torc in Ardnaglug bog
at Knock, Co. Roscommon. Internal
diameter 12.9 cm. Originally produced on
the Continent and subsequently imported
into Ireland, this ornament is a fine example
of early La Tène art. (Formerly known as
the Clonmacnoise torc.)

46 (*Left*) A decorated bronze mirror handle
with a stylized bird's head on the upper
loop; from Ballybogey bog, Ballymoney, Co.
Antrim. Length 11.5 cm.

Food production

42,43 These wooden ards originally had long shafts attached to a wooden frame which was drawn by oxen. (*Top*) Oak ard-head from Corlea, Co. Longford; about 45 cm long. (*Above*) From Gortygeeheen, Co. Clare; length 97 cm.

44 (*Below*) Decorated upper stone of a beehive rotary quern from Ticooly-O'Kelly, Co. Galway; max. width 33.6 cm. Turning the stone on a flat disc using a wooden handle, the user would have poured corn through the top hole and ground it to a fine flour.

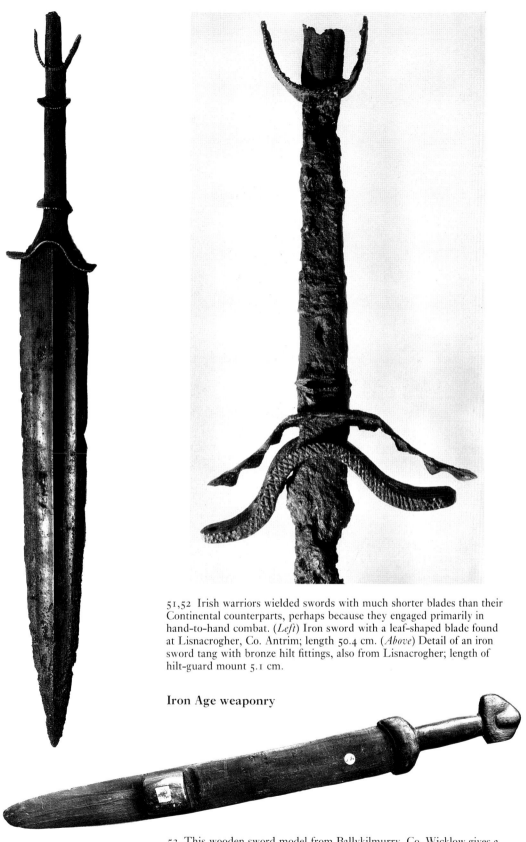

51,52 Irish warriors wielded swords with much shorter blades than their Continental counterparts, perhaps because they engaged primarily in hand-to-hand combat. (*Left*) Iron sword with a leaf-shaped blade found at Lisnacrogher, Co. Antrim; length 50.4 cm. (*Above*) Detail of an iron sword tang with bronze hilt fittings, also from Lisnacrogher; length of hilt-guard mount 5.1 cm.

Iron Age weaponry

53 This wooden sword model from Ballykilmurry, Co. Wicklow gives a good indication of the original appearance of a complete Iron Age sword in Ireland. Length 51 cm.

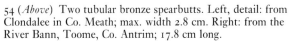

54 (*Above*) Two tubular bronze spearbutts. Left, detail: from Clondalee in Co. Meath; max. width 2.8 cm. Right: from the River Bann, Toome, Co. Antrim; 17.8 cm long.

55 (*Right*) Bronze scabbard chape (length 9.5 cm) and detail of a decorated scabbard-plate (max. width 4.5 cm), both from Lisnacrogher.

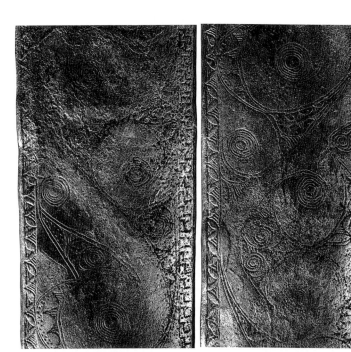

56 Details of a decorated bronze scabbard-plate from the River Bann. The engraved design is one of the finest of its kind. Max. width 3.5 cm.

75 Drawing of the gold buffer torc from Broighter, Co. Derry, and details showing the complexity of its decoration. c. 3/5.

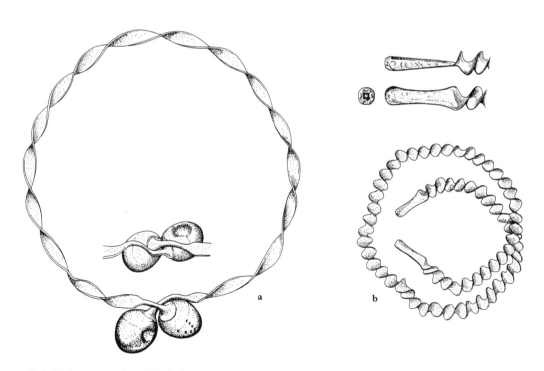

a

b

76 Gold ribbon torcs from Knock, Co. Roscommon (a) and Somerset, Co. Galway (b). c. 1/2.

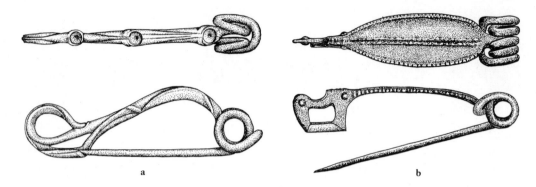

77 Irish bronze safety-pin fibulae. (a) From Clogher, Co. Tyrone; (b) no provenance. 3/4.

There are about thirty safety-pin fibulae of La Tène-type known from the country. These can be divided into two principal forms, those with a rod bow *fig. 77* and those with a bow of leaf shape. All are of bronze with the exception of two iron specimens. Some are made by hammering a metal rod to the required shape, others have been skilfully cast. The spring portion is of tightly coiled wire. This was the vulnerable point and several examples are broken here. In three instances a secondary spring was riveted in place after the original had snapped.

In several cases the foot section, into which the pin fitted, is cast in the form *pl. 49* of a stylized bird's head. This is an archaic Continental feature which was popular with the Irish brooch makers. Decoration is otherwise sparse. One *fig. 77* example stands out, however, from Clogher, Co. Tyrone. It is a beautiful casting, quite unlike any of the other Irish specimens, its bow curving in an

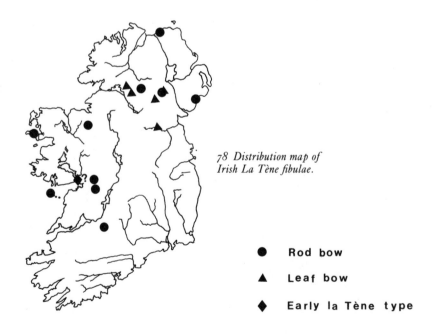

78 Distribution map of Irish La Tène fibulae.

● Rod bow

▲ Leaf bow

◆ Early la Tène type

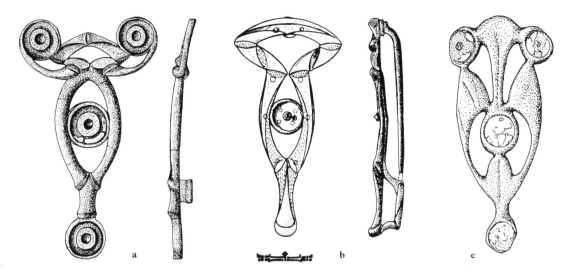

79 Bronze brooches of Navan type from (a) Somerset, Co. Galway, 2/3; (b) Navan Fort, Co. Armagh, 2/3; and Lough Ree, Co. Longford/Westmeath, 1/1.

elegant loop to a doubled foot. Three tiny circular settings on foot and bow once held inlays of red enamel and linking these are delicate, raised, sinuous trumpet curves. The object retains its golden patina, thus giving an impression of its former glory. Technically and artistically this is a special piece which was without doubt crafted to grace the cloak of a noble.

Safety-pin fibulae are thinly scattered across the La Tène regions of Ireland. *fig. 78* Apart from two examples from coastal sand-dunes of the northeast, they are unknown east of the Bann. In south-central Ulster, especially in the Clogher Valley, there is a significant concentration, especially of leaf-bow specimens, which were a speciality of this region, perhaps even of a single workshop. Otherwise, apart from one rustic-looking specimen from Co. Limerick, fibulae (though no leaf-bow types) are confined to areas west of the Shannon.

A small group of bronze dress fasteners – related to, but differing in form from, the safety-pin fibula – is the Navan-type brooch, so-called because two of *fig. 79: pls. 47, 48* the six known examples are recorded as coming from Navan Fort in Co. Armagh. These have an open-work bow with insets for red enamel in three instances. Four of the six had a pin attached at the back by means of a ball-socket mechanism. One has an imitation spring with the pin secured on a horizontal spindle. Raised trumpet ornament is a characteristic feature of these brooches. The type, which has been found in Armagh, Donegal, Galway and Westmeath, is unknown outside Ireland.

Ring-headed pins typically consist of a ring-head, an angled shoulder section *fig. 80* and a straight or curving shank. They are of bronze and, with one possible exception, are cast. Though inspiration for the development of this form of dress fastener may have come from southern or western areas of Britain the

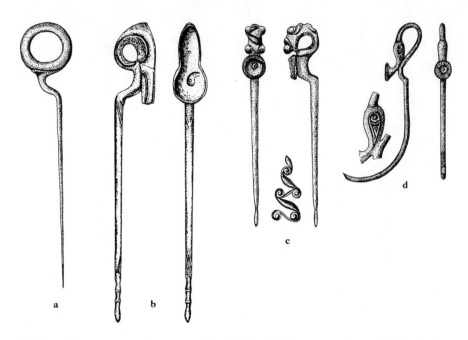

Irish craft centres, as always, rapidly devised their own variants. Indeed, pins of Irish type were occasionally exported to Britain. There are about 37 examples recorded from Ireland.

fig. 80: pl. 50

Simplest, and possibly the earliest, are those with a ring which, apart from being occasionally ribbed or knobbed, is plain. These are closest to the presumed British prototypes. Wholly Irish are those with spirals, bosses and leaf patterns cast in relief on the ring-head and which possess prominent

fig. 80: pl. 50

settings on the shoulder for red enamel inlays. Another Irish development consists of pins which originally had domed enamel studs riveted into settings

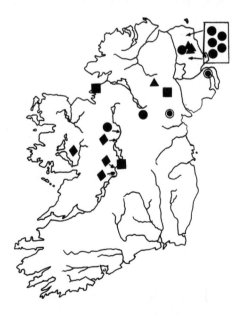

80 (*Above*) *Principal types of Irish bronze ring-headed pins. (a) No provenance; (b) 'Roscavey', Co. Tyrone; (c) Grange, Co. Sligo; (d) River Shannon. 1/2.*

81 (*Left*) *Distribution map of Irish ring-headed pins.*

●   **Type 1**

■   **Type 2**

▲   **Type 3**

◆   **Type 4**

◎   **Miscellaneous pins**

on head and shoulder. A range of miscellaneous forms including those with *fig. 80*: pl. 50
rings transformed into stylized bird heads and those with sharply curving pins
is also known.

Ring-headed pins are noticeably concentrated in Co. Antrim – an area in *fig. 81*
which the safety-pin fibula is virtually absent. In other parts of the country too,
particularly in the west, there is little distributional overlap between the two
forms of dress fastener. It is not clear, however, if this distinction is
chronological or cultural, or if it is to be explained in terms of regional fashions.

Personal ornament of demonstrably Iron Age date from Ireland is otherwise
scarce. A few bronze bracelets are known, at least one of which, from Newry in
Co. Down, is an imported piece. Bracelets of jet and glass are occasionally
found and there are a few spiral rings of bronze, for finger (or toe) adornment. A
female buried at Feerwore may have been wearing earrings. Glass beads were
certainly worn and a wide variety is known from Ireland ranging from tiny blue
examples to large beads with inlays of 'eyes', spirals and whirls. Beads of bone
and, occasionally, stone were also used. In one case, a burial at Carrowbeg
North, Co. Galway, a female skeleton wore an anklet of bone beads. On the
shoulder of the same skeleton lay a flattened cylindrical container of bronze. Its
purpose is unknown but it could have been a locket or charm perhaps originally
containing some perishable substance.

Weapons and warfare

The enduring image of Celtic society which emerges from the written sources,
both vernacular and Classical, is of a society dominated by a warrior caste
which is fierce and quarrelsome, recklessly brave in battle and exceedingly
prickly on points of personal honour. The Irish tales in particular present us
with a culture in which warfare is endemic, where fighting is based on
individual prowess, and where set-piece confrontations take place between
selected champions. Among these people warfare was almost a ritualized sport
with a well-defined code of conduct.

Across the European mainland, a warrior class is clearly recognizable in the
archaeological record. In all areas where La Tène cemeteries occur, burials of *fig. 3*
heavily armed adult males are a constantly recurring feature. The combined
evidence of archaeology and the written sources enables us to envisage, without
difficulty, the boastful, strutting warriors engaged in their lethal pursuits.

Scattered weapons, including swords, spears and spear-fittings, indicate that
a warrior class existed in Ireland, even though the quantity of such items is not
great. Slings are not recorded in the archaeological record (though they may
well have existed), and helmets are also unknown. Two horned bronze items of
headgear (see p. 155) were almost certainly intended for occasions of ceremony
rather than for use on the field of battle.

Swords of likely Iron Age date from Ireland now number around 30. Their *fig. 82*
blade lengths are surprisingly short, varying from a maximum of 46 cm to as
little as 37 cm. This is in sharp contrast with the long swords used by Celtic

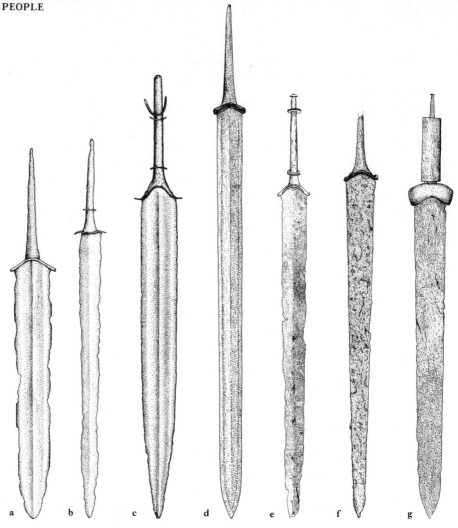

82 Examples of Irish La Tène swords from (a,b) Edenderry, Co. Offaly; (c) Lisnacrogher, Co. Antrim; (d) Ballinderry, Co. Westmeath; (e) Cashel, Co. Sligo; (f) Dún Ailinne, Co. Kildare; (g) no provenance. c. 1/4.

peoples abroad, and clearly indicates the local character of the Irish weapons. The shortness of the Irish swords may indicate their intended use for stabbing and hacking in close hand-to-hand combat.

The swords possess blades which are leaf-shaped, triangular or parallel-sided. The first are likely to be the earliest. Occasionally there are mid-ribs and a few have longitudinal grooves or ribbing. Hilts are of antler or, in one instance, sheep bone, and hilt-guards of antler are also known. Flattened oval pommels of antler are occasionally preserved. At the top of the blade there is a separately made hilt-guard-plate, usually of bronze, and normally bell-shaped. The best indication of the original appearance of a typical Irish La Tène sword is provided by a wooden model from Ballykilmurry, Co. Wicklow. This object, though possessing an enigmatic half-cylindrical projection on the blade, allows

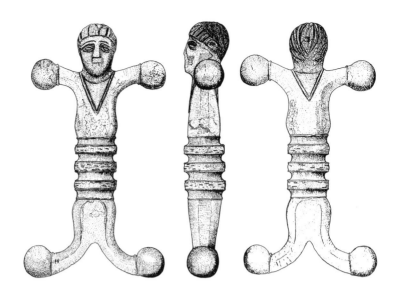

83 *Bronze anthropoid sword-hilt found in the sea at Ballyshannon, Co. Donegal. 1/2.*

us to observe in detail the original character of the hilt-fittings, most interestingly, the wooden version of the normally metal hilt-guard-plate which occurred between the organic hilt-guard and the blade.

Two swords stand apart from the rest as probable imports. One, surviving only as a series of rusted blade fragments, was recovered from the first-century cemetery at Lambay in Co. Dublin, and is part of a clearly intrusive assemblage. The other was raised from the sea in a fisherman's net at Ballyshannon Bay, Co. Donegal. It had a short, triangular iron blade, which is *fig. 83* now lost, and an elaborate grip of bronze, cast in the form of a stylized human figure. This type of anthropoid hilt is a late La Tène Continental type whose immediate origin is likely to have been western Gaul.

84 *Distribution maps of Irish La Tène swords (left) and scabbards (right).*

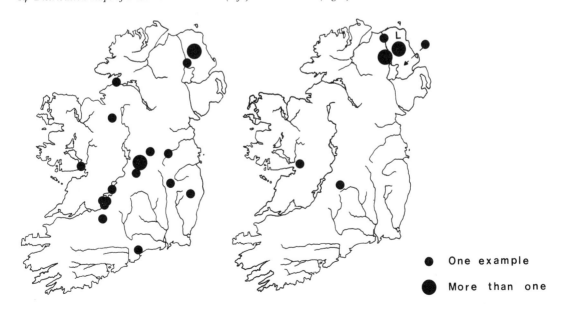

● One example

⬤ More than one

Of the scabbards in which the swords were carried only those of metal have survived. It is likely that examples of wood and leather also existed. Eight fragmentary scabbards have been found, four from Lisnacrogher, Co. Antrim, four from the River Bann (see pl. 55). Two scabbard chapes, which were fitted to the tips of the scabbards, have come from as far away as Galway and Tipperary. Only one scabbard is substantially complete (see *fig. 85*). It was made by folding the edges of one of the bronze sheets over the edges of the other with the cast-bronze, open-work chape fitted at the narrowed tip. Half way down the scabbard a suspension-loop was once attached. Three hollow, two-piece bronze rings from Lisnacrogher (see *fig. 86*) may have been part of the mechanism by which the scabbard was suspended from the belt: this is often the case on the European mainland. Six of the eight scabbard-plates bear engraved ornament along their length, and there can be little doubt that these objects are a product of specialist armouries established in the northeast of Ireland.

The spear was probably a weapon in widespread use during the Iron Age in Ireland. Unfortunately, as most examples are without archaeological context, an Iron Age dating for individual specimens is generally difficult to establish with confidence. A few, however, can be assigned to this period with little hesitation. These include several with leaf-shaped blades and a long iron specimen from Lisnacrogher, Co. Antrim, which has a blade length of 24 cm and a matted design of *rocked graver* ornament (see p. 157) on the base of the blade (see *fig. 87*). The same deposit produced a second iron spearhead and the remains of two wooden spearshafts, one of which, when found, is said to have been 2.4 m in length. Lisnacrogher also produced several cylindrical shaft mounts (see *fig. 87*), one of which was still attached to a spear-shaft (to which a knobbed bronze spearbutt was also fitted). In all, no fewer than 18 knobbed spearbutts came from this important site.

The total number of knobbed spearbutts from the country is now almost 50. They are a distinctively insular type known in parts of Britain, especially the north, as well as Ireland. Though moulds for the manufacture of such objects have been found in Scotland, the great numerical dominance of the type in Ireland argues strongly for an Irish origin. Two variants are known: a so-called Lisnacrogher type with ribbed socket, and a doorknob type with funnel-shaped socket (see *fig. 87*). The former is centred on the eponymous Lisnacrogher while the latter is most common west of the Shannon (*fig. 88*). Their function appears to have been to protect the base of the shaft from wear and breakage.

Other spearbutts in use during the Iron Age are in the form of long, tapering tubes of bronze which were either cast or hammered from sheet bronze (see *fig. 87*: pl. 54). These sometimes have cast or engraved decoration and a few originally had red enamel inlays. Most of these have been found in rivers, principally the Shannon and the Bann. The type appears to be an Irish development, as does the small group of cone- or trumpet-shaped butts which may also be of Iron Age date (see *fig. 87*). Tanged iron butts occur in a few instances but, while the type is known from Iron Age contexts abroad, in Ireland they continue later so that isolated specimens are undatable.

85 Bronze scabbard with chape attached, from Lisnacrogher, Co. Antrim. c. 1/3.

86 Hollow, bronze two-piece ring from Lisnacrogher. c. 3/5.

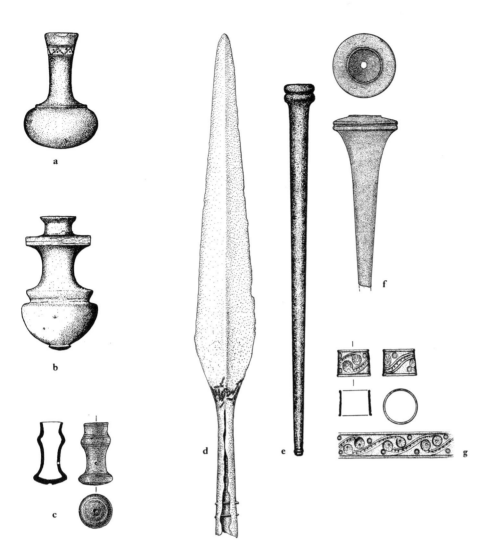

87 *Selection of Irish Iron Age spear fittings. (a–c) Knobbed spearbutts: no provenance; Coleraine, Co. Derry; and Lisnacrogher respectively. (d) Iron spearhead with rocked graver ornament from Lisnacrogher. (e) Tubular spearbutt, River Shannon. (f) Conical spearbutt from Ballybrit, Co. Galway. (g) Cylindrical spear ferrule found at Lisnacrogher. Various scales.*

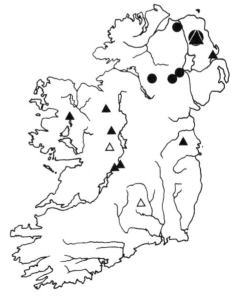

88 *Distribution map of knobbed spearbutts.*

▲ ● ◉   One example

▲ ● ◉ ▲   More than one

▲   Doorknob type
●   Lisnacrogher type

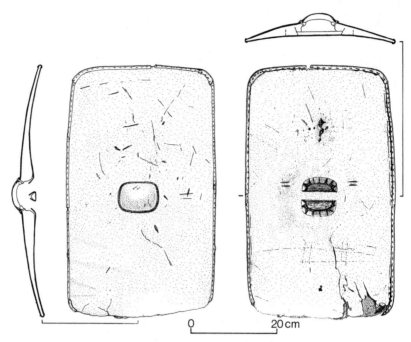

89 Leather-covered wooden shield discovered at Clonoura in Co. Tipperary. Battle scars are clearly visible on the front.

Shields are recorded in only two instances from Iron Age Ireland. The first survives as a bronze boss from the intrusive cemetery on Lambay Island, Co. Dublin. The other is a complete implement of wood and leather from Littleton

fig. 89 Bog, Clonoura, Co. Tipperary. It is a small, portable object, with dimensions of 57 by 35 cm, made of a gently convex board of alderwood covered on both sides by sheets of calf-hide. These are secured in position by strips of leather stitched around the edges of the object. A straight bar of oak, fitted across an oval opening at the centre of the shield, provided the grip and this was protected at the front by a domed wooden boss which was also held in place by a tight-fitting leather cover stitched to the alderwood board. At the back, on each side of the grip, a parallel pair of notches was cut into the leather for the attachment of thongs to carry it.

The front of the shield is scarred by ancient cuts and incisions which were doubtless sustained on the field of battle. Some are slash marks, others produced by stabbing. In several instances the point of a possible spearblade can be recognized. It is not unreasonable to assume that shields of this type were the norm in Iron Age Ireland, but these would rarely survive. Magnificent decorated implements such as those from the Witham and the Thames in England were never intended for practical defence in the vicious hacking and stabbing of Iron Age warfare. The Clonoura-type shield was light and manoeuvrable and would have effectively protected its owner from the blows of enemy weapons.

CHAPTER 7

Technology and Art

Gold is for the mistress – silver for the maid
Copper for the craftsman cunning at his trade.
'Good!' said the Baron, sitting in his hall,
'But Iron – Cold Iron – is master of them all.'
RUDYARD KIPLING (1865–1936)

Iron technology

One of the most important achievements of the Celtic peoples was the role they played in the widespread dissemination of iron technology across Europe. Even though this process was neither as sudden nor as dramatic as is sometimes assumed, there can be no doubt that the adoption of iron – for the manufacture of weapons and tools and eventually the construction of the iron ploughshare – had far-reaching implications for European society as a whole. There is thus some justification in retaining the old-established term 'Iron Age' to define this development though it is, of course, evident that a single technological criterion to define an entire cultural phase is oversimple.

The use in Ireland of the term 'Iron Age' is even more problematical (see p. 220) and the very small number of surviving iron artifacts of the period greatly exacerbates the difficulties. Factors such as the poor preservative qualities of this metal and the relative unlikelihood of its retrieval by chance finders have doubtless contributed to this dearth of evidence, but the possibility that ironworking was practised on only a limited scale for much of the so-called Iron Age in Ireland must be seriously considered. There is at any rate much we do not know about our earliest iron technology despite the pioneering work of Brian Scott whose studies form the indispensable basis for all modern considerations of Irish iron-working technology.

Iron ores would appear to have been reasonably plentiful in Ireland in early times. Bog ores were probably widely available and small outcrops would also have been at the disposal of the early blacksmiths. In the northeast of the country, in Antrim and extending into north Derry, the tropical weathering of the Lower Tertiary basalt flows produced important deposits of good quality iron ore.

Some information on the nature of the early iron-working industry in Ireland is available to us through an examination of the finished products and from the limited evidence of excavation. It is clear that the forge had to be a carefully organized place, well stocked with the necessary fuels, raw materials

90 *Heavily corroded iron sword of La Tène type, recovered from the River Corrib, Dangan Lower, Co. Galway.*

0   5 cm

and tools. For smelting the ores oak charcoal was probably preferred (though birch could have been used) because it is denser and longer burning than other, softer woods. Quite large quantities of the ore itself were needed, because at best only about 20 per cent of the total bulk was converted to usable iron. We can only guess at the complex social and economic infrastructure involved in the extraction of the ores and their transport from a bog or mountain source to the floor of an Iron Age smithy.

Focal point in the Iron Age forge, of course, was the smelting furnace, in which the ores were reduced to produce iron. The analysis of a small, open-air bowl furnace of second or third century AD date from Rathgall, Co. Wicklow and later evidence suggests that the bowl furnace was exclusively used for early smelting in Ireland. The Rathgall furnace was a small hemispherical, clay-lined pit which may have been covered by a clay dome or, more simply, by sods or soil. Its efficiency was limited, however, and only relatively small quantities of iron could be produced during each smelt.

How did it work? The smith would have placed charcoal in the furnace and heated it to a minimum temperature of 1100°C; then he would have added the ore. The high temperature would have caused the slag to sink to the bottom, leaving the bloom (a spongy mass of iron particles and slag) on top. Bellows were needed to achieve and maintain such temperatures and a clay tube, known as a *tuyère*, was used to protect the nozzle of the bellows from the red-hot charcoal. The bloom was then reheated to around 1200°C, after which it was hammered on an anvil to weld the iron particles together and to remove the remaining impurities.

To carry out his work the smith required specialist implements. He would certainly have had a range of hammers and fullers of different shapes and weights at his disposal, as well as various types of iron tongs. At the centre of the workshop the smith would probably have placed an anvil or a suitably shaped rock; and perhaps he used smaller anvils of iron for the finer aspects of his work. His toolkit would have consisted of cutting tools as well as various chisel types: the rocked tracer design on the base of a spearhead from Lisnacrogher was produced with just such a narrow-bladed implement. Files and punches were also employed, as were mandrels – round-sectioned bars used in the formation of the sockets of spearheads and other implements. Another tool to be found in the workshop was the swage: this was a two-part artifact with grooved faces which the smith would have used to reduce thickness and to provide a good rounded finish. A swage or something similar was almost certainly responsible, for instance, for creating the fine midribs of some spearheads and the longitudinal grooving and ribbing of sword-blades such as that from Dangan *fig. 90* Lower, Co. Galway. Above all, however, no forge could function without a bellows to maintain the temperature of the smelting furnace. While the only tool we have yet recovered from an Iron Age context in Ireland is an iron chisel from Feerwore, Co. Galway, the range of implements available to the craftsmen is evident from the fine artifacts they produced.

Scott's analysis of Irish iron artifacts has shown that the traditions of metalworking excellence so evident in the later Bronze Age were not lost with the earliest appearance of iron. Though the sample of early items is small, there are indications of a surprisingly high level of technical skill (see *fig. 91*) even at this initial stage of the Iron Age, as well as evidence of some quite understandable fumbling. The Rathtinaun axehead, for example, displays some basic deficiencies in its manufacture; but at the same time the deliberate carburization of its cutting edge to convert this functional portion to hardened steel (a feature also present on the axes from Toome and Lough Mourne, Co. Antrim), reveals an unexpectedly sophisticated knowledge of the techniques of iron manufacture. The twisting of the suspension rings of the Drumlane cauldron, by holding a heated iron bar with tongs at each end and twisting in opposite directions was also an achievement of no small significance.

The bulk of the surviving iron artifacts of the Iron Age belongs to the La Tène cultural horizon in the country. Inevitably, weapons – i.e. swords and spearheads – are the most numerous objects in this metal. As well as this there is a small handful of iron tools, two or three dress-fasteners and a few items of horse harness either wholly or in part of iron.

Scott's work has shown that the Irish La Tène blacksmiths, while experts in the shaping and the jointing of iron, were generally of only modest competence in the actual quality of the iron they produced. Spearheads were, for example,

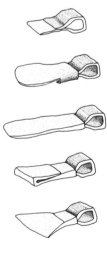

91 *Stages in the manufacture of the shafthole axehead from Rathtinaun, Co. Sligo. Not to scale.*

finely formed and several of the swords (notably examples from Lisnacrogher and Ballinderry, Co. Westmeath) are well-balanced, elegantly proportioned implements. But Scott points out that many of the swords were of limited effectiveness, and suggests that aesthetic considerations, linked to the prestige and symbolism of the weapons, were perhaps of greater relevance than their death-dealing abilities. The poor quality of the iron-work at this time could be the result of the wider dissemination of this metal throughout the community among craftsmen of modest competence. In bronzeworking, however, it is clearly evident that the outstanding skills of the earlier period were undiminished during the centuries of the Iron Age.

The craft of the bronzesmith

Without question it is the work of the bronzesmith which dominates our picture of the material culture of Iron Age Ireland. This picture is undoubtedly a biased one deriving from nothing more than the superior survival properties of bronze. However, the recent discovery of a knobbed spearbutt of iron from Co. Fermanagh and a pair of iron horse-bits from Co. Dublin, all three of which appear to be based on bronze prototypes, strongly argues for the continued pre-eminence of bronze in the metal technology of the Iron Age into the post-Christian era.

In every area of La Tène Ireland bronze-working was practised and the smiths responsible were proficient in all the techniques of high-quality craftsmanship. Their manufacturing skills, along with the superb ornament which often adorned the finished articles, establish them as equals of the best European bronzesmiths. Horse-trappings, ornate dress-fasteners, elaborately decorated discs and mounts and the great sheet-bronze trumpets testify in different ways to the technical and artistic sophistication of the Irish bronzesmiths. Several of these items are exceptional, created by master craftsmen working unquestionably under the patronage and protection of a powerful, aristocratic élite.

The variety of materials and specialist tools required for the manufacture of decorative bronzes implies, as in the case of the blacksmith, that the finest pieces must have been made by settled craftsmen operating in secure and permanent surroundings. Once more, it is through the finished products themselves that we can seek to reconstruct the varied and complex processes by which they came into being.

To what extent, for instance, did the blacksmith and the bronzesmith work together, or could a single individual practise both crafts? The latter must have been the case in the initial stages of iron-working, for it was the native bronzesmiths who carried out the first experiments in the new metal. But did the crafts diverge as time went on? Composite artifacts are known: bronze horse-bits with iron rings or with repairs in iron, for example, and there are iron swords with quillon-plates of bronze and bronze brooches with iron rivets. There are also iron objects, as noted above, which are clearly copies of bronze prototypes. Contact and collaboration between the crafts is thus evident, but we cannot say what this meant in practice. Nor do we know if the enamel-worker was a separate individual or if the bronzesmith was adept in this craft too. On all these points we can only speculate, bearing in mind the great complexity of metalworking practices in modern ethnographic contexts around the world.

Bronze is an alloy of copper and tin. The former is found in fairly abundant supplies in southern and western areas of Ireland, particularly in Wicklow and west Cork where mining is attested since the Early Bronze Age. Some tin may have been available in the country in prehistoric times but it seems likely that most of it was imported. The nearest source was Cornwall but Brittany could also have been a supplier. We can be sure that the mechanisms of distribution and exchange were efficient and streamlined, having been in operation, however intermittently, for the better part of two millennia.

No bronzesmith's workshop of the Iron Age has ever been found in Ireland nor can we point to a single surviving bronze-working tool, with the possible, though uncertain, exception of a lost compass-arm fragment from Lough Crew, Co. Meath, which might have been used in the creation of compass-drawn ornament. Even more surprising is the fact that not a single mould fragment from the casting of Iron Age bronzes has ever come to light in the country in sharp contrast to the thousands known from the later Bronze Age.

A number of unfinished objects has come to light. These include several horse-bit rings still preserving their jagged and irregular casting seams, and a Y-shaped horse pendant from which a conical accretion, the solidified bronze from the pouring gate, has not been removed. Clearly these objects are fresh from the mould, and were discarded before the final process of removing the irregularities had been carried out. The fragmentary link-end of a bronze horse-bit from an occupation level at Newgrange, Co. Meath has been deliberately cut at the end and may have been intended for melting and reuse. No solid evidence for bronze-working was, however, uncovered at that site.

One hoard of metal objects, found at Somerset, Co. Galway, probably dating to the period around the birth of Christ, may certainly be regarded as constituting the possessions of a bronzesmith. The hoard comprised a number of bronze mounts, a gold ribbon torc, a bronze brooch, a bronze cup-handle, part of a horse pendant, a cake and an ingot of bronze. One of the mounts had its original openwork centre cut away, perhaps following damage. It may have been intended to repair the damage. The cake had a series of parallel hammer marks upon it and it could be that this was to be worked up into a cup or bowl to which the handle could be attached. A closely similar cake of copper has come from the River Bann.

92 *Unprovenanced Y-shaped 'pendant'. The casting accretion at the lower end indicates that the object was never completed.* 1/4.

Techniques of bronze production

The two principal techniques involved in the manufacture of decorative bronzes were casting in the round and sheet-metalworking. Each required a

93 Portion of an unprovenanced Irish horse-bit. The object was clearly unfinished, for the inner link-end remains unperforated. 1/2.

high degree of expertise. From the finished artifacts there is no indication that moulds of stone were used but we cannot dismiss the possibility that, in some instances at least, casting in sand was practised. It is likely, however, that in the main casting was done in clay moulds.

The elaborate three-dimensional ornament which is often present on cast bronze items shows that the *cire perdue* or lost wax technique was widely employed. This technique involves the initial modelling of the desired form in wax on a clay core which is then covered by clay and baked, hardening the clay and allowing the melted wax to run out. Tiny bronze rods, known as chaplets, were inserted through the wax from the inner to the outer layer of clay so that when the wax had been evacuated the void, preserving the form modelled in the wax, remained intact. The latter was then replaced by molten bronze which hardened to the shape of the original wax model. The clay coating was finally removed and the object was completed by the removal of casting irregularities and the filing down of the ends of the chaplets which were now incorporated into the body of the cast bronze object. Artifacts produced in this way include the ringheaded pins with prominent curvilinear ornament, or the splendidly three-dimensional bird's head handles from Somerset, Co. Galway and the cup from Keshcarrigan, Co. Leitrim. Three-link horse-bits would have been similarly made, and in several of the earlier examples the clay casting cores remain *in situ* inside the hollow side-links.

94 Bronze discs with repoussé *ornament, from Monasterevin, Co. Kildare. 1/5.*

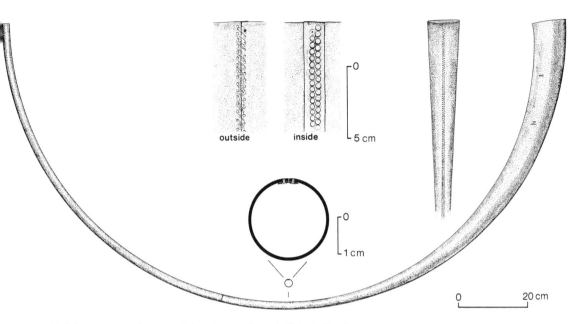

outside inside

95 *Tubular trumpet of hammered sheet bronze, from Ardbrin in Co. Down.*

The horse bridle-bits are particularly fine castings. In each case there are five units – the three-link mouthpiece and the cheek-rings – each one a complete casting which articulates within the other. A clue to the manufacturing procedure is provided by an incomplete, unlocalized example in the National Museum. This consists of a ring and a single side-link of the later type, the *fig. 93* inner end of which is unperforated. Clearly, this piece was discarded in the process of fabrication. The suggested sequence of construction would thus be to cast the two cheek-rings separately and then cast a side-link on to each ring. The openings through the inner link-ends had then to be drilled. The final stage would be to join each of the side-links to a common centre-link. To do this the bronzesmith had to construct a mould around the drilled end of each side-link thus creating the central-link. Considerable skill was needed to ensure that the points of articulation remained free to move after the completion of the casting process.

Sheet-bronzeworking was carried out with the same consummate skill as casting. The sheets were probably hammered from a cake or ingot of bronze and then cut to the required shape after which they were bent and decorated to their final form. The properties of bronze sheet were well understood and the technique of annealing – heating of the metal above its recrystallization temperature (perhaps as high as 650°C) to make it soft and malleable – was exploited to its fullest.

Sheet-bronzeworking was widely practised for the manufacture of cauldrons, tubular spearbutts and an extensive variety of mounts and fittings. Circular bronze discs such as those found at Monasterevin, Co. Kildare, are *fig. 94*: pl. 59 especially good examples of the sheet-bronzeworker's craft. These are characterized by high relief ornament surrounding a bowl-like hollow which was hammered to the back. In the best of these the hammerwork (known as *repoussé*) is of superb quality, the raised spirals and curves displaying almost flawless perfection in every detail. The bronzesmith must have placed the disc flat on a bed of pitch, or perhaps wet leather, to carry out the hammerwork. The delicate elements of the designs must have been achieved by using fine, round-ended punches of different types. On one unlocalized specimen the marks of punches have been deliberately arranged on the object to provide a matted background to the raised curves. The fact that the sheets were hammered both to the front and the back would have stretched the bronze almost to the limit, running the risk of cracking the delicate sheets. Frequent annealing, however, minimized this danger.

Some of the most splendid examples of Irish Iron Age sheet-metalwork are the bronze trumpets. The finest and best preserved of these was found early in *fig. 95* the nineteenth century in a lake at Ardbrin, Co. Down. It is an elegantly curved instrument measuring 1.42 m from tip to tip. It was made of two tubes of sheet bronze, one cylindrical, the other expanding towards the bell end. They were originally joined at the centre, presumably by inserting the ends into a hollow, biconical boss such as those which survive on several other examples.

To make the tubes, the sheets had first to be cut carefully to the required shape then bent by hammering the metal over carefully prepared mandrels, perhaps of polished wood or of iron, so that the edges exactly touched and the diameters of the two tubes at the points of junction matched each other exactly. To make them air-tight the tubes had to be sealed and this was a laborious task. It involved the insertion of two narrow strips of bronze, 1.1 cm wide and together totalling 2.40 m in length, along the seam on the inside of each tube. These had to be held securely, presumably by reinserting the tight-fitting mandrels into the tubes to wedge the sealing-strips in position. A series of closely spaced rivet-holes was then drilled on either side of the seam both through the tubes and the sealing-strips, along the entire length of the trumpet. No fewer than 1094 rivet-holes were drilled in this way.

The next stage involved placing 1094 expanded-headed rivets into the holes from the inside of the tube outwards. It is likely that these were put in at the ends first and secured in position by hammering their heads with a punch against the mandrel which had been reinserted into the tube. With the sealing strip securely in place the rest of the rivets could be inserted. The further from the ends, however, the more difficult it was to manoeuvre them into position. Obviously long, thin tweezers of some sort were needed for this; these could have been made of pliable withes. With the strips and rivets in place mandrels were once more inserted and the rivet-heads hammered to lodge them firmly in position. The ends of the rivets, exposed on the exterior, were then carefully filed smooth.

The final stage in the manufacture, and perhaps the most difficult, was bending the two sealed tubes so that together they created a regularly curving,

C-shaped instrument. To do this the tubes would have been tightly packed with a substance such as pitch, resin or sand after which it was slowly and carefully bent, constantly annealing the metal to avoid cracking or buckling.

Thus it is evident that the manufacture of these trumpets took time, patience, exceptional skill and a wide range of tools and materials. Sheet-metal had first to be hammered from the raw bronze. Chisels or other sharp-edged cutting implements were needed to cut the sheets to shape and a straight rule of some sort against which the edges were cut. The mandrels had to be carefully prepared. A variety of hammers was needed for forming the tubes, and punches were also necessary. The rivets were cast in clay moulds and, in view of the large number involved, this would have required no small amount of effort in preparing the moulds and casting the individual items. Files were used to smoothen the exterior surfaces of the rivets and a bow-drill of some sort must have been employed for the rivet-holes. Tweezers, if indeed they were made of long twigs, would have been readily available in the surrounding woodland but if pitch or resin instead of sand were used to fill the tubes before the final bending then again considerable effort would have been involved in gathering the required amount.

The trumpets show sheet-bronzework on a grand scale. Two horned head- *fig. 97* pieces – one from Cork, the other an unlocalized fragment often referred to as the Petrie Crown – consist of hollow bronze horns folded and sealed in exactly *fig. 96* the same way as the trumpets, but on an even finer level. The ornament decorating them, however, is of a type otherwise unknown in Ireland, with the single exception of a circular bronze disc from Loughan Island on the River *fig. 98* Bann in Co. Derry. It consists of fine curving lines raised in low relief above the surface of the bronze sheet. The detailed examination of these objects by Michael J. O'Kelly led him to believe that the relief was achieved by finely tooling away the background bronze by fractions of a millimetre. Such a technique would, however, have demanded quite incredible skill and the use of graving tools of exceptional fineness and sharpness. Thus we cannot discount the possibility that the designs were in fact cast and finished by fine tooling.

It is possible that craftsmen spun or polished their bronze bowls on a pole lathe in later Iron Age Ireland. Concentric striations are detectable on the interiors of several of the Irish bowls and tiny, centrally located holes or 'chuck-marks' on the bases of four examples (from Keshcarrigan, Co. Leitrim, from Co. Westmeath and two from the River Bann) indicate that at the very least the vessels were finished off by polishing. The two techniques are not the same. Spinning implies that a flat sheet was formed into a bowl over a rotating bowl-shaped former. The hole or chuck-mark indicates the spot at which the bronze was secured by a metal point against the wooden form. This technique is more elaborate than polishing which means simply that the hammered or cast bowl was smoothed off on a lathe. On finished objects it is often difficult to distinguish between the two methods.

While it does seem clear that a lathe was used on a number of the bowls found in Ireland, it is not certain that these were actually produced in Ireland itself: it

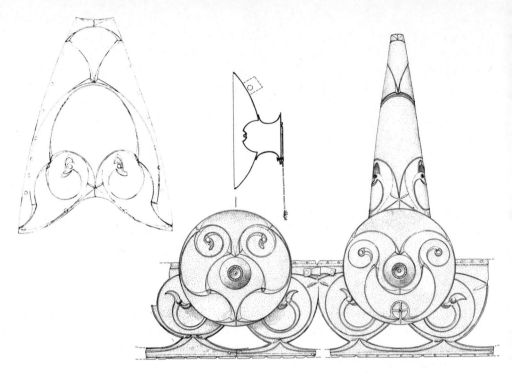

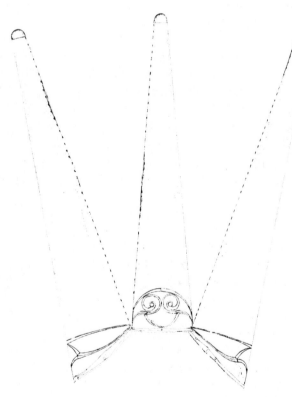

96 (Above) The Petrie Crown (see pl. 57).
Max. ht 15 cm.

97 (Left) The Cork Horns (see pls. 60, 61).
1/3.

98 (Below) Decorated bronze disc discovered at
Loughan Island, River Bann, Co. Derry. 2/3.

is frequently argued that such vessels were imported from Britain, where the technique was certainly known by the last century BC. It is nonetheless difficult to accept that the bird's head handle on the Keshcarrigan bowl is of non-Irish manufacture. We must thus conclude either that the handle was added in Ireland to an imported container or that the technique of lathe-finishing bronze vessels had indeed reached Ireland by the turn of the millennium.

A wide variety of tools would, as already noted, have been standard items in the workshops of all bronzesmiths engaged in the manufacture and embellishment of bronze artifacts. On the bronze scabbard-plates, for instance, we can recognize well the skilled, freehand use of fine graving tools. An example from the River Bann at Toome in particular, though of poor aesthetic quality, demonstrates with great clarity the technique of rocked graver, involving a hand-held graving tool which was gently rocked backwards and forwards over the surface of the bronze to produce a zig-zag line. This technique of engraving, widely known in Celtic contexts abroad, is found on other Irish objects, such as an iron spearhead from Lisnacrogher, several of the so-called 'spoons' of bronze (see below), and a bronze ring from a burial at Knowth, Co. Meath.

fig. 87
pl. 64

The use of fine chisels is also implied by the panels hand-cut for the retention of red enamel inlays present, for instance, on a mount from Ballycastle, Co. Antrim and on an unprovenanced horse-bit in the Scottish National Museum. The same sort of chisels were sometimes employed to cut openwork ornament into bronze. A magnificent example of this is the circular mount from Cornalaragh, Co. Monaghan. Tiny anvils might have been needed for such work.

pl. 63

The design on the Cornalaragh mount, though finished by hand, was laid out with a compass. The use of the compass is well attested by other items of bronze and the gold Broighter torc, but is especially clear on a series of bone flakes from Lough Crew, Co. Meath. The latter site, a reused passage tomb, did in fact produce the iron leg of a compass which has now been lost. It may be contemporary with the flakes, but its context within the mound was not recorded.

pl. 67
fig. 75: pl. 72

Hand-in-hand with bronze-working was the technique of enamelling. This is a form of glass (and is often difficult to distinguish from true glass) which in early Iron Age times was exclusively red. It replaced the red coral inlays of the earliest phases of the La Tène period in Europe and was initially attached to the metal as pre-shaped studs riveted in place. Later the technique of *champlevé* was introduced: this involved the preparation, either by chiselling or casting, of sunken settings in the bronze into which enamel was put in molten form to fill the panel in a shiny red sea.

Coral was not available in Iron Age Ireland but decoration both by *champlevé* and by the use of enamel studs was known. Two ringheaded pins from Lisnacrogher illustrate the method of riveting pre-shaped studs to bronze, and it could be that this technique predated the *champlevé* technique in Ireland. This cannot be demonstrated, however, and the fact that the two techniques

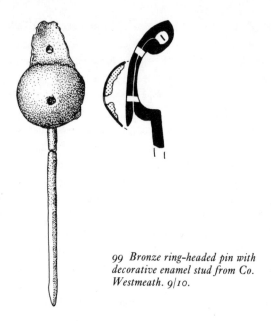

99 *Bronze ring-headed pin with decorative enamel stud from Co. Westmeath. 9/10.*

occur on two closely similar, and probably contemporary, brooches of Navan-type (from Navan itself and from Somerset, Co. Galway) indicates that they overlapped in time. Another method of using enamel is illustrated by one of the openwork mounts from the Somerset hoard. This object, thus far without parallel in Iron Age Ireland, has a domed boss at the centre composed of an openwork grille of bronze into which a correspondingly shaped filling of red enamel has been fitted from the back. On an unusual ringheaded pin, recently discovered in Co. Westmeath, the domed head of enamel is hollow at the back and may have been pre-formed in a mould before fixing it in place. It seems to *fig. 99* have had a clay backing when fitted to the pin.

It is possible that the enamel was imported in bulk and worked in local centres. Several large blocks have been found in the vicinity of Tara, Co. Meath in the last century, and these could be of Iron Age date. Analysis indicates a high lead content in the enamel, which inspired one commentator to suggest that the block was imported from Italy. Until the European enamels have been subjected to more detailed examination, however, this can be no more than an interesting hypothesis.

The art of repairing

As well as creating artifacts of bronze, the Iron Age bronzesmith would have been responsible for mending broken or damaged objects. These repairs sometimes display levels of quite considerable ingenuity, and remind us of the more mundane aspects of the bronzeworker's stock-in-trade. The almost obsessive determination to maintain the functionality of certain objects, despite repeated breakages (notably in the case of some horse-bits), underlines the perceived importance of such items.

The normal method of repairing damage to sheet-bronze was to rivet a patch of bronze across the defective area. Cauldrons, for example, were frequently treated in this way, and sometimes the entire base was replaced. Damaged trumpets were similarly repaired and on these, as occasionally on the cauldrons, patches seem to have been pre-shaped to enhance the appearance of the repair. In one instance, on a vessel from Ballyedmond in Co. Galway, a large break in the wall of the container was covered by riveting a pair of discarded D-shaped bucket escutcheons across the damaged area on both surfaces of the cauldron. Smaller breaks in the walls of cauldrons were sometimes filled by 'paper-clip' patches. Lesser cracks on other items were also repaired by riveting a narrow strip of bronze across the break in the manner of a splint. The snapped-off tip of one of the Lisnacrogher scabbards was repaired in this way and a cracked spearbutt socket from the same site was similarly strengthened. The same technique can also be observed on one of the so-called Monasterevin-type discs. Safety-pin fibulae were vulnerable at the point where the spring joined with the bow and they often snapped there. In several instances a secondary spring-unit was riveted in place. This involved drilling a fine rivet-hole through the bow-end and the replacement spring. The technique required no little skill, and of course the use of a sharp and narrow-bladed drill; the effort implied suggests again that these were items of some value.

The most frequently repaired objects were, however, the horse-bits. Obviously, these were particularly susceptible to damage as the intense pressure generated by the horses, whether ridden or in draught, must have caused severe friction wherever metal parts rubbed against each other or where the reins rubbed against the rings. Thus the outer ends of the link-loops, and especially the ring-pivots (the portion of the cheek-ring upon which the side-links articulated), became worn and often snapped. To remedy the damage the smiths inserted secondary pivots on to the rings between the stop-studs by filing away the broken ends of the original and riveting the replacement into position.

An extreme example of this sort of ring repair is illustrated by a horse-bit *fig. 100* from Gortgole, Co. Antrim. On this specimen the ring-pivots broke and were replaced, in the normal way, by secondary pivots which were held in place by tiny vertical rivets inserted through the stop-studs. Some time later one of the rings snapped immediately adjacent to one of the studs. This was repaired by riveting tiny strips of bronze, some 4 mm in width, across the break on two opposed surfaces of the ring. Because the fracture had taken place exactly at the point of junction of stud and ring, the only way the repair strip could effectively span the break was by making a horizontal incision into the base of the stud. The repair strip was then inserted into this and secured by three vertical rivets, one through the ring, the others through the undercut stop-stud. The latter was thus pierced by two minute rivets, one to hold the secondary ring-pivot, the other to hold the repair strip. We can only marvel at the fineness of the drill, perhaps with a steel bit, that was capable of making two rivet-holes with such precision through a single stop-stud.

100 Bronze horse-bit from Gortgole, Co. Antrim, showing the complex repair techniques. c. 4/5.

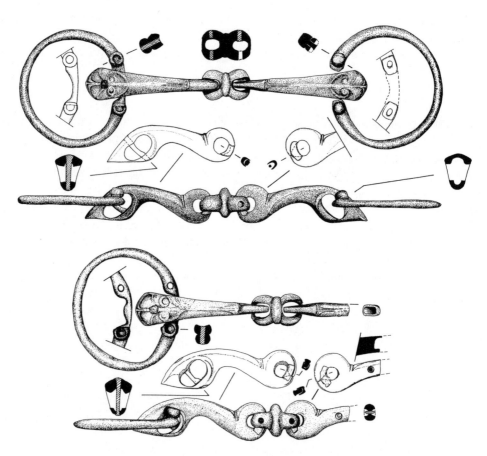

101 Pair of bronze horse-bits with multiple repairs; Streamstown, Co. Westmeath. c. 4/5.

The ring-pivot was the most vulnerable portion of the horse-bit, but the outer ends of link-loops were also frequently worn through. One remedy for this was to hammer the broken ends together and to seal the break rather crudely by the application of a small quantity of molten bronze across the crack. Alternatively holes were drilled into the broken ends and a secondary bar riveted across the break. The broken ends of central-links were similarly repaired.

In one instance, on a pair of bits from Streamstown, Co. Westmeath, the outer link-ends were worn to a thread but had not quite broken through. Here the craftsman wisely decided to preempt the inevitable break by inserting a vertical rod of iron through the link-loop thus shielding the frayed link-end *pls. 65, 66* from any further friction from the ring. Other repairs are evident on this pair of bits, including an attempt to fix a snapped side-link by means of a mortice-and-tenon join strengthened by riveted side-splints. These two horse-bits, displaying between them no fewer than twelve separate repairs, demonstrate better than anything else the high status of the horse-bit, and the skill and resourcefulness of the Irish bronzesmith. *fig. 101*

Goldworking

The amount of gold of demonstrably Iron Age date from Ireland is surprisingly limited and few of the surviving objects are of certainly native manufacture. This is in stark contrast to the exceptional wealth of such material from the later Bronze Age. Why the sudden drop in gold production? One possible explanation might be that the available native deposits of the raw material had by this time been worked out.

Gold ribbon torcs, notably those from Knock ('Clonmacnoise') and Somerset, are possibly products of local workshops. The latter in particular, with its non-functional straight rather than hooked terminals, could be an unfinished piece. Its presence in a bronzeworker's hoard perhaps suggests that the latter was also competent in the working of gold.

The decoration on the buffer torc from Broighter indicates that it was produced in Ireland. It has, however, been suggested that the terminals may be of foreign manufacture, added on in Ireland. The object is, at any rate, one of the finest examples of European Iron Age goldworking. The hollow tubes of sheet-gold may once have had a backing of iron or resin, as is the case with other contemporary torcs outside the country. The ornament consists of raised scrolls set against a background of engraved arcs. The relief patterns appear to *pl. 67* have been produced by chasing, i.e. by hammering the background to create the relief after the tubes had been folded. Some of the snail-shell spirals on the object are separately made units clipped into openings in the tube. The arcs illustrate once more the excellence of compass-work in Ireland around the turn of the millennium. On this object, traces of a ring-punch 1.75 mm in diameter have been recognized.

The Broighter collar is an exceptional piece and shows us that goldworking in Ireland, even though only sporadically practised, was of the highest order.

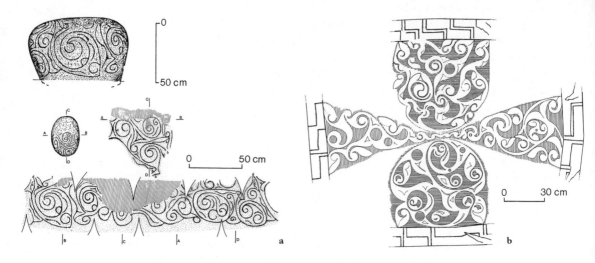

102 Decorated Iron Age standing stones. (a) Castlestrange, Co. Roscommon, with flattened-out detail of ornament. (b) Turoe, Co. Galway, showing the four-fold arrangement of the decoration.

From it we can once more assume an extensive range of specialist tools and a detailed knowledge of the properties of gold. It may be that the fragmentary bar-torc found at Newgrange is indicative of goldworking activity at that site some time after the birth of Christ (see below, p. 210).

Stoneworking

The high quality of some of the Iron Age stonework from Ireland strongly suggests that this was a specialist craft practised by professional artificers. The shaping, polishing and drilling of quernstones, for example, involved no little skill and technical expertise. Even more impressive are the decorated monoliths. These were, of course, made by craftsmen who were intimately acquainted with the stylistic intricacies of contemporary metalwork, but the translation of the finely cast and hammered metalwork designs to the obdurate

fig. 102 stone presented them with quite separate problems. Several of these – notably
pl. 69 the stones from Derrykeighan, Co. Antrim and Killycluggin, Co. Cavan – clearly demonstrate the use of large compasses in the layout of their decoration.
pl. 68 The stone at Turoe, Co. Galway is an especially fine piece. With its carefully executed quadripartite ornament and its expertly composed false-relief designs, this is unquestionably the work of a master mason. To carve this a range of iron chisels and heavy hammers must have been used.

La Tène art styles

The art of the La Tène Celts developed around the middle of the fifth century BC through the adaptation and development of Mediterranean plant motifs by the indigenous late Hallstatt peoples. Almost instantaneously, it seems, an abstract curvilinear ornament of great beauty and originality appeared which spread to all areas of La Tène influence in Europe. This art, described as the first great non-Classical art of Europe, represents one of the most enduring legacies of Celtic cultural expansion. La Tène art is an art of power and imagination which was lavished above all on high-status objects of metal. It is an art of waves and tendrils, scrolls and spirals which twist and turn with restless, sinuous grace across the surface to be adorned. It may be in two dimensions or in the round. Designs are often conceived to convey deliberate, contrived tension between symmetry and asymmetry and shapes constantly change as first one element of the design then another is allowed to take prominence in the eye of the beholder. It is an art of the oakwoods with a constantly flickering interplay between light and shadow. Faces too, or parts of faces, appear to lurk in the abstract undergrowth sometimes exuding fearsome menace, sometimes resembling cartoon characters. It is not always clear, however, if the perceived image was really intended by the artist or if it is no more than the accidental juxtaposition of abstract curves. Or is it all a deliberate ploy on the part of the craftsman to tantalize and mystify? La Tène art thus supplies us with insights into the Celtic personality which is laden with innuendo, contradictions and double meaning. The art reminds us of the words of the Greek ethnographer Poseidonius who wrote of the Celts in the century before Christ: 'They speak in riddles, hinting at things, leaving much to be understood'. La Tène art undoubtedly had a meaning, but that meaning is in most instances lost to us forever. Through the art, however, we can glance fleetingly into the Celtic soul.

The earliest stages of the European La Tène art style are absent from Ireland. The torc from Knock, Co. Roscommon (formerly Clonmacnoise), an import of the early third century BC, is the first clear indication of a La Tène presence in Ireland, but it is an isolated piece in the west of the country so its wider cultural significance should not be exaggerated. Some time in that century, however, or at the latest in the early second century BC, we can begin to recognize the existence in the country of native workshops producing a local version of La Tène decoration.

The style which emerges is recognizably Irish, though clearly rooted in foreign traditions. Throughout its development Irish La Tène art was in close touch with parallel developments in Britain, especially after the birth of Christ when the two insular traditions were closely linked and there was considerable cross-fertilization between them. The earliest stages of Irish craftsmanship also share many features in common with stylistic developments of directly European, probably Gaulish, origin, and it was through Gaul that ornamental ideas from as far away as the middle Danube found their way to Ireland. It continues to be a matter for debate as to how the art style was first introduced (p. 225).

Ireland certainly borrowed from abroad but the idiosyncratic genius of indigenous metalworkers left its mark right from the beginning. We can assume

103 Decorated bronze scabbard plates from (a–c) Lisnacrogher, Co. Antrim; (d,f) River Bann, Co. Toome; (e) River Bann. c. 1/3.

that there were centres of fine metal-working in different parts of the country, and as time went on a number of differing local styles of ornamentation are recognizable. It is not always possible to establish with certainty the locations of these centres, nor is the dating of the different styles securely based. Numbered among the craftsmen, however, were men of the highest quality who were fully acquainted with technical and artistic developments outside the country.

The earliest centres of high-quality metalwork in the country were almost certainly in the northeast, in Co. Antrim, where good iron deposits might well have been a factor enhancing the importance of this region in the earlier Iron Age. Eight bronze scabbards from the River Bann and from the important bog deposit of Lisnacrogher a short distance to the east of the river best represent this early school.

fig. 84

Six of the eight scabbards are lavishly decorated. This consists of engraved patterns of running waves or sequences of S-figures extending along the lengths of the scabbards. Apart from some initial marking out with the compass, the ornament is freehand and is produced for the most part with great flamboyance and vigour producing designs of vegetal character which swirl and writhe across the metal surface. A feature of the so-called Irish Scabbard Style is the great multiplicity of lesser motifs which are appended to the main figures: these fill the bodies of the figures and the spaces formed by them. Tightly drawn hair-spring spirals, leafy patterns, stippling, hatching, basketry and, in one instance, a tiny triple-dot motif repeated along the length of the scabbard, are the main filler motifs. These are produced in frequently changing combinations which, especially in the case of one of the Bann scabbards, provides us with patterning of at times startling complexity.

fig. 103

pls. 56, 70

These scabbards were produced by craftsmen with a detailed knowledge of all the finer subtleties of British and Continental scabbard engraving. There were, however, occasional lapses in quality: for instance, the graving tool slipped in several instances on one of the Lisnacrogher scabbards leaving unsightly scrapes. Especially poor in artistic quality, however, is another of the Bann scabbards which was decorated by a craftsman expert in the technique of rocked graver (in this instance the zigzag lines produced are termed 'walked scorper') but wholly incompetent in the execution of curvilinear ornament. Spirals and concentric circle motifs on this object are a travesty of what was intended and, in fact, so poor was the end product that the decorated surface of the scabbard, in its final phase of use, was turned inwards leaving an unadorned surface on view.

In the entire repertoire of Irish La Tène art, it is that on the scabbards which most resembles Continental traditions of La Tène decoration. Close stylistic links with early Yorkshire schools of scabbard engraving are also evident. Related to, or deriving from, the scabbards in style, but more decidedly insular, is the fine repoussé ornament on the bronze disc decorating the bell of the Loughnashade trumpet. The design, though filling a circular area, is produced in two perfectly matching halves – an approach described as fold-over symmetry. Curves and spirals, pseudo birds' heads and a proliferation of tiny

pl. 58

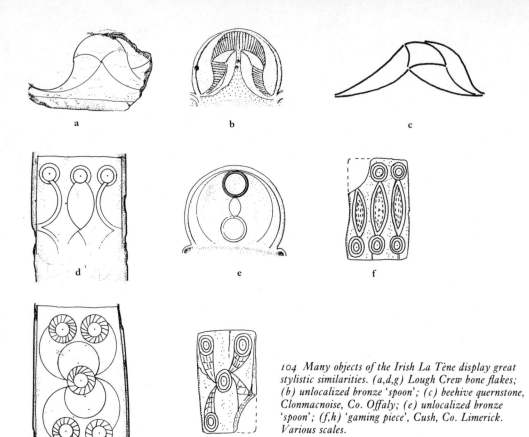

104 Many objects of the Irish La Tène display great stylistic similarities. (a,d,g) Lough Crew bone flakes; (b) unlocalized bronze 'spoon'; (c) beehive quernstone, Clonmacnoise, Co. Offaly; (e) unlocalized bronze 'spoon'; (f,h) 'gaming piece', Cush, Co. Limerick. Various scales.

domed bosses combine to provide a three-dimensional variant of the Scabbard Style. On this object, however, the stylistic development has moved somewhat from the more overtly vegetal character of the scabbard ornament.

The art on the first-century BC gold collar from Broighter bridges the gap between the vegetal approach of the earlier style and the more purely geometric character of the art of the later phases. The tendril scrolls and the leafy designs are still evident on this piece and the raised snail-shell spirals recall the two-dimensional spirals of the scabbards. Broighter is also stylistically related to the fine carved ornament on the roughly contemporary monolith from Turoe, Co. Galway. But on the Broighter collar new elements are present, for now the entire composition is geometric, planned and executed by means of a compass. The background web of overlapping arcs which highlights the raised ornament is also manifestly compass-drawn. This emphasis on the compass is an important innovation. Similarly new is the appearance of the so-called trumpet curve, a raised, expanding curve filled at its widest end by a tiny, pointed-oval boss, known as a lentoid boss. The motif on the collar described as a 'broken-backed curve' is also entirely insular in character, and now makes its appearance for the first time.

The trumpet curve and especially the emphasis on compass arrangements come increasingly to dominate the Irish La Tène style from the turn of the

fig. 75

pl. 71

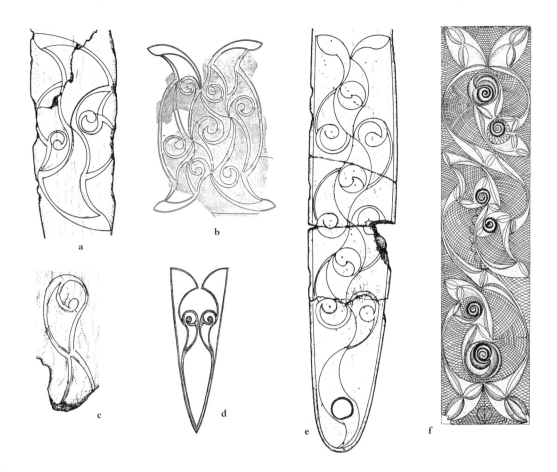

105 The Lough Crew style is characterized by superb compasswork. Bone flakes from Lough Crew (a,c,e) with some stylistic analogies: (b) Derrykeighan stone, Co. Antrim; (d) unprovenanced bronze spearbutt; (f) Broighter gold collar, Co. Derry. Various scales.

millennium onwards. Two major assemblages exhibiting objects with typical ornamentation are from Somerset, Co. Galway and Lough Crew, Co. Meath. The importance of these sites is emphasized by the use of the term Lough Crew-Somerset Style to describe technical and artistic developments of the years around the birth of Christ.

Objects of the Lough Crew-Somerset Style are widely dispersed throughout the country. There is great consistency in decorative approach, and a very considerable degree of uniformity in the motifs used, irrespective of the medium upon which they are found. Clearly the craft centres were working with a common grammar of ornament from which they scarcely deviated. The designs on the bone flakes from Lough Crew, the 'spoons' of bronze, the bone gaming piece from Cush, Co. Limerick, the beehive quern from Clonmacnoise and the standing stone from Derrykeighan all clearly illustrate the narrow homogeneity of this compass style, despite the wide geographical spread. The *figs. 104, 105* excellence of the compasswork is shown particularly at Lough Crew where the designs are crisply and accurately inscribed on to the surfaces of the polished

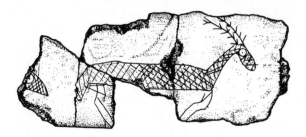

106 Bone flake fragment from Lough Crew, with an engraved representation of a stag. 1/1.

pl. 72   animal rib-bones. The curves are clean and pure and even very small circles are precisely drawn. It is difficult to envisage compasses small and delicate enough to inscribe some of the circles. On one flake in particular, the tiny circular eyes fig. 106 of two crudely drawn stags are a mere 2 mm in diameter. Even the most sophisticated modern instrument would have difficulty in matching such precision drawing.

    Later, some time in the early centuries AD, a variant of this style developed, characterized by raised, fine line ornament of great delicacy. Three master-figs. 96–98: pl. 61 pieces epitomize this style: the Cork horns, the Bann disc and the Petrie Crown. On all of these objects curving lines of infinite fineness adorn the bronze in compass-drawn patterns of outstanding quality. Each boasts a proliferation of trumpet curves, always ending in tiny lentoid bosses, and – especially on the Petrie Crown – there is a rare element of restraint leaving much of the bronze unadorned. This restraint enhances, rather than diminishes, the impact of the curving lines.

    Both on the Bann disc and the Petrie Crown bird-like forms occur. Each of the three arms of the triskele on the Bann disc, for example, terminates in a crested bird's head with bulging eye and upturned beak. On the Petrie Crown there are three separate renderings of the bird, one a crested head comparable with those on the Bann disc, one a bird with a more elaborate comb, and the third, more stylized and without a crest, made up of a series of trumpets. fig. 107 Similar birds' heads are found elsewhere, in more recognizably natural form, such as on the two plastic cup-handles from Keshcarrigan and Somerset. On many of the horse-bits, too, ornithomorphic shapes are detectable on the mouldings of the inner side-link ends and the same motif is sometimes present on the foot elements of safety-pin fibulae and on several of the ringheaded pins. Birds also appear on the cast-bronze mirror handle from Ballymoney, Co. Antrim. The little creature forming the suspension lug on the bowl from Fore, fig. 123 Co. Westmeath has a curling, gaping beak or snout. It is not entirely certain that this is a bird. It is quite unlike anything else from Ireland and it may be an import, perhaps from the south of England.

    Apart from birds the animal world is not extensively represented in the Irish La Tène decorative repertoire. Two bronze pigs, formerly thought of as Iron Age in date, may now safely be dismissed as late medieval sanders but, more recently, a genuinely Iron Age casting of a pig has been found. An unlocalized bovine mask is definitely Iron Age but is not certainly of Irish manufacture; a Belgic origin in southern England is possible. A small bronze ring with sheep

57,58 Masterpieces of the Irish Iron Age. (*Below*) The Petrie Crown, a fragmentary bronze headpiece of unknown Irish provenance. Decorated with elegant curves in low relief, this is one of the best examples of Irish La Tène art. Max. ht 15 cm. (*Bottom*) Decorative disc from the mouth of a tubular bronze trumpet; from Loughnashade, Co. Armagh. The fine *repoussé* design is perfectly symmetrical. Diameter 19.3 cm.

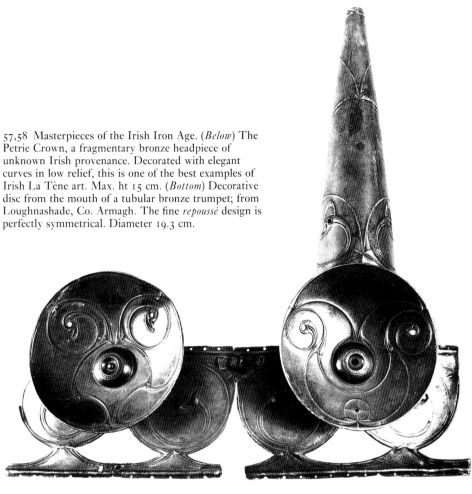

The art of bronze-working

59 (*Left*) Unprovenanced bronze disc of unknown purpose. Several such objects have been found and are sometimes called Monasterevin-type discs; the *repoussé* decoration was achieved by hammering the bronze on a bed of pitch or wet leather. Diameter 28 cm.

60,61 (*Right and below*) Found on wasteland in 1909 on the outskirts of Cork City, these three strange items are known as the Cork Horns; they probably formed part of a ceremonial headpiece. The technique and style of the designs are remarkably similar to those of the Petrie Crown (pl. 57). Max. length of central horn 26.2 cm.

62,63 Two bronze openwork mounts of unknown purpose. (*Above left*) This unique artifact from Somerset, Co. Galway has red enamel inlay at its centre; diameter 3.3 cm. (*Above right*) The decoration of this mount from Cornalaragh in Co. Monaghan was designed with a compass and then hand chiselled; diameter 7.4 cm.

64 (*Right*) Detail of engraved ornament on a bronze 'spoon'. The zig-zag lines produced by the technique of rocked-graver are clearly evident. Max. length 6.7 cm.

65,66 (*Left*) Repair details on a bronze horse-bit from Streamstown, Co. Westmeath. Above: the frayed inner ends of the side-links have been strengthened by applying irregular patches; length of central link 3.4 cm. Below: a bar has been inserted through the outer loop of the worn side-link to prevent further friction and eventual breakage.

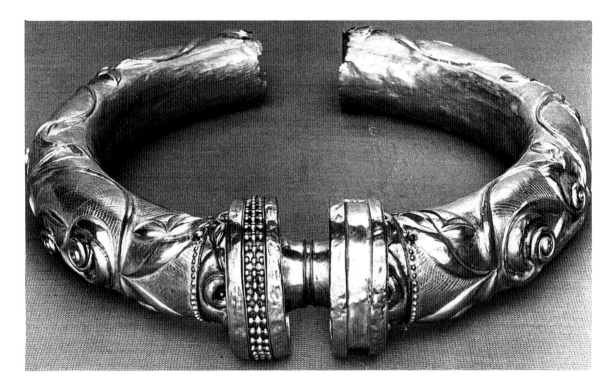

67 (*Above*) The gold buffer torc from Broighter, Co. Derry. Note the exquisite execution of the raised ornament and the detail of the background web of compass-drawn arcs. Internal diameter 13.4 cm.

68 (*Below left*) Granite monolith with carved relief decoration from Turoe, Co. Galway. The design is not dissimilar to that on the Broighter torc; indeed, the two are roughly contemporary.

69 (*Below right*) Carved face of a decorated standing stone found built into the gable end of a late medieval church at Derrykeighan, Co. Antrim. It probably dates from around, or shortly after, the birth of Christ; about 61 cm long.

71,72 The Lough Crew-Somerset style is typical of La Tène art in Ireland around the birth of Christ, and is characterized by trumpet curves and compass designs. (*Above*) The main design on this bronze mount from Somerset, Co. Galway is a *repoussé* trumpet curve ending in a lentoid boss, highlighted by background stippling and a series of compass-drawn arcs. Diameter 8.1 cm. (*Below*) Three polished bone flakes with expertly executed compass decoration, from Lough Crew, Co. Meath. A large number of such flakes was found in the chamber of a Neolithic passage tomb; they may have served a ritual purpose. Max. width of left-hand flake 2.7 cm.

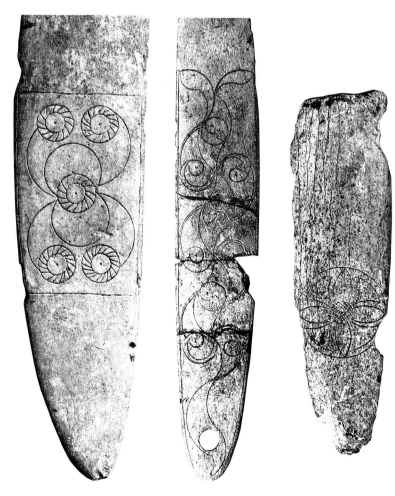

70 (*Above*) One of the elaborately decorated bronze scabbard-plates from Lisnacrogher, with designs in La Tène style. Width 4 cm.

73,74 (*Above*) Carved stone heads, generally regarded as representations of deities. Left: a carving with three faces from Corleck in Co. Cavan; such triplism is typical of Celtic religious beliefs. Right: from Cavan town.

75 (*Left*) The Tanderagee idol, Co. Armagh. This is either a horned god or a god wearing a horned helmet. Now on Cathedral Hill in Armagh, its original provenance is confused; it may be from the vicinity of Newry. Ht 60 cm.

76 (*Below*) Cathedral Hill, Armagh. Two (of an original three) carved stone bears. Between the legs of the left-hand carving the profile head of a dog or wolf is clearly visible.

77 (*Left*) An Iron Age bog body. Discovered in 1821 at Gallagh, Castleblakeney, Co. Galway (and subjected to several reburials and exhumations for the amusement of visiting officials), the remains were partially preserved by natural desiccation. Exactly how this young man died is not known, although one scholar suspects he was garrotted and ritually buried in the bog.

78 (*Below*) This bronze bowl was found within a fortified enclosure at Fore in Co. Westmeath. It is of British type and originally contained a cremation deposit. Max. diameter of rim 24.2 cm.

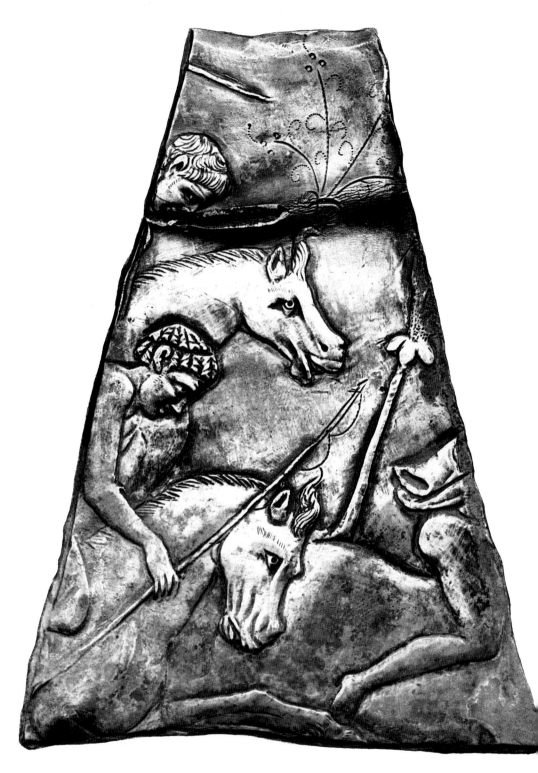

79 Fragment of a hacked, late Roman silver plate unearthed in a gravel ridge at Balline, Co. Limerick, together with silver ingots and other fragments of plate. Length 14 cm.

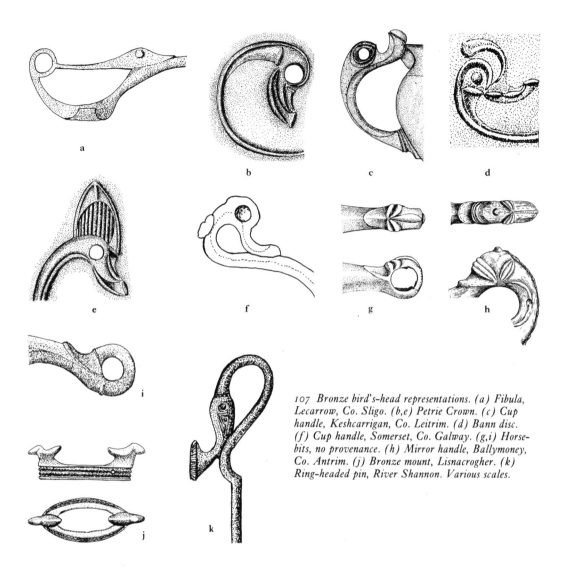

107 Bronze bird's-head representations. (a) Fibula, Lecarrow, Co. Sligo. (b,e) Petrie Crown. (c) Cup handle, Keshcarrigan, Co. Leitrim. (d) Bann disc. (f) Cup handle, Somerset, Co. Galway. (g,i) Horse-bits, no provenance. (h) Mirror handle, Ballymoney, Co. Antrim. (j) Bronze mount, Lisnacrogher. (k) Ring-headed pin, River Shannon. Various scales.

and goat heads is enigmatic. Finally of interest is the apparent snake head on the foot of an unprovenanced fibula of undoubted Irish fabrication. The absence of such creatures in Ireland indicates either that the craftsman was a foreigner from a country where such existed, or else he was a native who had encountered snakes on a trip overseas. pl. 49

The human faces which are such a feature of La Tène metalwork on the Continent are virtually absent in Ireland. Ireland did, of course, share the pan-Celtic veneration for the human head, and carvings in stone are not uncommon in northern areas of the country. In metal, however, we can point with confidence to only a single rendering of demonstrably native manufacture. This is the simple, yet impressive, visage created by four finely raised lines, cast on the end of an unlocalized bronze horse-bit. It compares well with the lurking, foliate faces of the European mainland. pl. 32

CHAPTER 8

Cult, Ritual and Death

> The whole of the Gallic people is passionately devoted to matters of religion.
>
> GAIUS JULIUS CAESAR (100–44 BC)

Like their Celtic cousins in Gaul, it is likely that the Irish were similarly concerned with religious affairs in the last centuries before Christ. There is much that the early Irish literature and the Classical writings have in common concerning Celtic beliefs and ritual practices, and together they give us important insights into the pagan Celtic preoccupation with the supernatural. The picture which emerges is of a people dominated by their religious beliefs, with deities and Underworld beings a continuous, lurking backdrop to their daily lives. There were lucky days and unlucky days, there was a right way and a wrong way of doing things, and there were strict rules of conduct in accordance with clearly defined taboos and prohibitions which must not be transgressed.

The gods were ever-present and there appears to have been no clear dividing line between the natural and the supernatural worlds. The Celts believed themselves at all times to be balanced precariously on the interface between the divine and the profane. All around lived the denizens of the Otherworld, in springs, in rivers and lakes, in forests and marshes, in caves and on mountain tops. The gods intruded into the affairs of men and often took sides in the disputes of mortals. They were capricious and moody, at times benevolent and helpful, at times malicious and spiteful. It was necessary to mollify and appease them constantly by means of offerings, by the correct rituals and by the proper manner of behaviour. You offended the gods at your peril.

There were many gods or, as has been suggested more accurately, god-types, for the general perception of divinity among the Celts was of an all-purpose, multi-faceted being possessing a variety of qualities and skills. Thus the numerous individually named gods worshipped in local cults across Celtic Europe may well represent no more than the local veneration of specific aspects of common pan-Celtic deities. There does, however, appear to have been a certain divine order which was comparable with the tribal hierarchy. Each tribe had its ancestral god and there are reasons for believing that certain gods were pre-eminent in the Celtic pantheon. In fact, Caesar tells us that the Gauls 'worship Mercury most of all. He has the greatest number of images.' It is generally held that this god is a Romanized version of Lugh, one of the greatest divinities encountered in the vernacular literature, and one whose name can be traced in placenames and inscriptions across the Celtic world. The antlered god Cernunnos is also found in many areas of Celtic Europe.

The nature-based character of Celtic religion is at all times evident. This is emphasized not merely by the recurring importance of natural places, but also by the prominent role played by birds and animals in ritual activities and by the frequency with which these figure in iconographical representations. Creatures of the water and the forest predominate. Most notable among the birds are ducks, geese and swans but the raven too is a recurring motif. Among the animals, the boar and the stag stand out.

On all matters of importance those professionally trained in the conduct of religious affairs – the Druids – were consulted. These were an important priestly caste who, according to Caesar, were 'concerned with the worship of the gods, look after public and private sacrifice and expound religious matters'. They were from high-born families and had to undergo lengthy oral training of up to twenty years. Divination was an important activity carried out by the Druids and associated with this was the practice of human sacrifice. Their influence was profound, in secular as well as in religious matters, and politically they were also a powerful force. They also seem to have had a judicial role and could settle disputes and decide on awards and penalties in criminal cases.

According to Caesar, the practice of Druidism developed in Britain and spread from there to Gaul. He stated that students travelled from Gaul to Britain to learn the secrets of Druidic art. A Druid centre existed on Anglesey in Wales, and the famous hoard of Iron Age metalwork found at Llyn Cerrig Bach on that island – dating from about 150 BC to AD 60 – may represent a succession of offerings by Druids in a sacred lake. The presence of Irish artifacts in this hoard suggests that people travelled from Ireland, too, perhaps to attend the sacred Druidic rites there. The Romans destroyed the Druidic centre on Anglesey in AD 61 and Tacitus, writing of their final stand in melodramatic terms, describes how the Druids 'lifting up their hands to heaven and pouring forth dreadful curses, scared our soldiers by the unfamiliar sight so that, as if their limbs were paralyzed, they stood motionless and exposed to wounds'. The Romans inevitably prevailed, however, and the sacred groves of the Druids were chopped down.

The complexity of Celtic religious beliefs and practices often defies easy reconstruction from material remains. For archaeology tends to uncover only the end-products of what were probably elaborate and long-drawn out ritual activities. Here, therefore, we enter the fascinating realm of speculation. For instance, is a particular building, represented in the archaeological record as an arrangement of postholes, a domestic residence – or was it too large, perhaps a temple? Were the objects disposed of in watery places (such as rivers or lakes) lost or discarded, or were they formally deposited as votive offerings to supernatural beings? Or, alternatively, were these valuable items deliberately disposed of or destroyed as part of an important activity to enhance the status of the upper echelons of Iron Age society? While we may never know the answers with absolute certainty, in trying to unravel the shadowy ritual world of the Celts the archaeologist must at least ask questions and offer tentative suggestions.

Ritual sites

In an earlier chapter we discussed the great internally ditched hilltop enclosures, and concluded that these were probably places where major religious assemblies occurred at key festivals during the annual cycle. Excavations at three sites – Dún Ailinne, Emain Macha and Raffin – revealed the former existence of enigmatic wooden structures. It is distinctly possible that these buildings had a primarily non-secular character, and it is widely held that the large Phase 4 circular structure at Emain Macha was, in fact, a temple. Indeed, Chris Lynn has recently put forward an elaborate hypothesis in which he suggested that the 'temple', the cairn and the covering earthen mound at Navan represent a deliberately planned, threefold cosmological construction laden with the most complex ritual meaning and dedicated to a Celtic version of the sky-god Jupiter. Intriguingly, a radiate pattern is recognizable in the stone arrangement of the cairn – a point of no small significance, for amongst the Celts the wheel is the symbol of the sky-god. Lynn further suggests that the central post could represent the sacred tree, the symbol of tribal integrity (see p. 83). His arguments are detailed and ingenious, and are not lightly to be dismissed.

Early prehistoric burial mounds were also sites of respect and veneration for the Iron Age inhabitants of Ireland, and were sometimes reused by them as burial places. Such might have been seen as enduring symbols of the ancient integrity of the tribe, emphasizing the stability of the people and their direct links with past generations. Neolithic and Bronze Age cairns and barrows were thus often an important element at sites which came to be ceremonial centres during the Iron Age. Cruachain and Tara are but two examples. We may also wonder if the frequent presence of prehistoric burial mounds within the ramparts of hillforts is part of this same preoccupation. It is interesting, at any rate, to note that ancient burial mounds retained their status as places of inauguration and ceremonial into the medieval period.

The larger mounds, notably the passage tombs in the Boyne Valley and at Lough Crew, Co. Meath, figure prominently in pagan mythology as places of supernatural mystery and as the abodes of Otherworld beings. Indeed, it has been suggested that the large collection of enigmatic bone flakes found in the chamber of passage tomb H at Lough Crew is in some way linked to ritual practices taking place on this remote hilltop site. Similarly, the Roman gold coins and jewellery found outside the Newgrange tumulus are sometimes seen as offerings placed there by provincial Roman visitors (p. 210). The stone carvings of presumed Iron Age date now housed in the Church of Ireland cathedral on the hilltop in Armagh city are thought by some commentators to indicate the former existence of a Celtic sanctuary of some sort which was replaced by the Christian foundation. Unfortunately, however, we cannot be certain that the stone sculptures are, in fact, originally from the site.

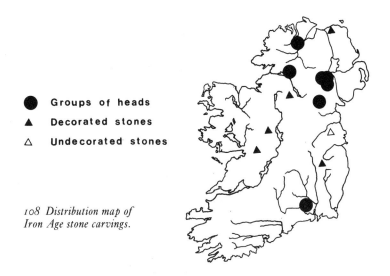

108 Distribution map of Iron Age stone carvings.

● Groups of heads

▲ Decorated stones

△ Undecorated stones

Standing stones

Few would doubt that the Irish Iron Age monoliths, both decorated and plain, served a votive or cult purpose. The *Lía Fáil* on the summit of Tara has already been commented upon (p. 67) and the written sources, however fanciful they might be, at least give an indication of the sort of ritual practices which might have been associated with these stones.

The decorated stones, of which five are known, are from widely scattered *fig. 109* locations in the country. None is in its original position and none is referred to *fig. 108* in the early literature. Information concerning original siting is available only in the case of the granite monolith now standing at Turoe in Co. Galway: before

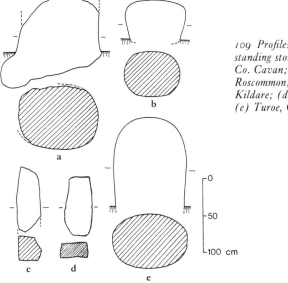

109 Profiles of five decorated Irish standing stones from (a) Killycluggin, Co. Cavan; (b) Castlestrange, Co. Roscommon; (c) Mullaghmast, Co. Kildare; (d) Derrykeighan, Co. Antrim; (e) Turoe, Co. Galway.

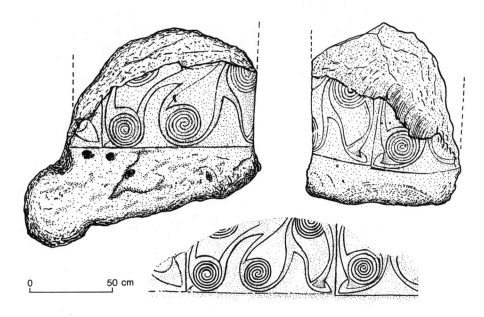

0   50 cm

110 Fragmentary decorated standing stone from Killycluggin in Co. Cavan.

removal to its present location in the 1850s it stood near the bottom of the low hillock of Feerwore, about 100 m to the west of the rath which was once situated on its summit. The stone at Killycluggin, Co. Cavan was extensively smashed *fig. 110* before the stump was buried near the foot of a small drumlin. We cannot say how far it was rolled before the attempt was made to dispose of it, nor indeed can we be sure if the damage was done in ancient or modern times. A small stone circle is situated on the nearby summit of the drumlin – so perhaps the stone was once associated with this monument.

It may reasonably be assumed that these stones were focal points in outdoor ceremonies of some sort. In the Rhineland, where decorated Iron Age stones also occur, they are often seen as having had a phallic significance and thus associated with a fertility cult. In Brittany, the majority of the Iron Age stones have been removed to new locations but when their original positions can be established it has been shown that they often served as the monumental focus of an Iron Age cemetery.

Wet sites: rivers, lakes and bogs

Iron Age finds from watery contexts are frequent in Ireland and, as already stated, it may well be that many of these items came to their last resting places in the course of ritual activities. Rivers figure prominently in Celtic mythology for the waters of rivers were inextricably bound up with the fertility of the soil. Each river had its tutelary goddess and many of today's river names – for example, the Shannon and the Boyne – derive directly from the names of such divinities. Springs and wells, too, had important supernatural properties, especially curative properties, and the many holy wells which are today dispersed across the Irish countryside are doubtless the Christianized descendants of places of pagan pilgrimage. A major hoard of Celtic metalwork from a well at Duchcov in Bohemia and the famous collection of Gallo-Roman wooden carvings found at the source of the Seine near Dijon in France (Fontes Sequana) are but two archaeological examples of the significance of such sites to the Celts.

Lakes, too, were sacred places among the Celtic peoples of Europe. As the Roman writer Seneca put it: 'the dark colour and unfathomable depth of their waters has conferred a sacred character upon some pools'. We can also point to the famous example of the lake at Toulouse which was the focus of a cult to the god Belenus by the local tribe the Volcae Tectosages. After the conquest of the tribe in 106 BC a great wealth of offerings was found there by the Roman consul L. Servilius Caepio. Indeed, as late as the sixth century AD, Geoffrey of Tours refers to a Gallo-Roman lakeside festival which included votive offerings thrown into the lake.

Archaeological evidence testifying to the sacredness of rivers and lakes is forthcoming but not always unambiguous. The eponymous site of La Tène, for example, a major deposit of material in Lake Neuchâtel in Switzerland, is usually accepted as having been a significant place of votive deposition in the last few centuries BC. The recent suggestion that it was a trading station on the lake which had suffered a natural catastrophe has received little support and seems unlikely. Comparable to La Tène is the collection of high quality metalwork found at Llyn Cerrig Bach, Anglesey in Wales earlier referred to. This is also usually interpreted as an accumulation of ritual offerings thrown into a sacred lake.

While large hoards of objects in watery places are likely to have been votive offerings, what about individual finds? On balance, it seems probable that these too were often deposited deliberately rather than lost, for once again they tend to display exceptional artisanship and are frequently of a military nature.

In Ireland, too, fine metalwork has been recovered from rivers and lakes. The River Bann, for example, has produced ornate bronze scabbard plates, spear ferrules, bridle-bits, spun bronze bowls and, from Loughan Island near Camus, the superbly crafted bronze Bann disc (Chapter 7). The Shannon, too, has produced swords, spear ferrules and brooches of high quality, and the magnificent bird-handled cup from Keshcarrigan, Co. Leitrim was recovered from one of the rivers flowing into the Shannon. Most of these items are not damaged, useless objects: the majority are in near perfect condition and a significant percentage is likely to have been thrown into the waters for votive purposes.

In this regard we should also remember the famous hoard of gold objects found at Broighter in Co. Derry. The find was discovered in the flood plain of the River Roe not far from the old coastline and must surely be regarded as a votive deposit. Indeed, on the Continent, such torcs are almost exclusively votive in character. It is particularly interesting to compare the find with that said to be from St Louis near Basle in Switzerland where a gold collar was found with other gold objects in the floodplain of the River Rhine.

The same applies to the fine metalwork often recovered from Irish lakes. For instance, a perfectly preserved, enamelled horse-bit from Lough Beg in Co. Antrim, a horse-bit and spearheads from Lough Inchiquin, Co. Clare, and two finely cast bronze yoke-mounts from Lough Gur, Co. Limerick, may also have come to their final resting places in non-secular contexts. Most telling of all, however, is the discovery in 1798 of four superbly made, sheet-bronze trumpets in the little lake of Loughnashade, situated at the foot of the hilltop upon which stands Emain Macha, the capital of ancient Ulster. Nobody can doubt that these great parade instruments were deliberately deposited in the lake. The reported discovery of human skulls in the same lake strongly supports the view that this was indeed a ritual deposition.

In Ireland, as elsewhere in Iron Age Europe, bogs have yielded significant items which could in many instances be interpreted as votive deposits. Thus the two gold collars found in a bog at Knock, Co. Roscommon (formerly Clonmacnoise), for example, or the many horse harness sets, might have been offerings. Perhaps too an element of votive intent lies behind the frequency with which beehive quernstones came to be discarded in bogs; and it is also difficult to envisage secular circumstances in which the large bronze cauldrons could have come to the bogs in which they were found. Indeed, the significance of the cauldron in Celtic mythology as a symbol of plenty and of rebirth is well known and the probable ritual deposition of cauldrons full of metal artifacts at sites as far apart as Duchcov in Bohemia and Carlingwark in Scotland emphasizes the cult importance of such containers among the Celts. Above all, the elaborate silver example from the Danish bog at Gundestrup shows, beyond reasonable doubt, the importance of the cauldron as a ritual object.

The most significant Iron Age bog deposit ever found in Ireland came to light in the last decades of the nineteenth century at Lisnacrogher in Co. Antrim, yielding the country's largest known collection of Iron Age metalwork. While no proper observations were made when the site was first discovered in the course of peat-cutting (before it was entirely obliterated by the actions of collectors and treasure hunters), early accounts refer to upright and horizontal timbers and to areas of brushwood. The site is thus frequently regarded as a crannóg. This is by no means certain, however, because the precise character of the wooden construction unearthed there is unclear. Moreover, the association of the La Tène metalwork with the so-called crannóg has never been demonstrated. Indeed, such an association was actually questioned by the renowned Scottish antiquarian Robert Munro, who visited the site in 1886.

It is thus possible, even likely, that Lisnacrogher – like Llyn Cerrig Bach or La Tène itself – was a site of votive significance rather than a settlement. It should not be forgotten that at La Tène, wooden structures existed (including two pile-supported bridges or jetties), from which offerings were probably thrown into the lake. Something similar might have existed at Lisnacrogher. In addition, the significant concentration of high status objects on the site, especially weapons and beautifully decorated scabbards (as at La Tène), allied to the essential absence of the more mundane trappings of domestic activity, lend support to the idea that this was not a secular habitation.

Human and animal forms

In stone a number of religious carvings of likely Iron Age date exists. Most are representations of the human form, principally of the human head, with the notable exception of three stone bears (one with a dog's or wolf's head carved between the legs) which once existed at Cathedral Hill in Armagh City. There *pl. 76* is clear evidence that the bear was venerated among certain Gaulish tribes on the Continent and the goddess Artio was especially associated with these animals. It is thus possible that a bear cult existed in the Armagh region, though there is no evidence that bears were present in Ireland at this time.

Heads of probably Iron Age date are mainly found in northern areas of the country, clustered in groups in the Raphoe area of Donegal, in the lower Lough Erne region of Co. Fermanagh, around Corleck in Co. Cavan and in three separate groups centred on Armagh city. There are also a few isolated examples *fig. 108* in other parts of the country. These heads underline again the Celtic character of Irish society, for the cult of the head was widespread in all areas of Celtic Europe. For the Celts the head was the seat of the soul, the very essence of the human personality which, in their iconography, came to represent the god. Heads of vanquished enemies were collected and preserved to be displayed as symbols of status and prowess and as a source of magico-ritual power. In this context, the human skulls found in the ritual lake of Loughnashade are significant and it is also important to note the concentration of skull bones and teeth, dated by radiocarbon to the Iron Age, which were found as secondary insertions in one of the Neolithic tombs at Carrowmore, Co. Sligo. The discovery prompted the excavator to suggest that 'an Early Iron Age tradition with deposition of skulls, as sacrifices or burials, cannot be excluded'.[11] This is even more strikingly suggested by the skull burial at Raffin (p. 80).

In Ireland, as elsewhere in the Celtic world, the realistic portrayal of the human form was of no great concern to Celtic craftsmen. In Europe this came late, following contact with the Mediterranean world, while in Ireland such realism was never achieved and archaic traditions of pagan Celtic figure sculpture were preserved. The best examples display an economy of detail and a deceptive simplicity, verging at times almost on crudeness, which manage, nonetheless, to evoke a deeply impressive feeling of the supernatural. The three-faced head from Corleck, Co. Cavan is one of the finest instances of Celtic *pls. 73, 74* stone sculpture in Ireland. In each case the human visage is indicated by circular eyes, glowering brow-ridge, rudimentary, spatulate nose and a straight, uncompromising split for a mouth. There is nothing else, no ears, no hair, nothing to soften the severity of the carving. Each face differs slightly from the next but in each we can sense the stern and brooding presence of an Otherworld being. Each embodies the unmistakable aura of power and of scarcely concealed menace. All that we know of the Celtic idea of the supernatural is encapsulated in this Co. Cavan carving.

pl. 75   Impressive too is the carving known as the Tanderagee idol. In this instance the carving is a human bust with the stumps of horns projecting from the forehead and a wide open, shrieking mouth. One arm, stretched stiffly across the chest, grips the other which seems to be severed. There is a hint of clothing. The figure has a terrifying appearance and must have been an object of awe and dread in its original setting – perhaps a centrepiece of cult activities.

There are other important carvings too but not all are as unequivocally Iron Age in date as the two described above. The janus figures on Boa Island in Co. Fermanagh, for example, display interesting details of clothing and facial hair, and could belong to the pre-Christian period. Similarly, the head from Beltany, Co. Donegal may well be pagan, especially if the indistinct carving around the neck is indeed a torc as has been suggested. It has also been argued that the presence of a tiny 'whistle-hole', bored into the mouth of several of the Irish heads, indicates an Iron Age date, for this feature has been noted on heads outside the country, from as far away as Bohemia.

The wooden figure from Ralaghan, Co. Cavan was once believed to be Iron Age in date. On the basis of recent radiocarbon evidence, however, it is now thought to belong to the earlier rather than the later part of the last pre-Christian millennium i.e. to the later Bronze Age (see above, p. 24). Certainly Iron Age in date is the strangely carved runner discovered under the roadway at

fig. 111   Corlea, Co. Longford (p. 101). It was a stout, more or less straight log of ash, 14 cm thick and about 5 m long. It had been trimmed of branches and chopped at one end to a blunted point. At the other end a deep notch had been adzed around the circumference of the log about 16 cm from its end. The knob thus formed was roughly flattened at the top and the edges were crudely rounded. The stump of a branch was left projecting upwards from the base of the knob and 12 cm below the notch the stump of a second branch was also left projecting in the same direction as the first. The impression created by the whole carving is crudely zoomorphic or perhaps even anthropomorphic.

The carving, however rough and unsophisticated it might seem, had been executed deliberately for a specific purpose. Is it possible that it once stood upright like a totem pole as a focus of some Iron Age ritual, as perhaps did the central oak post in the Phase 4 structure at Navan Fort (see p. 78)? Indeed, free-standing timber uprights were a feature of many Celtic sanctuaries and sacred sites in Britain, Gaul and as far east as Bohemia.

Inevitably the description of a sacred Gaulish grove, written by the first-century Roman poet Lucan, is called to mind:

A grove never violated during long ages, which with its knitted branches shut in the darkened air and the cold shade . . . From the black springs water wells up and gloomy images of the Gods, rough-hewn from tree trunks, stand there . . . The people do not frequent it to worship but leave it to the Gods.

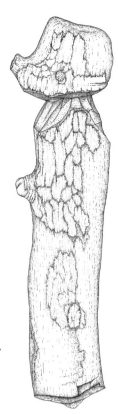

111 A zoomorphically carved ash stem used as a runner in the construction of the Corlea road. It perhaps originally served as a kind of totem pole. c. 1/8.

Of more direct relevance, however, are the tall wooden figures – believed to be of ritual character – which were erected in bogs in the last centuries BC and the early centuries AD in northern and eastern Germany and southern Scandinavia. Natural timbers with anthropomorphic features were chosen and these were then carved in varying degrees of crudeness to produce both male and female figures. Some scholars believe that these carvings figured in cult practices focused around a nature religion which placed specific emphasis on fertility, growth and reproductive cycles. Sacred trees were important, and one commentator has written that 'in spite of their sophisticated tools and skill as craftsmen, the awkward crudeness of all these figures is striking and must have been deliberate'.[12]

A bog in east Germany at Oberdorla near Mühlhausen has produced several carvings which are strikingly reminiscent of the knob-ended log from Corlea.[13] One in particular, though forked at the end to give the appearance of legs, has a 'head' produced by flattening the end of the log and cutting a deep notch around it exactly as on the Irish carving. At Oberdorla there is no question but that the carvings were intended to represent the human form.

Bog bodies

In southern areas of Scandinavia, in north Germany and occasionally in Britain, well-preserved human corpses of Iron Age date have been found in bogs. In many instances there is strong evidence to suggest that the individuals concerned were killed and buried in the course of ritual activities. We need only think of the famous Danish finds from Tollund (where the victim was hanged) and Grauballe (where his throat was cut) and, more recently, of the discovery made at Lindow Moss in Cheshire, England. Death by strangulation or hanging is a recurrent feature of these burials and, in the case of Lindow Man, a systematic death ritual took place which involved the initial pole-axing of the male victim, after which he was garrotted using a cord of sinew, and finally had his throat cut. In Ireland, a sizeable number of bodies has been recovered over the years in areas of bogland. The majority, however, are of fairly recent date, belonging to the early historic or the medieval periods, and until recently none has been regarded as dating to the Iron Age. But new radiocarbon dates have suggested that one of our best-known bog bodies may belong to this period. Even more intriguing is the possibility that the find may be the first Irish instance of Iron Age ritual deposition.

pl. 77   The body was found in 1821 at a depth of almost 3 m in a bog at Gallagh, near Castleblakeney in Co. Galway. The find was the subject of considerable local interest at the time and, after reburial, was dug up on a number of subsequent occasions to show to curious visitors. Eight years after its discovery it was presented to the Royal Dublin Society where it was displayed for many years before coming to the Royal Irish Academy (later the National Museum) in 1860. It was never conserved and is now in a shrivelled and shrunken state with few of the details originally present now surviving. Samples from the body recently analyzed, though in one instance suggesting a date in the Early Bronze Age, allow for the possibility that the body could belong to the latter part of the last millennium BC.

According to contemporary accounts, the Castleblakeney body was that of a young man with long, black hair and a beard. He was clothed in a tight dress or cape, stated to have been of deerskin, which extended as far as the knees. This was laced at the front and tied at the neck with a band of sally rods. At either side of the body, placed at an angle, was a pointed stake about 1.80 m in length. As Raghnaill O Floinn has recently suggested, the two flanking stakes imply that this was a deliberate burial and not an accidental drowning. He further suggests that the band of twisted sally rods could, in fact, have been a garrotte which was used to strangle the victim. Unfortunately the hazel band has not survived, nor is there any medical evidence to indicate that it was, in fact, used to dispatch the Castleblakeney man.

Burials

Death represents the ultimate confrontation between the human and the supernatural worlds. The surviving burial remains and the associated funerary monuments thus provide us with the clearest and most tangible surviving evidence of religious beliefs and practices.

A few dozen sites in scattered areas of the country have been investigated, and these show that throughout the centuries of the Iron Age there was considerable variety in the means of disposing of the dead. Of the recognizably Iron Age burials only a handful are likely to be the graves of intruders, for with rare exceptions, the burials of Iron Age Ireland are of decidedly local character and seem to reflect a long continuity of funerary practices extending back to remote antiquity. The few demonstrably foreign burials stand apart because of their obviously exotic grave goods.

Both cremation and inhumation were practised during the Iron Age in Ireland but there are some grounds for believing that cremation existed earlier. People continued to cremate their dead, at least sporadically, until well into the first Christian millennium, as suggested by a radiocarbon age determination of AD 430–580 for charcoal broadly contemporary with a cremation deposit under a mound at Furness, Co. Kildare.

The remains of the dead were sometimes covered by simple mounds or ringbarrows, or placed in the ground within embanked earthen enclosures. Sometimes older mounds were reused for burial purposes in the Iron Age. Simple cremations in pits, without a covering mound, may in some instances at least date to the Iron Age; and of the many flat inhumations – some in cists, some not – there are several which could also belong to this period.

It is possible, though not yet positively demonstrated, that ringbarrows are the earliest recognizable Iron Age form of burial in Ireland though, of course, their orgins lie in the Bronze Age. They appear at any rate to have been a dominant type, as hinted at by the presence of no fewer than thirty-five examples at the royal site of Cruachain in Co. Roscommon. Ringbarrows usually consist of a low, circular mound, generally less than 1 m in height and sometimes barely perceptible, enclosed by a fosse with low external bank. They rarely exceed 15 m in overall diameter. Evidence to date indicates that cremation was the exclusive rite practised by those burying their dead in ringbarrows, and individual mounds were used over a period of time, perhaps as family or tribal cemeteries. At Grannagh in Co. Galway, for example, a ringbarrow some 13.3 m in overall diameter, there were at least six interments, *fig. 112* the earlier ones in the centre and four in the silted fosse. Grave goods there were simple, consisting of bronze fibulae, beads of glass and bone and a few other *fig. 113* small items. At Oran Beg, not far from Grannagh in Co. Galway, three cremations were found in the ditch, one in the central mound. Principal grave goods were glass beads. At the classic ringbarrow of Carrowjames, Co. Mayo, no fewer than twenty-five burials occurred in the mound, concentrated towards *fig. 114* the centre in three main phases of burial activity. Only nine contained accompanying artifacts – and most of these were beads, metal rings and a variety of small objects of bronze. The mound was one of ten in a barrow cemetery. At least eight of these belonged to the Middle Bronze Age.

Tumulus II at Cush represents a different type of burial monument. This was a circular mound, 13.7 m in diameter and 2 m high, with a shallow external fosse. In the old ground surface under the mound, dug centrally into an area of fire-reddened soil (the probable site of the pyre), was a small pit which contained the burnt remains of a single individual. Accompanying the ashes

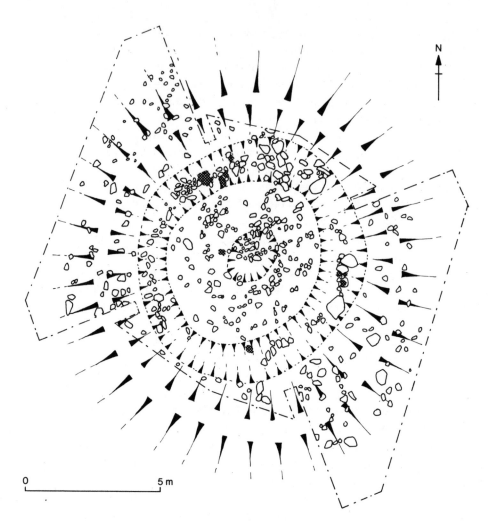

112 An Iron Age ringbarrow at Grannagh, Co. Galway. Cremation deposits are marked by cross-hatching. The depression at the centre of the mound was caused by early twentieth-century excavations.

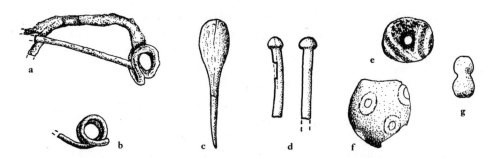

113 A selection of the grave goods from the ringbarrow at Grannagh. (a,b) Bronze fibulae; (c,d) bone pins; (e,f) glass beads; (g) bone bead. 1/1.

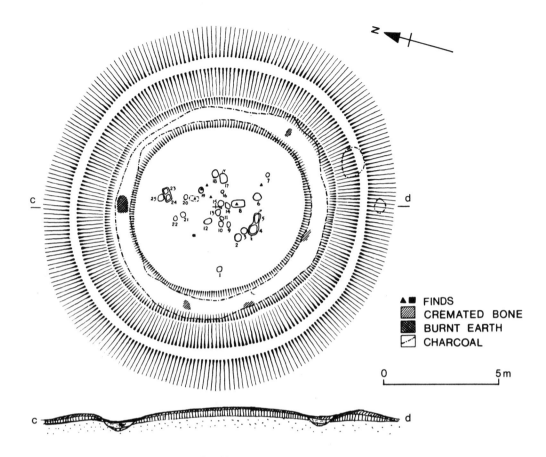

114 Iron Age ringbarrow at Carrowjames, Co. Mayo.

was a small, rectangular bone plaque with compass-drawn motifs adorning each face. Nearby stood a second, similar mound with an unaccompanied cremation (Tumulus III) which could also be of Iron Age date. A third mound in the vicinity (Tumulus I), which was found to contain urn-burials, clearly dates to the Early or Middle Bronze Age.

pl. 41

A low mound (Site C), one of three burial sites on the summit of Carbury Hill, Co. Kildare, was just over 8 m in diameter and some 90 cm in height. It covered a single cremation deposit which was without grave goods. The two other burial monuments on the hill, each formed by an enclosing bank with

fig. 115

fig. 116

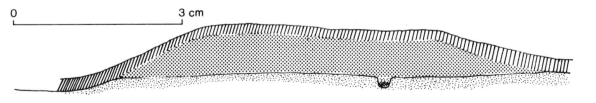

115 Site C at Carbury Hill, Co. Kildare. A burial mound with a cremation deposit is shown.

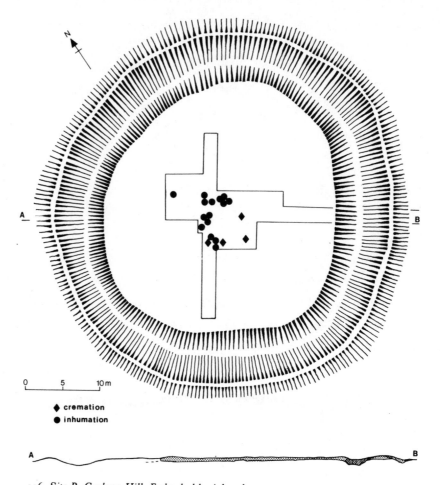

116 Site B, Carbury Hill. Embanked burial enclosure.

internal fosse (in one instance gapped at two opposed points on its circumference), may also belong to the Iron Age, perhaps late within the period, but firm dating evidence is again lacking. In one (Site A) there were two unaccompanied cremation deposits. In the other (Site B) there were four cremations and fifteen inhumations. In the latter instance it was interesting to note that the cremations preceded the inhumations. Nondescript grave goods *fig. 74* included a pair of iron shears, and a pair of iron rings which may have been part of a belt.

fig. 117 A unique Iron Age cemetery existed at Kiltierney, Co. Fermanagh. Initially a circular cairn of Neolithic date, probably a passage tomb, stood on the site. Some time around the birth of Christ the mound was reused as a place of burial and was substantially remodelled. During this period a ditch was excavated around the cairn and the material from this was used, partly to increase the height of the mound, partly to construct no fewer than nineteen small circular 'satellite' mounds around its perimeter. This secondary activity seems to have been conceived and carried out in a single phase. The encircling mounds were,

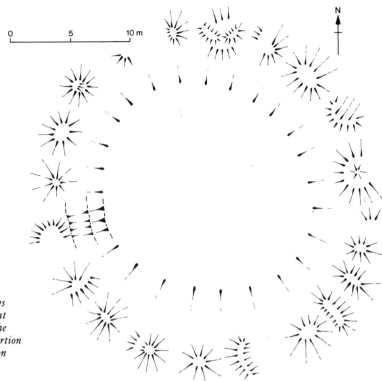

117 Iron Age 'satellite' barrows encircling a Neolithic tumulus at Kiltierney, Co. Fermanagh. The latter was also used for the insertion of secondary Iron Age cremation burials.

on average, 3 m in diameter and generally around 1 m in height. A series of cremations in small pits was placed in the main mound and the smaller mounds were also used to cover scatters of cremated human bones. Grave goods *fig. 118* included fibulae, glass beads and, under one of the satellite mounds, broken and burnt fragments of an enamelled bronze object which may be a portion of a decorated mirror handle.

Reuse of an earlier mound, in this instance of the Middle Bronze Age, also took place at Carrowbeg North, Co. Galway. During the Iron Age, and probably late in the period, four inhumations were inserted into the silted-up *fig. 119* ditch. Of these, three were extended, one was flexed. Grave goods were present

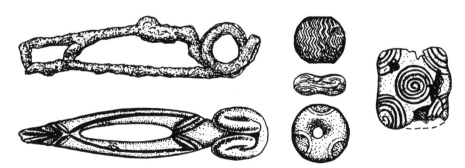

118 A selection of iron, bronze and glass grave goods from Kiltierney. 1/1.

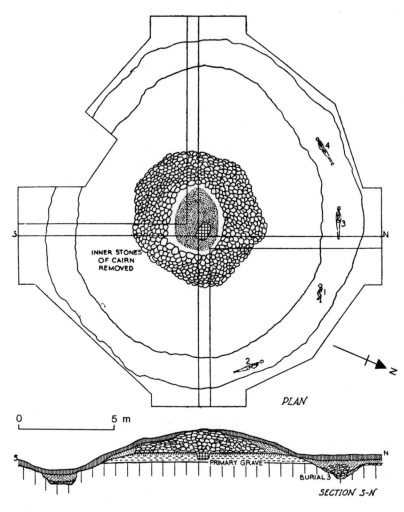

119,120 Four Iron Age burials were inserted into a Middle Bronze Age barrow at Carrowbeg North, Co. Galway (above). Only the flexed skeleton was found with any grave goods; these included a locket and a string of bone beads (left); 1/1.

in one instance only, that of the flexed skeleton, which was female. Around one ankle she wore a string of bone beads and in the upper chest or shoulder area she carried a bronze locket to which traces of textile were adhering (see *fig. 120*). At Pollacorragune, Co. Galway two mounds, again of probable Middle Bronze Age date, appear also to have been places of secondary burial in the Iron Age. The early excavations which took place there were unsatisfactory, so that details are extremely vague. It seems, however, that cremations were present and that these were accompanied by glass beads and amorphous iron objects.

As earlier noted, an interesting series of burials was discovered during excavations at the Rath of the Synods on the Hill of Tara in the 1950s. These clearly predated the ringfort on the site and are thus earlier than the Roman finds uncovered there. Their precise dating has not, however, been determined. The earliest burials occurred in a low mound with external ditch. Its maximum dimensions were 14.9 m by 16.5 m and it was preserved to a height of 85 cm. A total of ten burials was associated with this mound, five of which (or possibly six) were primary, four belonging to a slightly later phase. All were in unprotected pits. Apart from a single crouched inhumation belonging to the secondary phase, all were cremations. The only identifications consisted of a 'young adult' and a 'possible adult'.

This phase of burial was succeeded by a series of timber-built enclosures. There then followed a second period of sepulchral activity. This consisted of a small, flat cemetery of seven burials clustered together in an area measuring 6 m by 4 m. There were five inhumations and two cremations. An eighth burial, a cremation, 7.5 m to the east of this cluster, is probably contemporary with them. The interments were in simple pits, one of which appears to have been partly sealed by four small flags. Three of the inhumations were crouched, one extended and one disturbed. Identifications indicated the presence of a child and three adults, one of which may have been male. Some nondescript items of iron, bronze and bone may be grave goods but it is not certain if such items are primary in every instance. In at least one case, however, animal bones in the grave may be an original feature.

Simple, unaccompanied cremations are generally undatable, but it is likely that such methods of interment were widespread during the Iron Age and, no doubt, during the later Bronze Age as well. At Tara a series of secondary, unaccompanied cremations inserted into the earthen mantle of the Mound of the Hostages are generally regarded as dating to the Middle Bronze Age. Some could belong to a later phase of prehistory. Indeed, the presence at the site of a portion of a yellow, spiral-inlaid glass bead of probable Iron Age type, which may well have come from one of the burials there, strongly implies that burial activities on the mound continued into the Celtic period. Otherwise, the only probable Iron Age examples thus far recognized, apart from those at the Rath of the Synods, have been found at Cullen, Co. Tipperary where a series of pit-cremations (one accompanied by bone beads) formed the last of a long sequence of prehistoric burials on the site.

Unaccompanied inhumation burials are also, in most instances, undatable. While some of the many isolated examples known could well belong to some period (probably late) in the Iron Age, many could be substantially later than this while some could be earlier. On stratigraphic grounds a date around or shortly after the birth of Christ was established for the inhumation in a cist at the occupation site of Feerwore, Co. Galway. Some centuries later than this is the cemetery of unprotected inhumations, thirty in number, which has recently been excavated around the great Neolithic mound of Knowth in Co. Meath. *fig. 121* The majority of the skeletons were flexed, a few were extended. In four instances radiocarbon dates between 190 BC and AD 250 have been established. There are also two somewhat later dates. One interesting double burial (Nos. 8/9) was that of two adult males, both decapitated, who lay head to toe in a *fig. 122* single pit. Beads of bone and glass, metal rings, bone dice and other 'gaming

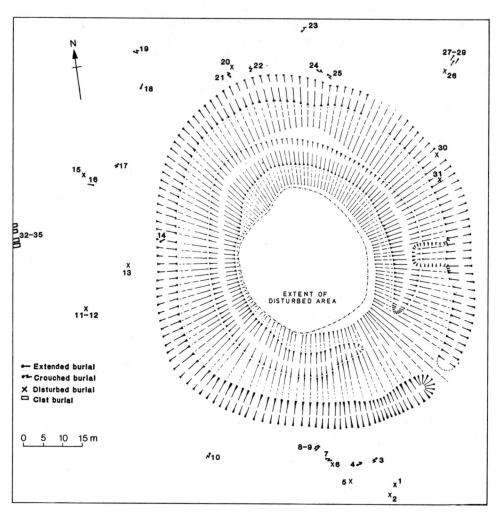

Extended burial
Crouched burial
X Disturbed burial
Cist burial

0   5   10   15 m

N

EXTENT OF
DISTURBED AREA

121 Some thirty inhumation burials of Iron Age and later date have been discovered around the Neolithic passage tomb at Knowth, Co. Meath. Note that burial 1 is Neolithic, while burials 32–35 belong to the Medieval period.

pieces' were the principal grave goods. This interment has a calibrated radiocarbon date of 40 BC–AD 100.

As stated earlier, the majority of Iron Age burials in Ireland are of essentially indigenous character. A small number, however, clearly reflect foreign influences and several are likely to be the last resting places of immigrants. The majority of these belong to a late phase of the Iron Age, and appear to indicate contact with the world of provincial Rome (pp. 200, 207, 209). One example, however – a cremation in a bronze bowl with ornithomorphic suspension-lugs, *fig. 123* recently found in a pit within a defended enclosure at Fore, Co. Westmeath – owes nothing to Roman traditions. The bowl is, in all probability, an import from southern Britain and is likely to date a century or more before the Roman conquest of that island.

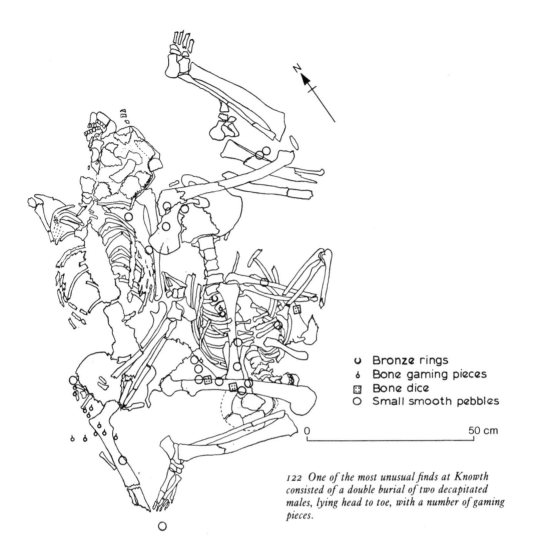

○ Bronze rings
◊ Bone gaming pieces
▦ Bone dice
◯ Small smooth pebbles

0   50 cm

122 One of the most unusual finds at Knowth consisted of a double burial of two decapitated males, lying head to toe, with a number of gaming pieces.

123 This bronze bowl was used as a container for a cremation deposit and was found within a fortified enclosure at Fore in Co. Westmeath. c. 1/3.

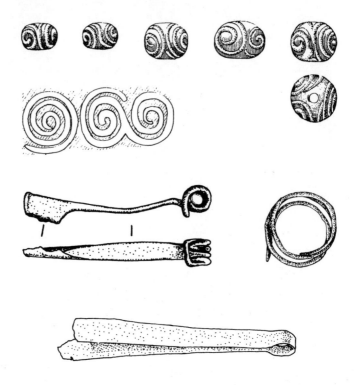

124 A selection of the grave goods accompanying the cremation burial at 'Loughey', Co. Down. 1/1.

The celebrated burial found in the middle of the last century near Donaghadee in Co. Down known as the 'Loughey' burial (though there is no known site of that name in the country) has until recently also been considered as the grave of a southern British immigrant. It appears to have been a cremation (though the original report does not make this clear) and was accompanied by a string of 150 beads and two bracelets of glass, a bronze fibula, two finger rings, a pair of tweezers and a straight, knobbed implement, all of *fig. 124* bronze. Other finds from the burial were lost soon after its discovery. Because the beads included a number of examples of yellow paste with inlaid spirals it was presumed that they derived from Meare in the English county of Somerset where similar beads were made. The fibula, belonging to the so-called Nauheim-derivative group, is also a type known in southern England in the years spanning the birth of Christ so that it was not unreasonable to view the Loughey material as an immigrant assemblage. However, recent scientific analysis of the beads by Julian Henderson has shown that their composition is quite distinct from that of the genuine Meare spiral beads. He also showed that the glass of the Loughey bracelets is Continental, so that it could be that the exotic elements at Loughey derive from the European mainland (where Nauheim-derivative fibulae are also known) rather than from southern Britain.

He did not rule out the possibility, however, that the beads from the Co. Down burial could have been locally made.

Pathological examination of human remains from Iron Age burials has produced some interesting information. Where size could be estimated, individuals were somewhat smaller than today's average. Females were under 1.50 m in height while males tended to be 1.70 m or less. It is scarcely surprising to observe that life expectancy was not high, but the almost total absence of individuals of advanced years is perhaps worthy of note. Only four of the twenty-nine burials from Knowth for which there is information are either 'middle-aged' individuals or of 'advanced age'. The older skeletons that do exist are often those of females. At Feerwore the woman was reportedly over thirty, probably over forty; and at Carbury Hill, Site B, a female in Inhumation 1 was described as rather elderly. But the average age of the deceased adults (where this could be determined) was between twenty and thirty.

Children represent a significant percentage of the burials, and the remains of children often accompany those of adults. This is readily explicable when, as in Cremation 18 at Carrowjames, the remains of an unborn foetus accompanied those of an adult, presumed to be female. But it is less clear in what circumstances children ranging from five to nine years of age came to accompany adults to the grave. In fact, at Carrowjames, apart from the unborn foetus referred to, children were exclusively buried with adults, with the sole exception of a six-year-old who was accompanied by the tiny bones of what may have been a new-born infant.

Such double-burials can be interpreted in several ways, but the possibility of human sacrifice cannot be excluded. There is ample evidence for this in other areas of the Celtic world. Human remains of suggested Iron Age date from two of the Neolithic tombs at Carrowmore, Co. Sligo could also be regarded in a similar light. Most startling, however, is the possibly Iron Age interment found within the embanked enclosure (Site 4) at the Curragh, Co. Kildare. There, buried centrally within the enclosure, lay the skeleton of a female whose strained and awkward position and unnaturally raised skull prompted the conclusion that she had, in all probability, been buried alive.

The bones thus far examined from Irish Iron Age burials reveal little about contemporary disease or disability. Only occasionally has arthritic deformation of the joints been noted and teeth are generally devoid of any traces of tooth decay, but are often exceptionally worn. Indeed, of the 168 teeth from the secondary Iron Age deposits in Grave 27 at Carrowmore, Co. Sligo (representing at least 23 individuals) only one tooth with caries was present – a lower molar. The extremely low degree of mineralization disturbance of the teeth from this site was taken to indicate that the individuals had not suffered from any serious children's diseases, nor had they been exposed to long or serious starvation periods. Thus it was concluded that their diet had been well balanced.

CHAPTER 9

Beyond the Empire

Writers of the present time have nothing to say of anything
beyond Ierne, which is just north of Britain. The natives are
wholly savage and lead a wretched existence because of the cold.
In my opinion it is there that the limits of the habitable earth
should be fixed.

STRABO (*c*. 63 BC–AD 21)

It was in AD 73 that Eleazar ben Yair, leader of the beleaguered zealot garrison
of Masada in Palestine, decided after seven years of rebellion on the ultimate act
of defiance against Roman rule. This was the mass suicide of every Jewish man,
woman and child on the encircled hilltop. Thus, no fewer than 960 souls chose
death rather than surrender to Rome.

The doomed defenders of Masada would not have known, nor indeed cared,
that at the other end of the empire, on the rain-soaked downs of northern
England, Roman legions were at the same time similarly engaged in containing
another revolt against the might of imperial Rome. In this instance it was the
Brigantes, one of the most powerful tribes of Celtic Britain, who waged war on
the Romans under their leader Venutius between AD 71 and 74. One year after
the fall of Masada, Venutius was defeated and the Brigantian uprising was at an
end.

Roman retribution in such circumstances was customarily swift and brutal,
and the situation in Brigantia can hardly have been an exception. Thus it is
likely that there were groups of survivors fleeing Roman vengeance in as yet
unconquered regions to the north and west. It may be that one such group
fig. 125 reached Lambay, a small island off the east coast of Ireland. Some of them
never left.

The burials at Lambay

At Lambay, in 1927, a number of inhumation burials was accidentally
fig. 125 uncovered in the course of harbour construction. In spite of the fact that these
were unfortunately destroyed without scientific investigation, we know that the
skeletons were flexed and they appear to have been in shallow pits covered by
clean silver sand. Among them must have been an important warrior burial, for
it is recorded that 'a sword, shield and ornaments' were found together under
'an iron disc'. The sword, fragments of which survive, had a long, heavy,
parallel-sided blade untypical of the normal short Irish weapon; and three

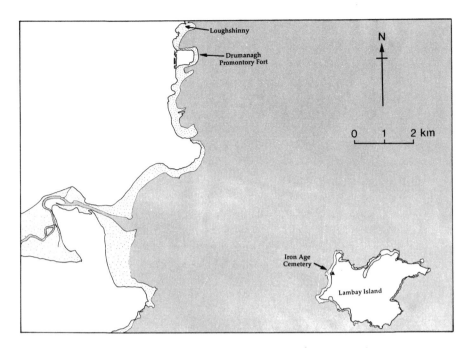

125 Location map of the Co. Dublin coast, showing Drumanagh promontory fort and the site of the Iron Age cemetery on Lambay Island.

bronze mounts from the site, two with openwork ornament, probably adorned a scabbard of leather or wood. The shield is represented in the preserved material by a bronze sub-conical boss with a disc-shaped projection at the end. Of the 'ornaments' Lambay produced five Roman fibulae, two bracelets, of jet and bronze, and a worn bronze torc of so-called beaded type. We do not know which of these accompanied the weapons. *fig. 126* *fig. 127*

Among the finds, too, were many pieces of decorative sheet-bronze, the majority of which seem to have been recovered from the spoil heaps left by the diggers. Rosette-headed studs of bronze are still attached to several of these. A number of the fragments have been successfully joined to produce two items. One of these is a circular disc with beaded edging and bears on its surface a raised, open-limbed triskele motif with central rosette stud. The second is triangular and has a separately made, cruciform boss riveted at the centre. A fragmentary iron mirror from the site may be the 'iron disc' referred to in the original account of the find. *fig. 128*

The assemblage of artifacts uncovered at Lambay is unique in Ireland. All the items are of decidedly foreign character and an origin for them in northern England has been convincingly argued. The beaded torc, in particular, is important for it is a type mainly concentrated in the territory of the Brigantes. The Roman fibulae, the rosette studs and the beading around the edge of the circular disc combine to emphasize the heavily Romanized milieu from which *fig. 129*

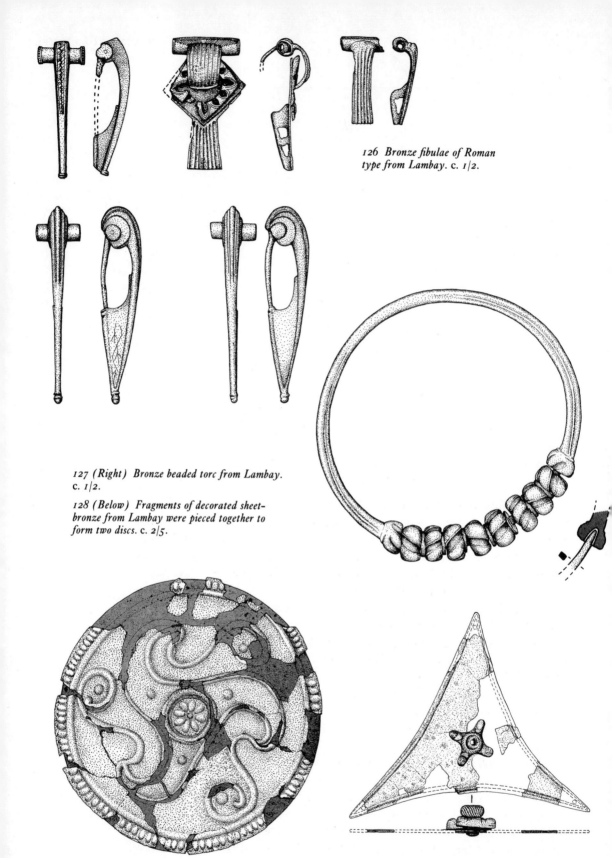

126 *Bronze fibulae of Roman type from Lambay.* c. 1/2.

127 *(Right) Bronze beaded torc from Lambay.* c. 1/2.

128 *(Below) Fragments of decorated sheet-bronze from Lambay were pieced together to form two discs.* c. 2/5.

129 Distribution map of bronze beaded torcs.

the Lambay settlers came. The finds probably date from some time in the latter part of the first century AD. Archaeology thus seems to be in agreement with the historical picture.

Ireland and the Classical authors

The extent of Roman influence in Ireland in the early centuries of the Christian era and the means by which Romanization might have taken place have long been a subject for debate. A variety of different mechanisms of introduction have been suggested, including the intriguing possibility of an attempted military incursion by Roman forces.

It is clear that a certain knowledge of Ireland existed in educated Mediterranean circles in the early centuries AD and occasional scraps of information have survived which give us a few insights into contemporary Classical perceptions of the country and its people. It is unlikely that any of the writers had ever set foot on the island, so their accounts are at best second-hand, based on those of earlier writers which themselves ultimately derive from the tales brought back by travellers such as sailors, merchants and adventurers. Many of the accounts are garbled and fanciful. Some are obviously migratory ethnographic motifs, many are rooted in Classical prejudices regarding *ultima thule* (remote countries) and the nature of barbarism. Ireland is thus often depicted as a cold and miserable place, peopled by wretched savages on the limit of the inhabited world, as the quotation from the Greek historian Strabo (above) admirably illustrates. Cannibalism and, indeed, endocannibalism (ritual eating of relatives), incest and all forms of fornication were reported to be rife. Such accounts are likely to have been based on travellers' tall tales though one author at least, Strabo, expressed reservations: 'I say this only with the understanding that I have no trustworthy witnesses for it'.

Fascinating though they are, most of these early writings can probably be dismissed as spurious – but they do contain some more reliable detail. The island was generally recognized to be smaller than Britain. Caesar, for example, referred to it as 'smaller by half', while Pomponius Mela, writing early in the first century AD, described Ireland as 'in shape oblong, with an equal length of coast on either side'. There seems to have been a general perception that Ireland lay midway between Britain and Spain.

As regards the island itself, Tacitus, writing late in the first century, notes that Ireland 'in soil, in climate and in the character and civilization of its inhabitants . . . is much like Britain'. Around the middle of the third century, Solinus repeated the standard account of the barbarism of the inhabitants, but makes interesting reference to the absence of snakes on the island (the first to do so) and refers also to the use by the natives of boats of wickerwork covered with the hides of oxen. He also retells a story which first appeared in the work of Pomponius Mela, concerning the richness of the pasture in Ireland: according to this account, if the cattle are not restrained at regular intervals from eating, the rich grass will cause them to burst! Interesting, too, is the late fourth-century account of Symmachus who refers to seven Irish dogs used for public amusement 'which on the day of the prelude so astonished Rome that it was thought they must have been brought in iron cages'.

A chance phrase by Tacitus is particularly important. He tells us that Ireland's 'approaches and harbours are tolerably well known from merchants who trade there'. This supports the general assumption that extensive trading contacts took place between Ireland and the Roman world, and it is likely that it was through such links that the Classical authors derived their information about the island. The famous map of Claudius Ptolemaeus (Ptolemy), undoubtedly the most important of the early documents on Ireland, was probably also essentially based on information gleaned from merchants.

Ptolemy's map

Ptolemy was born in Alexandria early in the second century AD, and was a noted mathematician, astronomer and geographer. Around the middle of the century he compiled his *Geography* which consisted of eight volumes. The greater part of the work comprises a series of tables of the different countries (there is no original map), in which such details as rivers, lakes, capes, tribes and important population centres are located by degrees of longitude and latitude. He systematically divided the surface of the known world into twenty-six fields, the first of which covers the area of Britain and Ireland. Much of the

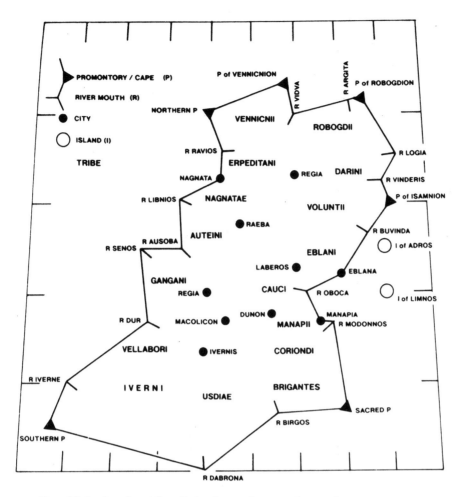

130 Map of Ireland as plotted from Ptolemy's second-century data on the country.

information goes back to Marinus of Tyre and ultimately, it seems, to the early first-century work of Philemon.

The precision of many of Ptolemy's measurements is indifferent, especially *fig. 130* for the countries of the east, but the map of Ireland, when drawn from the available figures, is surprisingly accurate along the northern, eastern and southern sides. The stormy Atlantic coasts of the west would have been less familiar to merchants and so less exactly surveyed. Some fifty-five tribal and placenames were listed by Ptolemy and these continue to be a source of great debate among scholars from the point of view of geography, philology and early Irish history. Only a few positive identifications can be made such as the rivers Shannon, Boyne, Lagan and Avoca and a number of tribal names seem recognizable in the early Irish sources – notably the Voluntii in the northeast, who are reliably equated with the Ulaidh of Ulster. The existence of a site called Isamnion located in the northeast of the country has been taken by some modern historians to refer to Emain Macha. There is, however, a *regia* site (literally 'royal place') in the area which could just as easily be the Ulster capital. The presence of Brigantes in the southeast is most interesting in view of the evidence of Lambay discussed above, but the existence in east-central Ireland of two north European tribes, the Cauci and the Menapii, is puzzling. It is also unclear precisely what is meant by the terms *regia* and *polis* which appear several times on the map.

The fact that some of the recorded names are written in the P–Celtic dialect, which was spoken in Britain and over much of the continent (as distinct from Q–Celtic which was the exclusive dialect of Ireland), has been commented upon, and some scholars have seen this as decisive evidence of intrusion from P–Celtic speaking areas abroad.[14] This is possible, but the likelihood that Ptolemy's informants were mainly seamen who themselves spoke P–Celtic dialects greatly diminishes the significance of the P–Celtic names on the Irish map (for they would inevitably have changed the local names to conform to their own linguistic practice). Furthermore, many alterations and errors would undoubtedly have crept in before the information was copied down in Greek and ultimately transposed into Latin in Italy in the late fifteenth century. The map does, however, confirm the presence of Celtic-speaking people in Ireland at the beginning of the Christian era.

Romans in Ireland

From Ptolemy's map it is reasonable to assume that commercial transactions with the natives took place in the vicinity of harbours and sheltered coastal inlets, and that merchants penetrated the interior along navigable rivers. The distribution of scattered archaeological material supports this picture. To

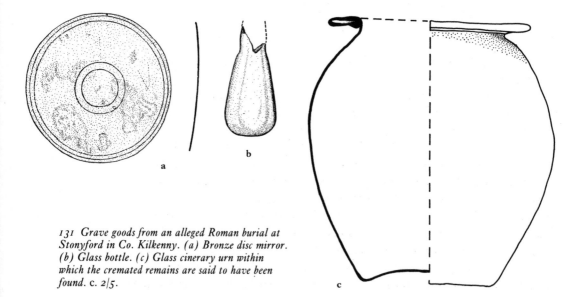

131 Grave goods from an alleged Roman burial at Stonyford in Co. Kilkenny. (a) Bronze disc mirror. (b) Glass bottle. (c) Glass cinerary urn within which the cremated remains are said to have been found. c. 2/5.

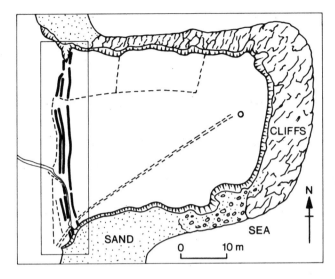

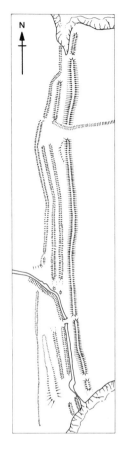

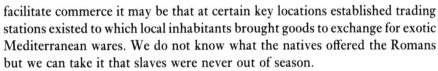

132 Site plan of the coastal promontory fort at Drumanagh, Loughshinny, Co. Dublin, with detail of its closely spaced multivallate defences.

facilitate commerce it may be that at certain key locations established trading stations existed to which local inhabitants brought goods to exchange for exotic Mediterranean wares. We do not know what the natives offered the Romans but we can take it that slaves were never out of season.

One such trading post may have existed in the vicinity of Stonyford, Co. Kilkenny. There, around the middle of the nineteenth century, a classic Roman cremation burial of the first or early second century was found. Details of the *fig. 131* discovery are contained within the sketches and hand-written notes of a scrapbook belonging to the antiquarian Henry Clibborn, now preserved in the Royal Irish Academy. The ashes of the deceased were contained in a glass cinerary urn which had been sealed by a polished bronze disc-mirror. It was accompanied by a small glass bottle, possibly a cosmetic holder. The objects are said to have been found in a rath and were 'protected by stones'. The grave goods suggest that this may well have been the burial of a woman.

Those who carried out the interment were obviously familiar with the processes of first- or second-century Roman burial ritual. This and the possibility that it was a female, along with the presence of a delicate and fragile glass urn, suggest that here we have evidence for a Roman presence more permanent than would be explained merely by occasional trading contacts. In this light, the location of Stonyford may be particularly significant, as Richard Warner suggested, for it lies not far from a crossing of the River Nore and within easy reach of Waterford harbour. The possibility that a Roman trading station existed somewhere in the area merits consideration.

In the context of Roman trade along the east coast the promontory fort at Drumanagh, close to the village of Loughshinny in north Co. Dublin is of great potential significance. Bounded by vertical cliffs on three sides, this extensive promontory, some 40 acres in area, is defended by three closely spaced *fig. 132* ramparts of earth with intervening ditches. There, in the 1970s, a sherd of first-century Gallo-Roman Samian ware was recovered from occupation soil revealed by deep ploughing. The recent discovery of two second-century Roman coins in ploughed land not far from the fort adds to the feeling that Drumanagh might have been a key site in the early centuries of our era.

The fort is beside an excellent, sheltered harbour and is an ideal landing place for merchants travelling up the Irish Sea. It could have been a native Irish settlement serving as a distribution centre for Roman produce, but it is also possible that it was a foreign, perhaps Romano-British, establishment. The closely spaced multivallation there hints at British or northwest French traditions of fortification so it could be that the occupants of Drumanagh were an intrusive grouping. In this regard, one translation of the name as 'the hill of the Menapii' is tantalizing, for this north European tribe is, as earlier noted, listed on Ptolemy's map. We should also remember that a settlement of *fig. 125* presumed north British immigrants existed in the first century on the island of Lambay opposite Drumanagh.

Not far from Drumanagh, in the townland of Damastown, Co. Dublin, a large typically Roman, bun-shaped ingot of copper was found. Directly across the sea in north Wales copper mining under the Romans was extensively carried out from the late first century AD onwards. At least eighteen ingots similar to that from Damastown have been found there. The Co. Dublin example may well have been traded from north Wales, and it is tempting to speculate that Drumanagh could have played a part in such trading activities.

Roman trade with Ireland assumes the regular presence of Roman ships in Irish ports. Our information of the nature of such boats is not extensive. The model gold boat from Broighter, Co. Derry with its mast and oars (p. 111) suggests that around the birth of Christ vessels of some sophistication were in use along Irish coasts. A recent discovery submerged under the waters of Lough Lene in Co. Westmeath gives us detailed insights into the nature of late *fig. 133* Iron Age or early Roman boating. The find is that of a fragmentary boat built in a clearly Mediterranean technique which became obsolete no later than the seventh century AD (and probably before this). A radiocarbon date for wood from the boat gives a range between 400 and 100 BC. It has been suggested, however, that as the dated sample was taken from a piece of yew, which is a slow-growing tree, allowance must be made for a possible old-wood effect. The boat could therefore date to the early Roman period.

Only a portion of the hull of the vessel survives. The prow and stern are missing, but it is evident that the boat was flat-bottomed with steep sides. It was carvel-built, which means that the oak planks (strakes) from which it was constructed are flush along their edges rather than overlapping as in the more usual clinker-built variety. The planks are held together by tenons inserted into matching mortices cut into the edges of the planks. Transverse pegs inserted through the thickness of the planks secure the tenons in place.

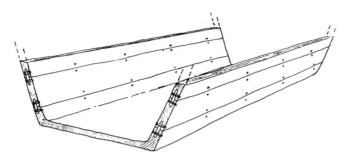

133 Sketch of a sunken boat of supposed Mediterranean type from Lough Lene in Co. Westmeath. Width of basal plank 1 m.

The method of manufacture displays considerable joinery skills and indicates a detailed knowledge of Mediterranean methods of boat-building. It seems that only someone with first-hand knowledge of Classical techniques could have created such a vessel. It is possible that an Irishman learned the technique abroad, but it is more likely that a Roman specialist built the boat locally for use on Irish inland waters. The slender, flat-bottomed vessel would not have been suitable for marine travel. Perhaps it was built by Roman traders to facilitate the transport of goods to the interior from some trading colony nearer the coast.

There are other indications in the Irish archaeological record of immigrants from provincial Rome. Early in the last century, for example, an unspecified number of extended skeletons in long stone cists was found (and destroyed) at Bray Head, Co. Wicklow. Each interment is said to have been associated with one or two Roman coins placed on or beside the breast. The coins have been attributed to Trajan (AD 97–117) and Hadrian (AD 117–138). The presence of coins in the burials reflects the Roman belief that such were needed to pay the ferryman Charon on the journey across the Styx to the Underworld. In classic Roman burials, however, the coins are in the mouth of the corpse, who needed both hands free to feed cakes to the two-headed dog Cerberus, the guardian of the Underworld.

Similarly, a series of inhumations, some in cists, some unprotected, excavated at Betaghstown, Co. Meath are likely to represent the remains of provincial Roman intruders. The unprotected inhumation burials discovered around the great Knowth tumulus might also be intrusive. At least some of the many inhumation burials in long stone cists discovered from time to time in the country, and never closely dated, might also belong to this intrusive horizon of the early centuries AD. Indeed, it may be that the change in burial customs (from cremation to inhumation) which seems to have been taking place in Ireland at this time could well reflect cultural influences from Rome where such a transition was taking place from the early second century onwards.

The people buried in these graves, like those at Lambay and Stonyford, came from abroad. They could, as perhaps at Lambay, have been refugees but equally they might have been returned emigrants, perhaps Irish auxiliaries with their Roman wives, who had adopted the manners and customs of their erstwhile paymasters. Mindful of the map of Ptolemy, it is possible that these are the burials of settlers from Britain or Gaul. We will never know for sure, but one thing is clear: Ireland was in no way isolated from the mainstream of Roman developments abroad during the early centuries of the Christian era.

The sacred mound at Newgrange

Among the visitors to Ireland, whatever their origins, were those who were attracted to some of the great monumental sites in the east of the country, sites which in the early centuries AD were still of major ritual and symbolic importance. The impressive tumulus of Newgrange, home of the all-powerful

fig. 134 Daghda, was certainly a magnet to travellers from the provincial Roman world.

fig. 135 While a scatter of tools and a few late Roman disc-brooches suggest the possibility that there might have been some short-term settlement at this time in the immediate vicinity of the tumulus, it seems likely that Newgrange was largely a centre of pilgrimage during Roman times.

The wealth and variety of the Roman finds discovered at Newgrange strongly support the view that ritual deposition took place on a grand scale. In 1842, a hoard of precious gold objects was found near the entrance, comprising a necklace, two finger rings and two bracelets. In addition, no fewer than twenty-five Roman coins have come to light over the years, ranging from the period of Domitian (AD 81–96) to Arcadius (AD 385–408). At least nine of the coins were of gold (two converted into pendants), while specimens of silver and copper were also found. They were noticeably concentrated in the vicinity of the three great standing stones which are situated in front of the entrance. These great monoliths would doubtless have been imbued with Otherworld significance and would thus have been a focus for ritual acts. (It should not be forgotten, however, that Iron Age visitors to Newgrange would not have known the location of the entrance to the passage tomb, and would have been unaware of the existence of the decorated kerbstones by then long covered by collapse from the mound.)

Among the more interesting finds from Newgrange is the cut-off terminal of a Middle Bronze Age gold bar torc discovered close to the foot of one of the

fig. 135 standing stones of the great circle surrounding the tumulus. Dating to the end of the second millennium BC, the torc had obviously been unearthed in Roman times, and had been cut up doubtless with a view to melting and reusing the gold. Its owner was certainly Roman for the letters SCBONS. MB were inscribed on it in *pointillé* Roman lettering. The significance of the lettering is unknown. This is a remarkable find, for the torc from which the terminal was cut is Irish and the lettering must thus have been executed locally. It is thus hard to escape the conclusion that here we have further tangible evidence of the presence on Irish soil of a literate Roman stamping his owner's mark on what was for him a gold ingot, ultimately to place it in the ground at Newgrange as an offering to a higher power.

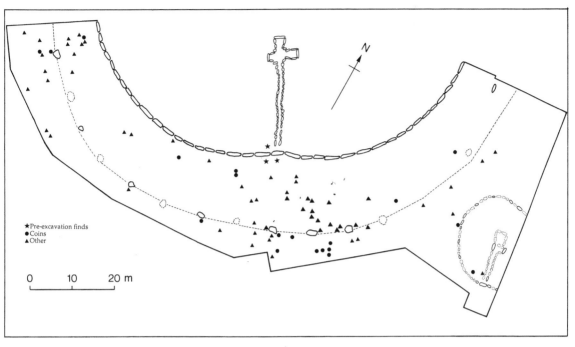

134 Distribution of Roman and related finds in the vicinity of the passage tomb at Newgrange, Co. Meath.

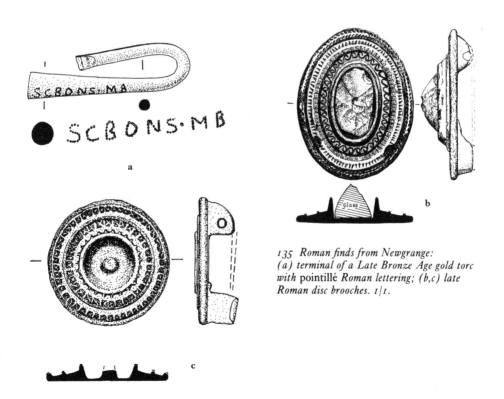

*135 Roman finds from Newgrange:
(a) terminal of a Late Bronze Age gold torc
with* pointillé *Roman lettering; (b,c) late
Roman disc brooches. 1/1.*

Roman finds at occupation sites

Not far from Newgrange, on the Hill of Tara, the impact of Rome is also clearly evident. Tara was, of course, a significant focus of tribal activity during the centuries of the Iron Age and there can be no doubt that the site was a major ceremonial centre. Inevitably, a Roman presence would have been attracted there. Excavations which have taken place on the hilltop at the so-called Rath of the Synods demonstrate this. Indeed, we may wonder whether the terms *regia* and *polis* on Ptolemy's map referred to sites such as Tara, for it is likely that at regular intervals throughout the year significant concentrations of the population would have gathered there.

The Rath of the Synods, in its final phase of use, was a triple-ramparted ringfort which appears to have been occupied in the late Roman period. Pits, postholes, cobbling and traces of wall-slots were found, but only a single hut-plan could be identified. This was oval with dimensions of 3.90 m by 3.50 m. Among the finds were pottery fragments of south Gaulish origin, including the remains of a goblet and sherds from several flagons. The majority could be dated to the first and second centuries AD. The site also produced a range of glass beads and what may have been part of a Roman glass inlay, the spring of a probable bow brooch, a pair of bronze dividers, two iron padlocks and a miscellaneous collection of iron and bronze objects. Of particular interest was the discovery of a lead seal bearing an oval impression which shows a raised figure of a bird holding something in its beak. This could have been for sealing documents but could equally have served for sealing merchandise. Perhaps it had been the possession of a private individual.

These imported items, concentrated together at a single site, are indicative of an affluent élite. The flagons indicate that the inhabitants could afford wine (a luxury commodity), and they had goblets for its proper consumption. The lead seal also suggests the presence at the site of a person of official standing whose mark carried weight. Even more intriguing is the dividers which could have been used in masonry work, fine joinery, or perhaps some form of draughtsmanship. Whatever function served by the tool, its presence at Tara, along with the other exotic material, emphasizes the considerable status of the occupants of the Rath of the Synods. In the apparent absence of any demonstrably native material from the excavations, it seems that they might have been settlers from the provincial Roman world.

At Dún Ailinne, Co. Kildare (another royal site comparable with Tara),
fig. 40 Roman bronze fibulae have also occurred, probably in association with one of the later phases of activity there. A more obviously secular occupation producing imported Roman material is the hillfort of Freestone Hill, Co. Kilkenny. The objects were found on the summit of the hill, within a small stone enclosure. As well as a range of domestic items of local character, two 'toilet implements' of bronze, some bracelet fragments of the same material and
fig. 136 a copper coin of Constantine II were recovered. The coin, a memorial issue, was minted in Trier between AD 337 and 340. It was in an unworn state. The

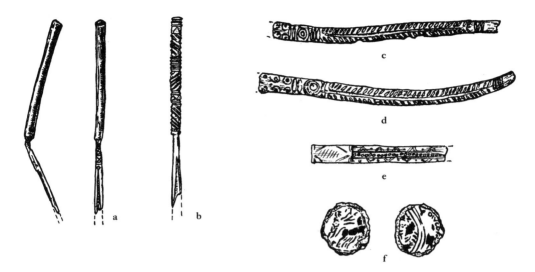

136 The Roman finds from Freestone Hill, Co. Kilkenny included: toilet implements (a,b); bracelet fragments (c,d,e); and a copper coin of Constantine II (f). 1/1

bracelets, simple strips of bronze bearing stamped ornament of the most mediocre quality, belong to a class of mass-produced ornament, widely distributed across the late Roman empire. The coin, useless in a society without currency, was perhaps a souvenir or a talisman.

Several other excavated settlement sites have yielded Roman artifacts. An imitation of the major issue of Constantius II (AD 324–361) came from under collapsed stones in a ringfort at Carraig Aille, Co. Limerick. However, the possibility that such coins continued to be made into the fifth century or later, and its uncertain association with the site, diminish its significance in the present discussion. Similarly uncertain are the contexts of an early fourth-century Roman coin and a heavy iron key of Roman type found at Uisneach in Co. Westmeath. The significance of Uisneach as a major ritual centre during the pagan Iron Age is well established, so the identification of early finds there is not surprising. The presence of a key, however, along with the padlocks from Tara, raises interesting questions about the social implications of such finds, especially if they are indicative of doors which were to be locked. Even if they were for securing chests rather than doors these items imply a certain attitude to wealth and possessions not readily apparent in earlier times.

At the hillfort of Rathgall, Co. Wicklow, probably long abandoned by the turn of the millennium, a second-century strap-tag of provincial Roman type was found; and another hillfort, Clogher in Co. Tyrone, yielded Roman pottery of the early centuries AD. Finally, a bronze fibula of the first century came from excavations in the vicinity of St Anne's well at Randalstown, Co. Meath. The well today is a holy well and until recently was the site of an annual pilgrimage. It may already have been sacred before Christianity reached Ireland.

137 Distribution map of Roman finds in Ireland.

Scattered evidence of Roman presence

Most of the Roman remains from Ireland consist of scattered finds, occasionally hoards, but generally isolated discoveries without archaeological association. The significance of such isolated finds is often difficult to assess since many Roman objects were brought to the country by eighteenth- and nineteenth-century antiquarians and collectors as mementoes of their foreign travels. In many cases these were subsequently discarded or lost and, with time, have found their way, without documentation, into museum collections. The problem is particularly acute in the case of coins. Thus Donal Bateson, in his study of Roman material from Ireland, rejected as spurious all but sixteen of the ninety recorded coin finds from the country. Bronze statuettes, lamps and other unprovenanced Roman items in the national collections are also unlikely to have been genuine ancient imports.

fig. 137   When all the acceptable Roman material in Ireland is examined, it transpires that they tend to fall into two distinct chronological groupings: a first/second-century group and one of the fourth/fifth century. Strangely, finds of the third century are scarcely present in the surviving remains. Material of both groups is clustered in the eastern coastal lowlands, between the Liffey and the Boyne, with finds occurring discontinuously from the Antrim coast northwards as far as Donegal. During the fourth and fifth centuries there is an additional spread inland in the south of the country. The coastal bias along the east and north is evident and this distribution is probably in large measure a product of the activity of merchants. The southern spread of Roman imports to the interior is less easily explained. It has been suggested that this may in some way be related to the historically attested Irish raids to western Britain in the years of the declining Roman empire.

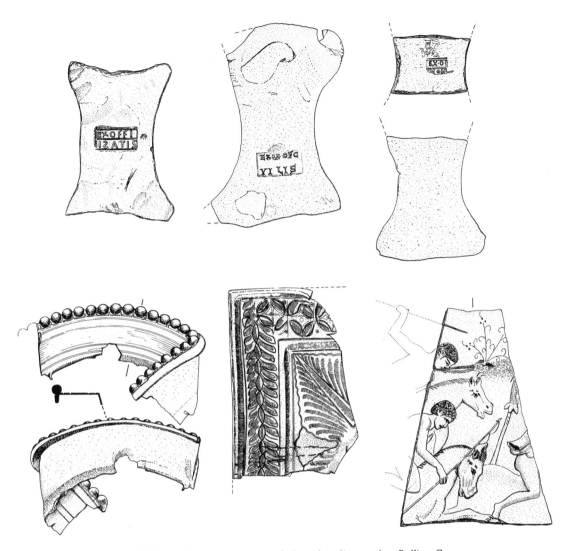

138 Late Roman hoard of silver ingots and fragments of silver plate discovered at Balline, Co. Limerick. 2/5.

Coins are the most common Roman finds from Ireland. As already noted, these have come from burials, settlements and sites of presumed ritual importance. A few individual specimens have been recovered from sandhills and during ploughing. Three large coin hoards from the north of Ireland are of special interest. Two of these, discovered in the early nineteenth century in north Antrim (one at Feigh Mountain the other at Flower Hill), contained an estimated 500 and 300 silver coins respectively. In each case the latest coins present are reported to have dated to the second century.

Another even larger hoard of silver, containing ingots and plate as well as coins, came to light in 1854 at Ballinrees, Co. Derry. The find contained no

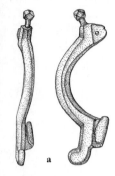

139 Miscellaneous Roman bronze fibulae from 'near Galway' (a); Dunfanaghy, Co. Donegal (b); Annesborough, Co. Armagh (c). c. 1/2.

fewer than 1506 coins and just over 200 ounces of silver ingots and cut plate. The coins, with one exception, are so-called *siliquae* ranging in date from Constantius II (AD 324–61) to Constantine III (AD 407–11) so that deposition in the early fifth century is likely. The plate includes fragments of bowls, dishes, platters and several spoons. There were also fifteen bar-shaped ingots, seven irregular lumps of silver, and two 'cow-hide-shaped' ingots, so-called because of their expanded ends and constricted centre. One (in two halves) weighs 314 g; the other is incomplete. Both of these hide-shaped ingots have official stamps, one bearing the letters CVR MISSI (which is either a personal name or, more likely, stands for CURATOR MISSIONUM), the other EX OF PATRICI – 'from the workshop (*officina*) of Patricius'.

Another silver hoard of the late fourth or early fifth century was found in 1940 in a gravel-pit at Balline in the Shannon estuary in Co. Limerick (see *fig. 138*: pl. 79). In this instance there were no coins. The hoard consisted of two hide-shaped ingots, similar to those from Ballinrees, and parts of two others, as well as three pieces of silver plate. Official Roman seals are present on three of the four ingots. These carry the letters EX OFFI ISATIS, EX OFC VILIS and EX O NON. As well as the official stamp, the second of the three bears the Christian Xhi Rho symbol. The two complete ingots are of almost identical weight, weighing 317 g and 318 g respectively. In one instance, to achieve the required weight, two additional pieces of silver have been crudely riveted through two holes, one near each end.

A Romano-British background for these ingots is firmly established by the existence of a hide-shaped ingot at the Roman fort of Richborough in Kent bearing the same ISATIS stamp as one of the Irish examples. The discovery in Kent of a hide-shaped silver ingot bearing a CVR MISSI stamp on it, precisely as on one of the Ballinrees ingots further strengthens the Kentish connection for the Irish silver, and strongly suggests that the immediate source of this Irish material lies in southern England. The fragments of plate – the remains of once beautifully decorated platters hacked into conveniently sized pieces for melting – are probably also from the same quarter, though at least some of the platters could be of Mediterranean manufacture.

Various suggestions have been put forward to explain the accumulation of such large quantities of Roman silver. Inevitably the image of Irish raiders returning with booty from plundered Roman villas in Britain is widely held. It is equally possible, however, that the silver was acquired abroad by Irish auxiliaries for service under the Roman standards. The presence of ingots supports this view – especially since the three complete specimens are within a few grammes of the official Roman pound (325 g) – because in the later fourth century, unlike in earlier times, the Roman Treasury required large sums in gold and silver for payment to its soldiers and officials. A well-attested fourth-century practice of payment was in the form of Imperial donatives, of which Julian's promise of five gold *solidi* and a pound of silver to each man on the occasion of his accession in AD 361 provides a good example. Quantification was, in fact, increasingly important in the late Empire, and strict official control was kept over the weighing of quantities of precious metals which became ever more dominant as units of currency.

Less dramatic, but certainly more commonplace, are the bronze fibulae of Roman manufacture which occur from time to time in Ireland (see *fig. 139*). We do not know if these were items of trade or were worn on the garments of visitors from overseas. More puzzling are the finds of pottery sherds, both of Samian ware (ultimately Gaulish in origin (see *fig. 140*)) and Arretine ware, which was made in Italy (chiefly in Arretium). These sometimes come from occupation sites thought to be later in date than the sherds. Some scholars argue, therefore, that these have nothing to do with early Roman influences, but were imported to Ireland – as souvenirs and amulets, or for dye-making or medicinal purposes – many centuries after their original period of manufacture. In several instances, however, notably at Tara and Drumanagh, there can be little doubt that the Roman sherds were indeed imported in Roman times. The first- or second-century Roman *olla* (storage jar) dredged from 150 fathoms of water off the Porcupine Bank 250 km northwest of Ireland may well have been on a ship destined for Ireland, but pottery of this type has never been found in the country.

There are other chance finds of Roman origin from Ireland. These include a bronze ladle from Bohermeen, Co. Meath and a *patera* (saucepan) handle from Rathlin Island, Co. Antrim. Several of the so-called toilet implements – small pronged implements of bronze – are also occasionally found in the country, but not all are necessarily of Roman manufacture and some, indeed, might be native copies. A jet spoon from Carbury Hill, Co. Kildare may also be a local copy of a well-known class of late Roman silver spoon with swan's-neck handle. It was found in disturbed soil in one of the burial mounds on the hill but may once have been part of a grave deposit. A small bronze hand-bell, found with a Y-shaped object and other bronzes at Kishawanny in Co. Kildare, might also be of Roman manufacture.

140 Fragments of Samian ware found at Lagore, Co. Meath. c. 1/4.

141 A bronze ladle from Bohermeen in Co. Meath. 1/4.

142 *Stone oculist's stamp recovered from a
dike at Golden, Co. Tipperary. 1/1.*

fig. 142

One of the most interesting of all the Roman finds from Ireland is an oculist's stamp found, it is said, in a dike at Golden, Co. Tipperary in 1842. Some human bones are also said to have been found in the same place. The object is a carefully made rectangular tablet of fine-grained slate, with an inscription of letters along one edge incised in the negative. The letters, in two lines, read MIVVENTVTIANI (?)C/DIAMYSVSADV which has been translated as MARCI JUVENTUTI TUTIANI DIAMYSUS AD VETERES CICATRICES. If the last letter of the top line is in fact a C it may stand for COLLYRIUM. In English translation the inscription, somewhat enigmatically, reads 'For the son of Marcus Tutianus an eye salve misy for his old scars'. Misy was a yellow translucent substance described as a 'yellow copperas' which was especially suited to eye complaints.

Across the Empire there were numerous oculists who cured eye diseases with salves of two types, solid (which was most common) and liquid. The former was sold in small sticks on which the oculist, using his stone stamp, impressed the name of the preparation, the purpose for which it was prescribed and always his own name as a guarantee of quality. The eye-salve was made of vegetable substances such as myrrh or saffron, or of powdered minerals. Oculists' stamps are rare in Italy but are common in the provinces, especially in the northwest (i.e. Britain and France), where the cold damp climate may have contributed to an increase in eye diseases. The presence of such an object in Ireland offers intriguing possibilities. The owner of the stamp was evidently a skilled specialist professionally concerned with curing eye disorders. Can we take it that he was practising in southern Ireland at some period in the early centuries of the Christian era? Is it thus possible that the stamp, as in the case of Stonyford, implies a settled Roman presence of some substance in the country?

Another suggestion, even more intriguing, has sometimes been mooted. Oculists' stamps are not infrequently associated with Roman military outposts. The occurrence of one in Ireland, in possible association with human remains, has caused some historians to wonder whether here we have archaeological evidence for an abortive Roman military intrusion which came to grief in Co.

Tipperary. This theory, based on the Golden find alone, would scarcely be considered at all were it not for two enigmatic literary references. The first of these concerns the Roman general Agricola who, late in the first century, certainly contemplated the possibility of invading Ireland. His biographer Tacitus, in a passage referring to Agricola's ideas about Ireland's occupation, tells us that having reached the narrow isthmus between the estuaries of the Clyde and Forth, Agricola 'crossed over in the first ship and conquered hitherto unknown peoples, and fortified the coast of Britain facing Ireland . . .' Some scholars have asked where could he have crossed to by ship except Ireland? The other reference is in Juvenal Satire 2 dating early in the second century. He writes 'We have taken our arms beyond the shores of Ireland and the recently conquered Orkneys, and Britain of the short nights'. Again, it is argued, since the capture of the Orkneys and Britain are historic facts, why should not the reference to Ireland be taken at face value?

The matter rests there. It is evident that in the first centuries AD there was considerable movement between Ireland and the Roman world, and that the Romans had a good knowledge of Ireland. A small-scale landing of Roman legions may well have taken place – one which, if unsuccessful, would not necessarily have been recorded. It has also been noted that for just this period there is a dearth of surviving historical documentation. An attempted military intervention in Ireland is not proven but such a possibility cannot be completely dismissed.

CHAPTER 10

Celts, Culture and Colonization

The gods did not reveal, from the beginning,
all things to us; but in the course of time,
through seeking we may learn, and know things better.
But as for certain truth, no man has known it,
nor will he know it; neither of the gods,
nor yet of all the things of which I speak.
And even if by chance he were to utter
the final truth, he would himself not know it;
for all is but a woven web of guesses.

XENOPHANES (*c*. 570–475 BC)

The later prehistoric centuries were crucial, formative years in Ireland. These witnessed the beginnings of new movement – cultural, artistic, technological, perhaps even religious – and after more than a thousand years of bronze-using, a new metal, iron, came to replace bronze for the manufacture of tools and weapons. During these centuries Ireland edged gradually towards the light of history, to emerge in the earliest written records as a country of recognizably Celtic character. An indelible mark was left on the evolving pattern of Ireland's social geography which was to endure almost to modern times.

Definition and terminology

In Europe the period we define as the Iron Age is well represented in the archaeological record and our ever more detailed knowledge of society there is enhanced by the written accounts of Classical commentators. The chronology of Iron Age Europe is subject to increasingly fine precision. For Ireland, however, the contemporary situation is much less clear and the Iron Age is seen as a vaguely defined era, following on a Bronze Age and assumed to end at some (as yet undefined) point in early historic times. Neither the beginning nor the end of this Iron Age can be satisfactorily established, but it is not unlikely that the period involved may have spanned as much as a millennium.

There are, in fact, several ways in which a population group can, in the archaeological sense, be described as belonging to the Iron Age. A minimum basic criterion, however, must be the possession by the community not merely of iron objects but of the technology involved in their manufacture. The means by which knowledge of the new technology was acquired, as well as the reactions of the community to iron-using, are also important. Such factors will influence the speed and the extent of the adoption of the new technology, and in any given area it is clear that the spread will be uneven as a consequence of geographic conditions and the conservatism or otherwise of individual groups. It is important to note, however, that the dissemination of the new technology need not necessarily imply any population change. Indeed, at such a transitional stage between bronze- and iron-using, the terms Bronze Age and Iron Age could, in certain circumstances and in a cultural sense, be deemed interchangeable.

It seems increasingly likely that the gradual introduction of iron-working occurred around the middle of the last millennium BC, although hard archaeological evidence for this continues to be somewhat elusive. Nonetheless, on the assumption that iron-working techniques were not invented independently in Ireland, it follows that the relevant knowledge was introduced from abroad. There is only one means by which such information can have been carried to Ireland: in the human mind. Whether the mind, or minds, involved were those of traders, prospectors, colonizers, raiders or returning emigrants is unknown. But somebody, for some reason, must have crossed the sea to Ireland with the new technology.

The presence in the country of Hallstatt-derived or Hallstatt-influenced objects may be a clue to the cultural source whence came the new knowledge. It may be that this Hallstatt material belongs to the same archaeological horizon as the potentially early iron objects we discussed. The temptation might even be to regard the Hallstatt presence in the country as a distinct element in our blanket term 'Iron Age', one with cultural and possibly even ethnic undertones. The Hallstatt material in Ireland is, however, extremely limited in extent and essentially insular in character. It may very well be that the concept of a Hallstatt 'Iron Age' in the country is illusory. We should not, however, dismiss the possibility that future discoveries could alter this impression.

It is only with the appearance of La Tène material that radical and wide-ranging innovations are detectable in the Irish archaeological record, which give greater substance to the idea of an Irish Iron Age. In fact, some commentators have gone so far as to regard 'La Tène' and 'Iron Age' in Ireland as synonymous. This cannot, however, be the case. Not only are there increasing hints of a pre-La Tène 'Iron Age', but it seems also that in southern areas of the country, where La Tène influences are all but absent, an 'Iron Age' of non-La Tène character – as yet scarcely recognized – must have existed. An 'Iron Age', heavily permeated by elements emanating from the provincial Roman world, might even be taken to indicate a developed- or post-La Tène 'Iron Age' in the country. Nonetheless, the very use of such terms implies that it is the La Tène component which is pivotal in any considerations of the Iron Age in Ireland.

Care is necessary in the use of the term 'La Tène' in Ireland. Here, the La Tène horizon is represented by only a limited number of elements of the pan-European La Tène tradition, the majority rendered in native form. Much of what is standard abroad is absent in Ireland, and conversely there are significant aspects of the native tradition which are not found outside the country. The finer chronological subdivisions of the European La Tène culture have thus only the most general relevance for Ireland as the impact of La Tène arrived late and lasted, in developing insular form, for many centuries after it had elsewhere become largely obsolete.

In discussing La Tène remains in Ireland there is frequently a tendency on the part of some scholars to regard this body of material as an essentially homogeneous entity and its introduction into the country is often, by implication, taken to reflect a single historical event. Reference is made to a 'La Tène culture' in Ireland and distribution maps are used as if all the objects plotted were contemporary pieces. This is misleading, for the Irish La Tène material has a potential date range of up to half a millennium. In addition, it must be borne in mind that a wide range of diverse strands of influence, emanating from widely scattered areas of the outside world, are detectable in the Irish La Tène horizon. Just as the term 'Iron Age' requires further qualification, so too our use of the term 'La Tène' must be carefully defined.

Reference is frequently made in the archaeological literature to the existence of a La Tène 'culture' in the country. But how far is this justified? What do we understand by 'culture'? We have few burials and practically no domestic sites which may be related unequivocally with the Irish La Tène horizon, a horizon composed for the most part of scattered artifacts. The surviving remains are dominated by ornate metalwork, often of outstanding quality, which must represent the trappings of an élite and exclusive stratum of society. The humbler, more mundane aspects of everyday life, the simple, utilitarian objects, unadorned and without diagnostic form, scarcely impinge as yet on the surviving archaeological record.

Clearly, therefore, no matter how we seek to define 'culture', there are undoubted difficulties in applying the term to the Irish La Tène material. Gordon Childe's requirement that an archaeological culture is an 'assemblage of artifacts that recur repeatedly associated together in dwellings of the same kind and with burials of the same rite'[15] applies only in a limited way to the Irish evidence. Used in an anthropological sense the term 'culture' seems to apply even less comfortably to the Irish La Tène material. Thus we may ask if the meagre La Tène remains in Ireland combine to fulfil Clyde Kluckhohn and William Kelly's definition of culture as 'all those historically created designs for living, explicit and implicit, rational, irrational and non-rational, which exist at any given time as potential guides for the behaviour of man'.[16] However, for the material here under discussion, D.W. Harding's more pragmatic approach to the problem of culture has much to commend it. He felt that the term was archaeologically acceptable 'provided we do not expect it to be anything other than that which we have defined it as'.[17] As long as we avoid the temptation to regard our archaeological culture as the automatic material expression of an ethnic or linguistic unit we may use the term as a convenient label to describe a given set of archaeological data.

Archaeology and philology

The spread of Iron Age influences across Europe brings the whole question of the meaning of 'culture' into critical focus, for this is the period when that group of people we know as the Celts emerge in the historical record. Few European archaeologists would hesitate to relate the spread of La Tène cultural elements across Europe to the historically attested Celtic migrations, while recognizing of course, that migration is not the only mechanism by which La Tène influences were widely disseminated across the Continent. Inevitably, the appearance in Ireland of a body of artifacts displaying clear and obvious affinities with the La Tène horizon outside the country has often been interpreted as 'the coming of the Celts' to Ireland.

This last is a major archaeological, historical and philological statement, one laden with far-reaching assumptions. It implies that a population group, speaking a Celtic language and with a distinctive culture and way of life came to Ireland from a specific area at a specific time and established itself in sufficient numbers to render 'Celtic' significant areas of the country which had hitherto been non-Celtic. In other words, the statement is a classic expression of the invasion hypothesis. With it the parameters of archaeological discussion are broadened to enter the realms of philology and protohistory.

Linguists have always taken it for granted that the presence of a Celtic-speaking population in Ireland at the dawn of history can only be explained by invoking colonization on a substantial scale. Accordingly, they have sought from archaeology the physical evidence of this assumed event. Archaeologists, for their part, have often looked to philology and the written sources to support a series of postulated invasions deemed to be indicated by specific changes in the archaeological record. The interaction of the related disciplines has not always been successful. Because of the almost inevitable lack of familiarity with the subtleties of each other's fields of research, scholars have all too often over-emphasized the significance of the available evidence or have failed to notice the pitfalls.

A basic defect inherent in many studies of the Irish Iron Age is the imposition, often unconscious, of historical interpretations on the archaeological evidence. An assumption is made, itself non-archaeological, that a Celtic language can have been introduced to Ireland only through the agency of large-scale folk intrusion, from which it follows that appropriate evidence for such an event must, of necessity, be forthcoming in the archaeological record. Any apparent change or cultural break in the archaeological sequence at a more or less suitable date is thus interpreted in the context of what linguists assume to have happened. Any defects or seeming contradictions in the material evidence are either ignored or dismissed as weaknesses inherent in the nature of the subject. Implicit or explicit, such thinking has underlain most interpretations of Irish Iron Age archaeology for the better part of this century.

It seems, however, that this approach is at variance with the fundamental principles of archaeological interpretation. It is wrong to start with an answer and then arrange the archaeological evidence accordingly. On the contrary, the archaeological picture must be established on its own merits and must stand on its own before correlation with evidence from related disciplines is attempted. As Leonard Palmer put it when referring to the problems of archaeology and philology in Iron Age Greece: 'the techniques of the two sister disciplines are so diverse that each group of scholars would do well to advance to the frontiers of its competence and then ask questions'.[18]

For archaeologists, therefore, the problem of the Celts should be treated primarily as archaeological. This is a critical point because, in the final analysis, it is the philologists and historians who depend on archaeology for confirmation or otherwise of their hypotheses about the question of the origins of the Celts in Ireland. Thus it is evident that archaeological interpretation should not be determined by information from sources which themselves depend on archaeology for corroboration.

The invasion problem

For linguists, the problem has not been *whether* a Celtic migration took place, but rather *when*, and widely varying dates have been suggested by them. For archaeologists, burdened with the responsibility of actually demonstrating in the material remains tangible evidence for such a migration, the problem has been more complex.

Use of the term 'invasion' inevitably conjures up images of the large-scale military movements of recent history, but such can have nothing in common with any movements of people who crossed the seas to Ireland in ancient times. Indeed, it might with justification be written that one of the problems with the invasion hypothesis is the use of the term 'invasion'. For, technically speaking, in the context of possible impact on the archaeological record, 'invasion' has a wide range of meanings and can vary from large-scale, conscious and organized colonization at one extreme to the appearance on the coast of a handful of ship-wrecked sailors on the other.

The key problem for archaeologists is not whether during prehistory people moved from time to time, in varied numbers and for varied reasons, from area to area: it would be absurd to deny this. The problem is rather to determine the means by which any such movements can be identified in the archaeological record.

In Ireland, evidence relating to immigrant cultural groupings displays far greater ambiguity than elsewhere. The island has always imposed its personality on incoming cultural traditions, rapidly metamorphosing the innovating elements so that they acquire, or appear in, a distinctively Irish form. Furthermore, for most periods of prehistory, but especially for the La Tène Iron Age, the innovating archaeological horizon lacks significant and extensive elements which characterize it in the areas of its supposed origin. To what extent, therefore, are we justified in using an invasionist model to explain the presence in the country of La Tène cultural elements?

The introduction of La Tène

The Irish La Tène horizon represents the most plausible physical manifestation of an imported Iron Age presence in the country. The La Tène remains appear to represent a major break with previous cultural traditions, in art and aspects of technology, and in all forms of weapons, ornaments and domestic equipment. It is not surprising that this material is so often regarded as evidence of incoming Celtic peoples.

Let us examine the problems with this theory. In the first instance, almost every object of La Tène type which survives is of undeniably native manufacture. The very scarcity of extant material should also be taken into account: even allowing for loss or destruction of artifacts over the centuries and for the unknown percentage of as yet undiscovered material, there is still a striking disparity between the quantity of Late Bronze Age objects from the country and the meagre tally for the La Tène Iron Age. It thus seems strange that a warrior aristocracy supposedly responsible for imposing so many aspects of its culture on the indigenous population (language, customs, and method of social organization) should have had almost no impact on the archaeological record. Only the bridle-bits occur in any sort of significant numbers. Furthermore, there is an almost total absence from the Irish La Tène horizon of so much that is typical and diagnostic in La Tène areas outside the country. Virtually the whole range of normal La Tène domestic material is missing from Ireland, as are the belt-fittings, the varied mounts and fittings for horse and cart so common abroad, the great majority of personal ornament types, the coinage and, above all else, the pottery. The burial record and the almost negligible settlement evidence do not in any way conform to what was normal in any of the areas from which the Irish La Tène tradition is said to have originated.

If a colonization of Ireland had taken place, it ought to be possible to isolate a chronologically defined horizon of imported objects (or objects closely related to or derived from those in the alleged homeland). It should also be possible, in an ideal situation, to indicate the region outside the country from which came the innovating influences and traditions. There have, of course, been attempts to establish the source or sources of the La Tène presence in Ireland. In no instance, however, has the existence of an intrusive horizon been demonstrated. All that has been possible is to point to an occasional import and to isolate areas of stylistic or typological similarity between artifacts in Ireland and those abroad. Thus scholars have interpreted the Knock, Co. Roscommon (formerly 'Clonmacnoise') torc and a few other items as indicating an 'infiltration' into the west of the country from the Continent. The earliest Irish horse-bits and the decorated scabbards have also, on more than one occasion, been seen as a product of folk intrusions from eastern England, as has the introduction of the beehive quern to Ireland.

It is evident that the Roscommon torc, and somewhat later, the Ballyshannon sword, demonstrate links with the European mainland. Similarly, it is probable that in details of the horse-bits and the scabbards we may recognize contacts between metal-working centres in Ireland and in eastern England, even though there is a strong likelihood of directly Continental involvement in the ornament and the chape form of the Irish scabbards. But such introduced elements seem scarcely extensive enough to support the notion of significant immigration from either area. Material of demonstrably Continental origin is far too limited in quantity to demonstrate this, and the La Tène horizon in eastern England is almost wholly distinct from that in Ireland. Above all, the inhumation burials with square-ditched enclosures, which are such a widespread and characteristic feature of the Iron Age in Yorkshire, are unknown in Ireland.

There is no denying that the Irish La Tène tradition came from outside: the art style, the technology, the new method of grinding corn and the inspiration to cast and forge new artifact types are all innovative. But if large-scale population movements were not responsible for this, what was? Irish emigrants – craftsmen perhaps – returning from abroad might have played a part in bringing about such changes. Or, if foreigners were indeed involved, these are likely to have been a small élite that appeared in Ireland in the last centuries BC, whose presence could have facilitated the introduction of the changes which are visible in the surviving record. It remains an open question whether such a hypothetical group could be held to have made the island 'Celtic'.

The positive dating to 95/94 BC of the Navan temple and its broad contemporaneity with one of the constructional phases at the Dorsey, along with the 148 BC dating of the Corlea road, strongly suggest that during the second and early first centuries BC significant events on a tribal scale were taking place in Ireland. Radiocarbon dates for the building of the Black Pig's Dyke and the Dun of Drumsna suggest that these earthworks, too, could belong to the same phase of monumental construction. It was at exactly the same time that La Tène cultural elements spread across the land – indeed, this occurred in those very areas where there is evidence for such large-scale communal works. There may well be a connection. Tribal expansion and the growth of tribal power might have created conditions which were receptive to innovating La Tène traditions from abroad. Thus, it could have been the burgeoning ambitions of rival rulers which lay behind such public displays of communal power and influence and which provided the impetus for the initial reception and subsequent patronage of exotic metalworkers. Conversely, it could be argued that small bands of intruders, as suggested above, imposed themselves upon the native peoples to carve out new dynasties whose basic material culture was largely subsumed by that of the numerically dominant natives. It is difficult to choose between such alternatives but it seems that it is to answer such questions that future research should be directed.

The enigma of southern Ireland

As has been noted, it is clear that the terms 'La Tène' and 'Iron Age' in Ireland are not synonymous. This is especially so for the south of the country. Here, the

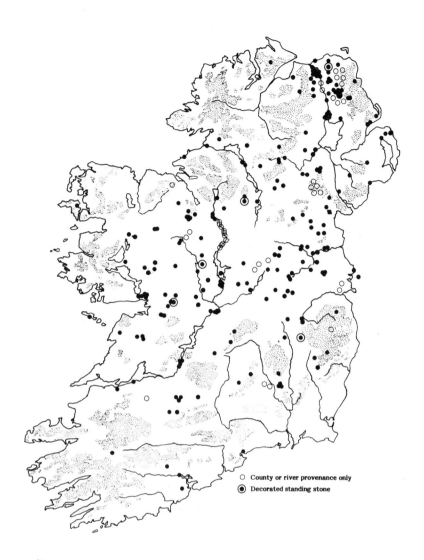

○ County or river provenance only

◉ Decorated standing stone

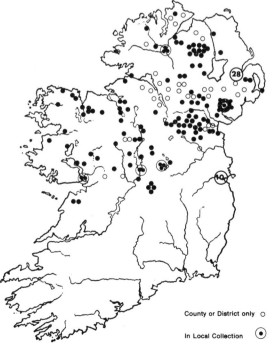

*143 (Above) Distribution of La Tène
material (excluding quernstones) in Ireland.*

*144 (Left) Distribution of beehive
quernstones in Ireland.*

County or District only ○

In Local Collection ◉

figs. 143, 144

marks of La Tène cultural traditions are scant, and in most of Munster and south Leinster La Tène remains are entirely absent. The total absence of beehive querns south of a line drawn from Dublin to the mouth of the Shannon is particularly striking in this regard. But the south must surely have experienced an 'Iron Age' at some stage in prehistory.

The nature of southern Irish society in the last centuries BC has been a matter of great uncertainty for many years. Some writers, baffled by the apparent southern vacuum, have considered the possibility of a long survival there of later Bronze Age traditions. Yet the earliest historical documents do not indicate that the south was any less 'Celtic' than other parts of the country. If there are no La Tène remains in the south, and precious few of Hallstatt character, what then *was* the material culture of the inhabitants of southern Ireland in the centuries immediately preceding their emergence as 'Celts' in the earliest historical sources?

It has been suggested above (p. 60) that an apparent southern concentration of large hillforts may shed light on this conundrum, but this can only come about by extensive excavation. In Chapter 3 we saw that some scholars believe that certain aspects of the southern forts – notably the *chevaux de frise* defences – betray Iberian influence, and have speculated whether the elusive southern Iron Age could in some way embody traditions of Iberian origin (while undoubtedly 'Celtic' in many ways, Spain too largely lacked La Tène material culture). In this regard the fact that Q-Celtic dialects were common to both Spain and Ireland was seen as significant. Modern linguists, however, are reluctant to postulate a direct relationship between early Celtic dialects in Ireland and Iberia and there is, in fact, no conclusive archaeological evidence for cultural contacts between the two areas. The ape skull recovered at Navan Fort does, however, show that there were links of some sort in later prehistory between Ireland and the western Mediterranean.

In conclusion

Archaeology presents us with a perplexing picture, one which is largely at variance with that presented by philology, early Irish history, folklore and tradition. It seems almost heretical to insist that a Celtic invasion of Ireland never happened. In this regard, however, the archaeologist should bear in mind the deficiencies of his discipline. Perhaps, as in the field of religion, he should adopt a stance akin to that of the agnostics rather than one of outright atheism. Perhaps there was, indeed, a migration of 'Celts' to Ireland. The only problem is, archaeology cannot prove it. As J.R.R. Tolkien wrote:

To many, perhaps to most people outside the small company of the great scholars, past and present, 'Celtic' of any sort is . . . a magic bag, into which anything may be put, and out of which almost anything may come . . . Anything is possible in the fabulous Celtic twilight, which is not so much a twilight of the gods as of the reason.[19]

Appendix: Radiocarbon Dates Used in the Text

The fullest summary of Irish Iron Age dates occurs in R.B. Warner, J.P. Mallory, and M.G.L. Baillie, 'Irish Early Iron Age Sites: A Provisional Map of Absolute Dated Sites', *Emania* 7, 1990, 46–50. Other dates have been published in C. Earwood, 'Radiocarbon dating of late prehistoric wooden vessels', *Journ. Irish Archaeol.* 5, 1989/90, 37–44; R.B. Warner and J.P. Mallory, 'The Date of Haughey's Fort', *Emania* 5, 1988, 36–40; J.P. Mallory, 'Further Dates from Haughey's Fort: 1989–1990', *Emania* 9, 1991, 64–65; B. Coles, 'Anthropomorphic wooden figurines from Britain and Ireland', *Proc. Prehist. Soc.* 56, 1990, 315–33; T.B. Barry, 'Archaeological excavations at Dunbeg promontory fort, Co. Kerry, 1977', *Proc. Roy. Irish Acad.* 81C, 1981, 295–329; E. Grogan, 'Excavation of an Iron Age Burial Mound at Furness', *Journ. Co. Kildare Archaeol. Soc.* 16:4, 1983/84, 298–316; D. Sweetman, 'Reconstruction and Partial Excavation of an Iron Age Burial Mound at Ninch, Co. Meath', *Ríocht na Midhe* 7:2, 1982/3, 58–68; A.T. Lucas, 'Prehistoric Block-Wheels from Doogarymore, Co. Roscommon, and Timahoe East, Co. Kildare', *Journ. Roy. Soc. Antiq. Ireland* 102, 1972, 19–48; T. Condit and V. Buckley, 'The "Doon" of Drumsna', *Emania* 6, 1989, 11–14; G. Burenhult, *The Archaeological Excavation at Carrowmore, Co. Sligo, Ireland*, G. Burenhults Forlag, Stockholm 1980; A.L. Brindley and J.N. Lanting, 'Concerning the boat, the track and the sword', *Archaeol. Ireland* 4:4, 1990, 6. Thanks are due to Raghnaill ÓFloinn for supplying the unpublished dates for the Gallagh bog body.

Site name	Site type	Provenance of sample	Uncalibrated Years BP	Calibrated Years BC/AD	Lab #
Gortgill (Antrim)		Dugout canoe	2060 ± 60	350 BC–AD 70	UB 2681
Near Cloughmills (Antrim)		Handled wooden bowl (UM A.415.1935)	1985 ± 70	180 BC–AD 140	OxA-2430
Haughey's Fort (Armagh)	Hillfort	Wood from basal layer of inner ditch	2923 ± 50	1300–990 BC	UB 3050
			2855 ± 55	1160–920 BC	GrN 15480
		Charcoal from hearth	2865 ± 25	1120–940 BC	GrN 15481
		Charcoal from pit	2920 ± 25	1260–1030 BC	GrN 15482
		Charcoal from pit	2833 ± 55	1200–850 BC	UB 3049
			2850 ± 20	1070–940 BC	GrN 15483
		Charcoal from hearth	2850 ± 35	1130–920 BC	GrN 15484
		Charcoal from middle ditch	2852 ± 55	1254–900 BC	UB 3388
		Charcoal from outer ditch	2889 ± 27	1205–998 BC	UB 3387
		Charcoal from hearth	2865 ± 25	1211–932 BC	GrN 15481
		Charcoal from pit	2920 ± 25	1289–1013 BC	GrN 15482
		Charcoal from pit	2833 ± 55	1213–834 BC	UB 3049
			2850 ± 20	1208–929 BC	GrN 15483
		Charcoal from pit	2877 ± 60	1260–910 BC	UB 3386
		Charcoal from pit	2221 ± 26	386–198 BC	UB 3385
			2253 ± 26	394–209 BC	UB 3384
The Dorsey (Armagh)	Linear earthwork	Charcoal under north bank	2020 ± 45	170 BC–AD 80	UB 2219
			2240 ± 45	400–180 BC	UB 2220
			2015 ± 45	160 BC–AD 80	UB 2221
Navan Fort: Site A (Armagh)	Hilltop enclosure	Charcoal from outermost wall slot	2175 ± 45	380–100 BC	UB 752
Navan Fort: Site B (Armagh)		Charcoal from slot W (phase 3)	2185 ± 55	390–100 BC	UB 782
		Burnt plank from slot R (phase 3)	2110 ± 45	360–20 BC	UB 784
		Charcoal from slot Z (phase 3)	2105 ± 70	370 BC–AD 50	UB 790
		Charcoal from slot C1 (phase 3)	1785 ± 230	370–670 AD	UB 973
		Charcoal from slot A2 (phase 3)	1785 ± 45	120–370 AD	UB 976
		Wood from slot C3 (phase 3)	2045 ± 35	180 BC–AD 50	UB 978
		Charcoal from peripheral pit 16 of ditched enclosure (phase 3)	2085 ± 75	370 BC–AD 70	UB 971
		Branch from destruction layer of 40m structure (phase 4)	2100 ± 60	370 BC–AD 50	UB 467
		Twigs from central post packing of 40m structure (phase 4)	2150 ± 70	390–20 BC	UB 469
		Branch from packing of central post of 40m structure (phase 4)	2130 ± 65	380 BC–AD 1	UB 470
		Central post of 40m structure (phase 4)	2175 ± 45	380–100 BC	UB 772
		Straw from destruction of 40m structure (phase 4)	2020 ± 35	150 BC–AD 70	UB 773
		Charcoal from destruction layer of 40m structure (phase 4)	2160 ± 65	390–40 BC	UB 774
		Charcoal from post pit 75 of 40m structure (phase 4)	2170 ± 70	390–40 BC	UB 972
		Bones from Barbary ape	2150 ± 70	390–20 BC	OxA 3321

Site name	Site type	Provenance of sample	Uncalibrated Years BP	Calibrated Years BC/AD	Lab #
Navan Fort: Site B (Armagh)		Peaty material from enclosing ditch	2420 ± 40	766–398 BC	UB 3091
Co. Armagh		Handled wooden bowl (NMI W34/Wk.159)	2070 ± 65	174–86 BC	OxA 2417
Ralaghan (Cavan)		Wooden figure	3046–2856 (Cal)	1096–906 BC	OxA 171
Gallagh, Castleblakeney (Galway)		Bog body	2220 ± 90	410–50 BC	Ha 6908
			2320 ± 90	770–180 BC	OxA 2923
			3480 ± 70	2020–1640 BC	OxA 2756
Dunbeg (Kerry)	Promontory fort	Charcoal from ditch, partly sealed by rampart	2530 ± 35	800–500 BC	UB 2216
Dún Ailinne (Kildare)	Hilltop enclosure	Occupation phases 5, 6 or 7	2165 ± 70	390–30 BC	SI-977
		Occupation phases 5, 6 or 7	1950 ± 80	160 BC–AD 240	SI-979
		Posthole phases 4 or 5	2075 ± 80	370 BC–AD 80	SI-986
		Posthole phases 4 or 5	1855 ± 50	AD 30–320	SI-987
		Palisade (phase 3)	1755 ± 90	AD 70–520	SI-985
		Palisade (phase 3)	1900 ± 85	100 BC–AD 330	SI-980
		Palisade (phase 3)	1935 ± 85	160 BC–AD 250	SI-978
		Palisade (phase 2)	2200 ± 50	390–110 BC	SI-984
Furness (Kildare)	Burial mound	Charcoal from central stake under mound	1540 ± 30	430–580 BC	GrN 10472
Knowth (Meath)	Passage tomb	Inhumation burial 4 near main passage tomb	1830 ± 30	AD 90–240	GrN 15369
		Inhumation burial 7 near main passage tomb	1920 ± 60	70 BC–AD 240	GrN 15370
		Inhumation burial 8/9 near main passage tomb	1960 ± 30	40 BC–AD 250	GrN 15371
		Inhumation burial 10 near main passage tomb	2095 ± 20	190–50 BC	GrN 15372
Ninch (Meath)	Burial mound	Charcoal over inhumation I in mound	1820 ± 115	70 BC–AD 440	UB 2425
Raffin (Meath)	Hilltop enclosure	Bone from skull burial	1975 ± 50	100 BC–AD 120	AA 10281
Black Pig's Dyke, Scotshouse (Monaghan)	Linear earthwork	Charcoal from north Bank	2240 ± 90	490–90 BC	GrN 12616
		Charcoal from palisade slot	2165 ± 55	390–70 BC	UB 2600
Black Pig's Dyke, Aghnaskew (Monaghan)		Charcoal from palisade slot	2190 ± 55	390–100 BC	UB 2601
Clonsast (Offaly)		Wooden trackway	1910 ± 130	200 BC–AD 410	D-26
Daithi's Mound, Rathcroghan (Roscommon)	Ringbarrow	Charcoal from under and low in bank	2120 ± 25	350–70 BC	GrN 11220
		Charcoal from under and low in bank	1940 ± 70	100 BC–AD 230	GrN 11429
		Charcoal from top of bank	1825 ± 30	AD 90–320	GrN 11430
Doogarymore (Roscommon)		Wooden wheels: wheel fragment, 1968 find	2315 ± 35	410–260 BC	GrN 5990
		Complete wheel, 1969 find	2400 ± 35	760–390 BC	GrN 5991
Dun of Drumsna (Roscommon)	Linear earthwork	Wood fragment from bank	2105 ± 35	338–44 BC	GrN-18564
Carrowmore (Sligo)	Secondary burials in megalithic tomb	Charcoal from intrusion in chamber (Grave 27)	1730 ± 70	AD 130–440	Lu 1630
			2260 ± 80	490–110 BC	Lu 1631
		Charcoal from Pit 4 (Grave 26)	1860 ± 110	100 BC–AD 410	Lu 1628
Lough Gara, Rathtinaun (Sligo)	Crannóg 61	Twigs from 'fire basket, LBA level'	2070 ± 130	390 BC–AD 230	D-53
		Twigs from 'fire basket, end of LBA'	2140 ± 130	410–120 BC	D-54
		Wooden outer pile	2150 ± 130	410 BC–AD 100	D-55
		Wooden house-post of 'EIA'	2100 ± 130	400 BC–AD 140	D-57
		Wood from outer revetment pile 'EIA'	1630 ± 130	100–660 AD	D-58
		Twigs from 'fire basket, LBA level'	2150 ± 130	410 BC–AD 130	D-59
		Charred cereals, 'end of LBA horizon'	2160 ± 130	490 BC–AD 90	D-60
Clogher (Tyrone)	Ringbarrow	Charcoal from low ring-ditch fill	1770 ± 65	AD 90–410	UB 838
		Charcoal from ring-ditch fill	1710 ± 75	AD 130–530	UB 2036
		Charcoal from ring-ditch fill	2185 ± 45	390–110 BC	UB 2037
		Charcoal from ring-ditch fill	1770 ± 90	AD 60–440	UB 841
		Charcoal from ring-ditch fill	1670 ± 70	AD 230–550	UB 2034
		Charcoal from ring-ditch fill	1725 ± 115	AD 60–560	UB 2033
		Charcoal from top of ring-ditch fill	1635 ± 65	AD 250–560	UB 842
Lough Lene (Westmeath)		Portion of carvel-built wooden vessel	2195 ± 25	400–100 BC	GrN 17263
Rathgall (Wicklow)	Hillfort	Charcoal from smelting pit	1685 ± 70	AD 180–540	SI-1480

Notes to the Text

1 D. Greene, 'Táin Bó Cúailnge', in M. Dillon (ed.), *Irish Sagas*, Mercier Press, Cork 1968, p. 98.

2 See for instance J. Carney, *Studies in Irish Literature and History*, Institute for Advanced Studies, Dublin 1955, p. 279; K. McCone, *Pagan Past and Christian Present in Early Irish Literature*, An Sagart, Maynooth 1990, p. 5; and K.H. Jackson, *The Oldest Irish Tradition: A Window on the Iron Age*, Cambridge University Press, Cambridge 1964.

3 J. P. Mallory, 'The Sword of the Ulster Cycle', in B.G. Scott (ed.), *Studies on Early Ireland: Essays in Honour of M.V. Duignan*, Belfast 1982, pp. 99–114.

4 H.N. Savory, *Guide Catalogue of the Early Iron Age Collections*, National Museum of Wales, Cardiff 1976, p. 21.

5 J.D. Cowen, 'The Hallstatt sword of bronze: on the Continent and in Britain', *Proc. Prehist. Soc.* 33, pp. 377–454.

6 C. Burgess, 'The Bronze Age', in C. Renfrew (ed.), *British Prehistory: A New Outline*, Duckworth, London 1974, p. 213.

7 T. Champion, 'The End of the Irish Bronze Age', *N. Munster Ant. Journ.* 14, 1971, pp. 17–24.

8 C.F.C. Hawkes, 'Hillforts', *Antiquity* 5, 1931, pp. 60–97.

9 P. Harbison, 'Wooden and Stone *Chevaux-de-frise* in Central and Western Europe', *Proc. Prehist. Soc.* 37, 1971, pp. 195–225.

10 Quoted in A. Walsh, 'Excavating the Black Pig's Dyke', *Emania* 3, 1987, p. 6.

11 G. Burenhult, *The Archaeological Excavation at Carrowmore, Co. Sligo, Ireland*, G. Burenhults Forlag, Stockholm 1980, p. 67.

12 H. Schutz, *The Prehistory of Germanic Europe*, Yale University Press, Newhaven and London 1983, p. 333.

13 B. Krüger (ed.), *Die Germanen*, Akademie-Verlag, Berlin 1988, pp. 382–83, Taf. 52, 53.

14 The terms P-Celtic and Q-Celtic have been coined by linguists to describe the differing ways in which the primitive Celtic form of the k^w sound was treated. In Ireland (whose Celtic speech is termed Goidelic) this sound was exclusively retained as 'q', which later became 'c'. On the other hand, in Britain (Brittonic) the 'q' sound was transformed into a 'p' sound. Thus, for example, we might compare the Irish *ceathair* for 'four' with the Welsh *pedwair*. This p/q dichotomy is by no means confined to Britain and Ireland and its significance as an index of wider cultural differentiation receives far less emphasis today than it did in earlier studies.

15 V.G. Childe, *Prehistoric Migrations in Europe*, Instituut for Sammenligende Kulturforskning, Ser. A: Foresninger XX:V, Oslo 1950, p. 2.

16 See H. Hoijer, 'The Relation of Language to Culture', in A.L. Kroeber (ed.), *Anthropology Today: An Encyclopedic Inventory*, University of Chicago Press, Chicago 1953, p. 554; C. Kluckhohn and W. Kelly, 'The Concept of Culture', in R. Linton (ed.), *The Science of Man in the World Crisis*, Columbia University Press, New York 1945, p. 97.

17 D.W. Harding, 'Iron Age Attitudes: A Postscript', in J. Collis (ed.), *The Iron Age in Britain: a review*, University of Sheffield, 1977, p. 65.

18 L.R. Palmer, *Myceneans and Minoans: Aegean Prehistory in the Light of the Linear B Tablets*, Faber and Faber, London 1961, p. 254.

19 J.R.R. Tolkien, 'English and Welsh', in *Angles and Britons – O'Donnell Lectures*, University of Wales Press, Cardiff 1963, pp. 29–30; the quotation is taken from M. Chapman, *The Celts: The Construction of a Myth*, St. Martin's Press, New York 1992, p. xiii.

Further Reading

The following bibliography makes no claim to be comprehensive but is intended as a selective guide to further research for the general reader. To a large extent reference to specific primary source articles in books and specialist journals is avoided and emphasis is placed, as much as possible, on more synthetic works which contain extensive bibliographies. Specialist articles are cited only when they deal with information not found in the general texts or represent very recent work.

Chapter 1: Introduction

The literature on the Celts is extensive. Only a selection is cited here. A useful, extended summary of the most important sources is given in R. and V. Megaw, *Celtic Art from its beginnings to the Book of Kells*, Thames and Hudson, London 1989, 26off. The most recent major synthesis of Celtic culture and civilization is V. Kruta, O.-H. Frey, B. Raftery, M. Szabo (eds), *The Celts*, Thames and Hudson, London 1991, Rizzoli, New York 1991. Other useful general summaries are S. James, *Exploring the World of the Celts*, Thames and Hudson, London and New York 1993; B. Cunliffe, *The Celtic World*, Constable, London 1992; V. Kruta and M. Szabo, *Les Celtes*, Hatier, Paris 1978; J. Collis, *The European Iron Age*, Batsford, London 1984; T.G.E. Powell, *The Celts*, Thames and Hudson, London 1958 (reissued 1980); J. Filip, *Celtic Civilization and its Heritage*, Wellingborough and Academia, Prague 1977 (first published 1962); N. Chadwick and M. Dillon, *The Celtic Realms*, Weidenfeld and Nicholson, London 1967; A. Ross, *The Pagan Celts*, Batsford, London 1986; K. Spindler, *Die frühen Kelten*, Reclam, Stuttgart 1983; P. Jacobsthal, *Early Celtic Art*, Oxford 1944; J.V.S. Megaw, *Art of the European Iron Age*, Bath, London 1970; P.-M. Duval, *Les Celtes*, Gallimard, Paris 1977; B. Raftery (ed.), *Celtic Art*, Unesco/ Flammarion, Paris 1990; C. Eluère, *The Celts: First Masters of Europe*, Thames and Hudson, London 1993, Abrams, New York 1993; F. Schlette, *Kelten zwischen Alesia und Pergamon*, Urania, Leipzig 1977; for the significance of the Irish tales see K.H. Jackson, *The Oldest Irish Tradition: A Window on the Iron Age*, Cambridge University Press, Cambridge 1964; K. McCone, *Pagan Past and Christian Present in Early Irish Literature*, An Sagart, Maynooth, 1990; J.P. Mallory (ed.), *Aspects of the Tain*, The Universities Press, Belfast 1992; P. MacCana, *Celtic Mythology*, Newnes Books, Feltham 1983 (first published 1968); see also J.P. Mallory, 'The Sword of the Ulster Cycle' in B.G. Scott (ed.), *Studies on Early Ireland: Essays in Honour of M.V. Duignan*, Belfast 1982, 99–114.

Chapter 2: From Bronzesmith to Blacksmith

Important source works on the Irish later Bronze Age include G. Eogan, 'The later bronze age in Ireland in the light of recent research', *Proc. Prehist. Soc.* 30, 1964, 268–351; G. Eogan, *Hoards of the Irish Later Bronze Age*, Dublin 1983; useful summaries in M. Herity and G. Eogan, *Ireland in Prehistory*, Routledge and Kegan Paul, London 1977, 148–221; M.J. O'Kelly, *Early Ireland*, Cambridge University Press, London 1989, 147–214; P. Harbison, *Pre-Christian Ireland*, Thames and Hudson, London and New York 1988, 133–54; J.P. Mallory and T.E. McNeill, *The Archaeology of Ulster*, The Institute of Irish Studies, Belfast 1991, 115–42. For Britain and Ireland (including Hallstatt) see J.V.S. Megaw and D.D.A. Simpson (eds), *Introduction to British Prehistory*, Leicester University Press, Leicester 1979, 242–344; see also C.B. Burgess, 'The bronze age', in C. Renfrew (ed.), *British Prehistory: a new outline*, Duckworth, London 1974, 165–232. For Clonfinlough see A. Moloney, Irish Archaeological Wetland Unit, Transactions Vol. 2, Crannog Publication, Dublin 1994. For Navan Fort, Co. Armagh, and for hillforts, see below. For Ralaghan, see B. Coles, 'Anthropomorphic wooden figurines from Britain and Ireland', *Proc. Prehist. Soc.* 56, 1990, 315–33; for King's Stables see C.J. Lynn, 'Trial excavations at the King's Stables, Tray Townland, County Armagh', *Ulster J. Archaeol.* 40, 1977, 42–62. For early Iron Age in Britain see B. Cunliffe, *Iron Age Communities in Britain*, Routledge and Kegan Paul, London 1974, 129–51; D.W. Harding, The Iron Age in Lowland Britain, Routledge and Kegan Paul, London 1974, 134–56; see also Megaw and Simpson (eds), *op. cit.* For bronze swords in Ireland see G. Eogan, *Catalogue of Irish Bronze Swords*, Stationery Office, Dublin 1965. For Bronze Age/Iron Age transition in Ireland see T.C. Champion, 'The end of the Irish bronze age', *N. Munster Ant. Journ.* 14, 1971, 17–24; B. Raftery, *La Tène in Ireland*, Marburg 1984, 7–14; B.G. Scott, *Early Irish Iron Working*, Ulster Museum, Belfast 1991 (with extensive bibliography). Rathtinaun, Co. Sligo is unpublished; information here presented is based on a typescript report prepared by excavator, J. Raftery. For climatic problems see G.F. Mitchell, *The Irish Landscape*, Collins, London 1976, 158–59; S. Piggott, 'A note on climatic deterioration in the first millennium BC in Britain', *Scottish Archaeol. Forum* 4, 1972, 109–13; T. Champion, C. Gamble, S. Shennan, A. Whittle (eds), *Prehistoric Europe*, Academic Press, London 1984, 277–79.

Chapter 3: Hillforts

Recent and ongoing work on the national aerial survey in Ireland by M. Gibbons and T. Condit of the Sites and Monuments Record in the Office of Public Works continues to reveal hitherto unknown hillfort sites. An up-to-date evaluation of all this information remains to be written. Early summaries include B. Raftery, 'Irish Hill-Forts', in C. Thomas (ed.), *The Iron Age in the Irish Sea Province*, Council for British Archaeology, Research Report 9, 1972, 37–58; B. Raftery, 'Rathgall and Irish Hillfort Problems', in D.W. Harding (ed.), *Hillforts: later prehistoric earthworks in Britain and Ireland*, Academic Press, London 1976, 339–57; B. Raftery, 'Freestone Hill: an Iron Age Hillfort and Bronze

Age Cairn', *Proc. Roy. Irish Acad.* 68C, 1–108. For Spinans Hill complex see T. Condit, 'Ireland's Hillfort Capital', *Archaeol. Ireland* 6:3, 1992, 16–20. For Dun Aenghus and *chevaux de frise*, see P. Harbison, 'Wooden and Stone *Chevaux de Frise* in Central and Western Europe', *Proc. Prehist. Soc.* 37, 1971, 195–225, esp. pp. 203–5. For Haughey's Fort see *Emania* 4, 1988 and *Emania* 8, 1991; J.P. Mallory and T.E. McNeill, *The Archaeology of Ulster*, The Institute of Irish Studies, Belfast 1991, 120–23. For Donegore see J.P. Mallory and B.N. Hartwell, 'Donegore', *Current Archaeol.* 92, 1984, 271–75; Mallory and McNeill, *op. cit.*, 35–36. For coastal promontory forts see M.J. O'Kelly, 'Three Promontory Forts in Co. Cork', *Proc. Roy. Irish Acad.* 55C, 1952, 25–59.

Chapter 4: King and Tribe

The definitive synthetic work on early Irish kingship, with full bibliography, is F.J. Byrne, *Irish Kings and High-Kings*, Batsford, London 1973; the literature on Tara is extensive. Important publications include R.A.S. Macalister, *Tara, a pagan sanctuary of ancient Ireland*, Charles Scribner's Sons, London 1931; S.P. ÓRíordáin, *Tara, the monuments on the Hill*, Dundalgan Press, Dundalk 1971; D.L. Swan, 'The Hill of Tara, Co. Meath: the evidence of Aerial Photography', *Journ. Roy. Soc. Antiq. Ireland* 108, 1978, 51–66. For Cruachain see J. Waddell, 'Rathcroghan – a royal site in Connacht', *Journ. Irish Archaeol.* 1, 1983, 21–46; M. Herity, 'A Survey of the Royal Site of Cruachain in Connacht – 1, Introduction, the Monuments and Topography', *Journ. Roy. Soc. Antiq. Ireland* 113, 1983, 121–42; M. Herity, 'A Survey of the Royal Site of Cruachain in Connacht, II', *Journ. Roy. Soc. Antiq. Ireland* 114, 1984, 125–38; J. Waddell, 'Rathcroghan in Connacht', *Emania* 5, 1988, 5–18. For Dún Ailinne see B. Wailes, 'Dún Ailinne: An Interim Report', in D.W. Harding (ed.), *Hillforts, Later Prehistoric Earthworks in Britain and Ireland*, Academic Press, London 1976, 319–57; B. Wailes, 'Dún Ailinne: A Summary Excavation Report', *Emania* 7, 1990, 10–21, and other related papers in same volume. For Navan Fort (Emain Macha) the fullest report as yet is by C.J. Lynn, 'Navan Fort: A Draft Summary of D.M. Waterman's Excavations', *Emania* 1, 1986, 11–19; almost every volume of *Emania* (Vols 1–10, 1986–1992) contains important papers pertaining to Navan Fort. For an idiosyncratic interpretation of Site B at Navan see C.J. Lynn, 'The Iron Age Mound in Navan Fort: A Physical Realization of Celtic Religious Beliefs?', *Emania* 10, 1992, 33–57 and also C.J. Lynn, 'Navan Fort – home of gods and goddesses?', *Archaeology Ireland* 7:1, 1993, 17–21; a general overview is in J.P. Mallory and T.E. McNeill, *The Archaeology of Ulster*, The Institute of Irish Studies, Belfast 1991, 116–23, 146–50. For the dating of the central post at Navan see M.G.L. Baillie, 'The Central Post from Navan Fort: the first step towards a better understanding of the Early Iron Age', *Emania* 1, 1986, 20–21; also M.G.L. Baillie, 'The Dating of the Timbers from Navan Fort and the Dorsey, Co. Armagh', *Emania* 4, 1988, 37–40. For Knockbrack enclosure see D. Keeling, 'A Group of Tumuli and a Hill-Fort near Naul, county Dublin', *Journ. Roy. Soc. Antiq. Ireland* 113, 1983, 67–74. For Giraldus Cambrensis see J.J. O'Meara, *The First Version of the Topography of Ireland by Giraldus Cambrensis*, Dundalgan Press, Dundalk 1951, esp. pp. 93–94. For *óenachs* see F.J. Byrne, *Irish Kings and High Kings*, Batsford, London 1973, 30–31. For Tailtiu and Carman see M. MacNeill, *The Festival of Lughnasa*, Oxford University Press, London 1962, 311–49. For *bile* see A.T. Lucas, 'The Sacred Trees of Ireland', *Journ. Cork Hist. Archaeol. Soc.*

68, 16–54. For linear earthworks see C.J. Lynn, 'The Dorsey and Other Linear Earthworks', in B.G. Scott (ed.), *Studies on Early Ireland: Essays in Honour of M.V. Duignan*, Belfast 1982, 121–28; C.J. Lynn, 'An Interpretation of the Dorsey', *Emania* 6, 1989, 5–9; A. Walsh, 'Excavating the Black Pig's Dyke', *Emania* 3, 1987, 5–19; T. Condit and V. Buckley, 'The "Doon" of Drumsna – Gateways to Connacht', *Emania* 6, 1989, pp. 11–14. For a summary report on Raffin, see C. Newman, 'Sleeping in Elysium', *Archaeology Ireland* 7:3, 1993, pp. 20–23.

Chapter 5: The Road to God Knows Where

For Corlea excavations see B. Raftery, *Trackways Through Time*, Headline, Dublin 1990. For Doogarymore wheels see A.T. Lucas, 'Prehistoric Block-Wheels from Doogarymore, Co. Roscommon, and Timahoe East, Co. Kildare', *Journ. Roy. Soc. Antiq. Ireland* 102, 1972, 19–48. For a general consideration of Celtic chariots and extensive literature see S. Piggott, *The Earliest Wheeled Transport*, Thames and Hudson, London 1983, 195–238. Irish archaeological evidence on transport is discussed in B. Raftery, *La Tène in Ireland*, Marburg 1984, 57–61; and B. Raftery, 'Horse and Cart in Iron Age Ireland', *Journ. Indo-European Studies* 19:1,2, 1991, 49–71. The literary evidence is covered by D. Greene, 'The Chariot as described in Irish Literature', in C. Thomas (ed.), *The Iron Age in the Irish Sea Province*, Council for British Archaeology, Research Report 9, London 1972, 59–73. For horse-trappings see B. Raftery, *La Tène in Ireland*, Marburg 1984, 15–57. For Broighter boat see Raftery, *op. cit.*, 181–82; also A.W. Farrell and S. Penny, 'The Broighter Boat: a Re-assessment', *Irish Archaeol. Research Forum* 2:2, 1975, 15–28. For Lough Lene boat see below, Chapter 9.

Chapter 6: The Invisible People

Most of the material considered in this chapter is illustrated, described and discussed, along with full bibliography, in B. Raftery, *A Catalogue of Irish Iron Age Antiquities*, Marburg 1983 and in B. Raftery, *La Tène in Ireland*, Marburg 1984. For Feerwore see J. Raftery, 'The Turoe Stone and the Rath of Feerwore', *Journ. Roy. Soc. Antiq. Ireland* 74, 1944, 23–52. For wood see M. Taylor, *Wood in Archaeology*, Shire Archaeology, Aylesbury 1981; and C. Earwood, *Domestic Wooden Artifacts in Britain and Ireland from the Neolithic to the Viking Period*, Exeter University Press, Exeter, 1993. For Red Bog and Littleton Bog see G.F. Mitchell, *The Irish Landscape*, Collins, London 1976, 134–38, 158ff; G.F. Mitchell, 'Littleton Bog, Tipperary: an Irish agricultural record', *Journ. Roy. Soc. Antiq. Ireland* 95, 1965, 121–32. For Dún Ailinne palaeobotanical remains see P. Crabtree, 'Paleoethnobotany at Dún Ailinne, Co. Kildare, Ireland', *MASCA Journ.*, University of Pennsylvania, 2:1, 1982, 3–5; faunal remains from Dún Ailinne are discussed in P. Crabtree, 'The Mammalian Fauna from Dún Ailinne, Co. Kildare, Ireland', *MASCA Journ.* 3:6, 179–81; P. Crabtree, 'Dairying in Irish Prehistory', *Expedition* 28:2, 1986, 59–62; P. Crabtree, 'Subsistence and Ritual: The Faunal Remains from Dún Ailinne, Co. Kildare, Ireland', *Emania* 7, 1990, 22–25. For a counter-view on dairying see F. McCormick, 'Evidence of Dairying at Dún Ailinne?', *Emania* 8, 1991, 57–59. For beehive querns see S. Caulfield, 'The Beehive Quern in Ireland', *Journ. Roy. Soc. Antiq. Ireland* 107, 1977, 104–39. The fields at Cush are analyzed in S.P. ÓRíordáin, 'Excavations at Cush, Co. Limerick,' *Proc. Roy. Irish Acad.* 45C, 1940, 139–45. For textiles see L. Bender Jorgensen, *North European Textiles until AD 1000*, Aarhus University

Press, Aarhus 1992, 18–41, 215. For the Castleblakeney bog body see below, Chapter 8. For the Broighter gold torcs see R.B. Warner, 'The Broighter Hoard: A Reappraisal and the Iconography', in B.G. Scott (ed.), *Studies on Early Ireland: Essays in Honour of M.V. Duignan*, Belfast 1982, 29–38. For the reprovenancing of 'Clonmacnoise' torc, A. Ireland, 'The Finding of the "Clonmacnoise" Gold Torcs', *Proc. Roy. Irish Acad.* 92C, 1992, 123–46.

Chapter 7: Technology and Art

The basic source work for early Irish iron technology is B.G. Scott, *Early Irish Ironworking*, Ulster Museum, Belfast 1991; see also H. Maryon, 'The Technical Methods of the Irish Smiths in the Bronze and Early Iron Ages', *Proc. Roy. Irish Acad.* 44C, 1938, 181–228. An important general work on prehistoric metallurgy is R.F. Tylecote, *The Prehistory of Metallurgy in the British Isles*, The Institute of Metals, London 1986. For scabbard engraving techniques see P.R. Lowery, R.D.A. Savage and R.L. Wilkins, 'Scriber, Graver, Scorper, Tracer: Notes on Experiments in Bronzeworking Technique', *Proc. Prehist. Soc.* 37, 1971, 167–82. For general considerations of European La Tène art, see above, Chapter 1. For Britain and Ireland see C. Fox, *Pattern and Purpose*, National Museum of Wales, Cardiff 1958; I.M. Stead, *Celtic Art*, British Museum Publications, London 1985; R. and V. Megaw, *Early Celtic Art in Britain and Ireland*, Shire Archaeology, Aylesbury 1986; B. Raftery, *La Tène in Ireland*, Marburg 1984, 319–24; and L. and J. Laing, *Art of the Celts*, Thames and Hudson, London and New York 1992, 93–137.

Chapter 8: Cult, Ritual and Death

Out of the huge selection of works on Celtic ritual and religion the following may be suggested: P. MacCana, *Celtic Mythology*, Newnes Books, Feltham 1983 (first published 1968); M. Green, *The Gods of the Celts*, Alan Sutton, Gloucester 1986; M. Green, *Dictionary of Celtic Myth and Legend*, Thames and Hudson, London and New York 1992; M. Green, *Animals in Celtic Life and Myth*, Routledge, London 1992; A. Ross, *Pagan Celtic Britain*, Routledge and Kegan Paul, London 1967; A. Ross, *The Pagan Celts*, Batsford, London 1986; J.L. Brunaux, *The Celtic Gauls: Gods, Rites and Sanctuaries*, Seaby, London 1987; S. Piggott, *The Druids*, Thames and Hudson, London 1968 (reprinted in London and New York 1991). The site of La Tène is examined in P. Vouga, *La Tène*, Hiersemann, Leipzig 1925; while a new interpretation appears in H. Schwab, 'Entdeckung einer keltischen Brücke an der Zihl und ihre Bedeutung für La Tène', *Archäologisches Korrespondenzblatt* 2, 1972, 289ff; a description and discussion of the differing views is available in A. Furger-Gunti, *Die Helvetier, Kulturgeschichte eines Keltenvolkes*, Verlag Neuer Zürcher Zeitung, Zürich 1984, 58–70. For Llyn Cerrig Bach see C. Fox, *A Find of the Early Iron Age from Llyn Cerrig Bach, Anglesey*, National Museum of Wales, Cardiff 1946. St. Louis, Basle and related gold finds are discussed in A. Furger-Gunti, 'Der "Goldfund von Saint-Louis" bei Basel und ähnliche keltische Schatzfunde', *Zeitschrift f. Schweiz. Archäologie und Kunstgeschichte* 39, 1982, 1–47. For Loughnashade see B. Raftery, 'The Loughnashade Horns', *Emania* 2, 1987, 21–24. The most recent assessment of the Gundestrup cauldron is in F. Kaul, I. Marazov, J. Best, N. De Vries, *Thracian Tales on the Gundestrup Cauldron*, Najade Press, Amsterdam 1991; see also R. Hachmann, 'Gundestrup-Studien. Untersuchungen zu den spätkeltischen Grundlagen der frühgermanischen Kunst',

Bericht Röm.-Germ. Kommission 71, 1990, 565–903. For Lisnacrogher see B. Raftery, *A Catalogue of Irish Iron Age Antiquities*, Marburg 1983, 287–88. For Ralaghan see above, Chapter 2. For the Corlea carving see B. Raftery, *Trackways Through Time*, Headline, Dublin 1990. For the north European wooden carvings see H. Schutz, *The Prehistory of Germanic Europe*, Yale University Press, Newhaven and London 1983, 332–36; B. Krüger (ed.), *Die Germanen*, Akademie-Verlag, Berlin 1988, Tafeln 52, 53; B. Coles, 'Anthropomorphic wooden figurines from Britain and Ireland', *Proc. Prehist. Soc.* 56, 1990, 315–33. For iconic stone carvings in Ireland see E. Rynne, 'Celtic Stone Idols in Ireland', in C. Thomas (ed.), *The Iron Age in the Irish Sea Province*, Council for British Archaeology, Research Report 9, 1972, 79–98; H. Hickey, *Images of Stone*, Blackstaff, Belfast 1976. For stone carvings in general see A. Ross, *Pagan Celtic Britain*, Routledge and Kegan Paul, London 1967. Carrowmore is covered in G. Burenhult, *The Archaeological Excavation at Carrowmore, Co. Sligo, Ireland*, G. Burenhults Forlag, Stockholm 1980, 64–67. For European bog bodies see P.V. Glob, *The Bog People*, Faber and Faber, London 1965. For Britain and Ireland with a good general summary and catalogue see I.M. Stead, J.B. Bourke, D. Brothwell, *Lindow Man, The Body in the Bog*, British Museum Publications, London 1986. For the Castleblakeney body see R. Ó Floinn, 'Irish Bog Bodies', *Archaeol. Ireland* 2:3, 1988, 94–97; for burials in general see B. Raftery, 'Iron Age Burials in Ireland', in D. ÓCorráin (ed.), *Irish Antiquity: Essays and Studies Presented to Professor M.J. O'Kelly*, Tower Books, Cork 1981, 173–204; E. O'Brien, 'Pagan and Christian Burial in Ireland during the First Millennium AD: Continuity and Change', in N. Edwards and A. Lane (eds), *The Early Church in Wales and the West*, Oxbow Monograph 16, 1992, 130–62. For recent work at Kiltierney, Co. Fermanagh burials see C. Foley in A. Hamlin and C. Lynn (eds), *Pieces of the Past*, DOE for Northern Ireland, Belfast 1988, 24–26. The Fore, Co. Westmeath burial is as yet unpublished; for a drawing of bowl see P. Wallace, 'My Plans for the Museum', in *The New Nation*, No. 5, April 1989, 19.

Chapter 9: Beyond the Empire

For a summary of Masada history and excavations, a good introduction is Y. Yadin, *Masada: Herod's Fortress and the Zealots' Last Stand*, Weidenfeld and Nicolson, London 1966. For Classical sources to Ireland see J.F. Kenney, *The Sources for the Early History of Ireland*, Vol. 1, Columbia University Press, New York 1929; J.F. Killeen, 'Ireland in the Greek and Roman Writers', *Proc. Roy. Irish Acad.* 76C (Colloquium on Hiberno-Roman Relations and Material Remains), 1976, 207–15. The most recent summary and catalogue of Roman material in Ireland is in J.D. Bateson, 'Roman material from Ireland: a re-consideration', *Proc. Roy. Irish Acad.* 73C, 1973, 21–97; while a good general summary can be found in R. Warner, 'The earliest history of Ireland', in M. Ryan (ed.), *The Illustrated History of Ireland*, Country House, Dublin 1991, 112–16; see also R. Warner, 'Some observations on the context and importation of exotic material in Ireland, from the first century BC to the second century AD', *Proc. Roy. Irish Acad.* 76C (Colloquium on Hiberno-Roman Relations and Material Remains), 1976, 267–92. For Lambay see E. Rynne, 'The La Tène and Roman Finds from Lambay, Co. Dublin: a re-assessment', *Proc. Roy. Irish Acad.* 76C (Colloquium on Hiberno-Roman Relations and Material Remains), 1976, 231–44. For Ptolemy see M. Grant, *Greek and Latin Authors, 800 BC to AD 1000*, H.W. Wilson, New York 1980, 368–70. For Ptolemy's map and summary of sources see F.J. Byrne, Map 14, in T.W. Moody, F.X. Martin, F.J. Byrne (eds), *A New History of Ireland*, Vol 9, Part 2, Clarendon Press, Oxford 1990, 98; see also J.P. Mallory, 'The Origins of the Irish', *Journ. Irish Archaeol.* 2, 1984, 65–69; J.P. Mallory and T.E. McNeill, *The Archaeology of Ulster*, Institute of Irish Studies, Belfast 1991, 143–46; J.J. Tierney, 'The Greek Geographic Tradition and Ptolemy's Evidence for Irish Geography', *Proc. Roy. Irish Acad.* 76C (Colloquium on Hiberno-Roman Relations and Material Remains), 1976, 257–65. For a recent assessment of the Stonyford burial see E. Bourke, 'Stonyford: a first-century Roman burial from Ireland', *Archaeol. Ireland* 3:2, 1989, 56–57. For the Lough Lene boat see A.L. Brindley and J.N. Lanting, 'A Roman boat in Ireland', *Archaeol. Ireland* 4:3, 1990, 10–11. For Roman finds at Newgrange see R.A.G. Carson and C. O'Kelly, 'A Catalogue of the Roman Coins from Newgrange, Co. Meath and Notes on the Coins and Related Finds', *Proc. Roy. Irish Acad.* 77C, 1977, 35–55. For the Ballinrees hoard see H. Mattingly and J. Pearce, 'The Coleraine Hoard', *Antiquity* 2, 1937, 39–45. For Balline see S.P. ÓRíordáin, 'Roman Material in Ireland', *Proc. Roy. Irish Acad.* 51C, 1947, 43–53.

Chapter 10: Celts, Culture and Colonization

The concepts of archaeological and anthropological 'cultures' and related topics have been extensively discussed in the modern literature. A random selection of significant publications includes V.G. Childe, *Piecing Together the Past*, Routledge and Kegan Paul, London 1956, 16, 48–49; H. Hoijer, 'The Relation of language to culture', in A.L. Kroeber (ed.) *Anthropology Today: An Encyclopedic Inventory*, University of Chicago Press, Chicago 1953, 554–73; D.W. Harding, *The Iron Age in Lowland Britain*, Routledge and Kegan Paul, London 1974, 3–5; and B.M. Fagan, *Archaeology: A Brief Introduction*, Harper Collins, New York 1991, 35–50. For 'Celtic' problems in Ireland see G. MacEoin, 'The Celticity of Celtic Ireland', in K.H. Schmidt (ed.) *Geschichte und Kultur der Kelten*, Heidelberg 1986, 161–74; see also papers by J. Waddell, J.T. Koch, B. Raftery, G. Cooney and E. Grogan, R.B. Warner and J.P. Mallory in *Emania* 9, 1991; J. Waddell, 'The Celticisation of the West: an Irish Perspective', in C. Chevillot and A. Coffyn (eds), *L'Age du Bronze Atlantique*, Beynac-et-Cazenac 1991, 349–66; S. Caulfield, 'Celtic Problems in the Irish Iron Age', in D. ÓCorráin (ed.) *Irish Antiquity: Essays and Studies presented to Professor M.J. O'Kelly*, Tower Books, Cork 1981, 205–15. A general consideration of 'invasion' problem in Ireland can be found in J. Waddell, 'The invasion hypothesis in Irish prehistory', *Antiquity* 52, 1978, 121–28. For suggested La Tène 'infiltrations' into Ireland see E. Rynne, 'The introduction of La Tène into Ireland', *Bericht über den V Internationalen Kongress für Vor- und Frühgeschichte Hamburg 1958*, Berlin 1961, 705–9. For recent thought-provoking consideration of the 'Celtic' problem see M. Chapman, *The Celts: The Construction of a Myth*, St. Martin's Press, New York 1992.

Sources of Illustrations

Index

Numerals in *italics* refer to line drawings; numerals in **bold** refer to plates

Abbeyshrule 104
acculturation 26
adze 97, 100, 101, 118, 119; adzing 186
Africa 79
Agricola 219
agriculture 121, 122; decline in 122; techniques 123
Ailill 15, 70
alder 99, 116, 117, 120; shield 146
Alexandria 204
All Cannings Cross, Wilts., England 26
Allia, Battle of 9
alloy, copper/gold 25
Alsatian 126
Altartate Glebe, Co. Monaghan 115, 118; *64*
amber, beads 22; necklace 34
Ammianus Marcellinus 11
Anglesey 105
animal bones 80; rib 120, 123
animal forms 108, 185
animal husbandry 125
anklet 127, 141; of bone beads 194
annealing 22, 153–55
Annesborough, Co. Armagh *139*
Annlore, Killeevan, Co.Monaghan 34
anthropomorphic carving 186, 187
antler hilts 142; hilt-guards 142; picks 44, 120; pommels 142
Antrim 147, 165; coast 214; horse-bit *59*; terret *57*
anvil 149, 157
ape 62, 79, 126, 228
Aran Islands 44; Inis Mean 45; Inishmore 44
Arcadius 210
arcs 166
ard 21; head 101, 123; *72*; *42*, *43*
Ardbrin, Co. Down 154; *95*
Ardennes, Belgium 12
aristocratic elite 150
Ark of the Covenant 68
Armagh 74, 83, 85; City 185; County 116, 139; heads 185
armlets 127
armouries 144
Arretine ware 217
Arretium, Italy 217
art, La Tène 162; *see also* ornament, La Tène

arthritis 199
Artis 180
ash 19, 99, 102, 117; board 118; carving 186; pollen 19; shaft 34
Asia Minor 10
assemblies, religious 82, 83, 180
assembly, places of 81; *47*
Athboy, Co. Meath 82
Athenaeus 11
Atlantic 205
Attavally, Co. Mayo
Attymon, Co. Galway 107; *33*
Aughinish, Co. Limerick 21, 32
auxiliaries 209
Avoca, River 205
axeheads *67*; bronze 26, 31; iron 118, 149; looped and socketed 22, 26, 31, 35; *16*; shafthole 34, 35; *91*; unlooped and socketed 118

badger 17, 126
bags 120
Balashanner, Angus 26
ball, hollow gold 23
ball-socket mechanism 139
Ballinderry, Co. Offaly, No. 2 19; sword from 150; *82*
Balline, Co. Limerick 216; *138*; **79**
Ballinrees, silver hoard 215, 216
Ballybeen, Dundonald, Co. Down 25; *11*
Ballybrit, Co. Galway, spearbutt *87*
Ballycastle, Co. Antrim, mount 157
Ballyedmond, Co. Galway, cauldron 115, 159; *64*; **38**
Ballykilmurry, Co. Wicklow, model sword 142; **53**
Ballykinvarga, Co. Clare 61
Ballylin, Co. Limerick 43
Ballymoney, Co. Antrim, cauldron *64*, *107*; **37**; mirror 127, 168; **46**
Ballyshannon Bay, Co. Donegal, sword 143, 225; *83*
Baltic 17
Banagher Glebe, Co. Derry 39
Bangor, Co. Down 14
bank-and-ditch 85
Bann Disc 155, 168, 183; *107*
Bann, River 14, 28, 183; bowls, bronze 155; disc

155; scabbards 144, 157, 165, 183; *103*; **56**; spearbutt 54
Banqueting Hall, *Teach Miodhchuarta* 69, 70, 82
Barbary ape 62, 79, 126
bark 117
barley, grains 122, 123
Barrow, River 82
barrows 66, 69, 70, 71, 180
basket 117
basketry 105; ornament 165
Bateson, Donal 214
battles, Roman customs 57
beads 189, 198; amber 22, 34, 127; bone 141, 189, 194, 195; *113*; glass 22, 74, 127, 141, 189, 193–95, 212; *113*; Iron Age 195; stone 141
bear, brown 17; cult 185; stone 185
beard 188
bees 126
Belenus, god 183
Belgae 57
bell, hand 217
bellows 148, 149
belt 119,120, 128, 144; fittings 127,128; iron 192
Beltaine 83, 104
Beltany, Co. Donegal 186
Benagh, Mount Brandon, Co. Kerry 46, 47; *30*; **14**
Betaghstown, Co. Meath 119, 126, 128, 209
bile 83
binding strips 116
birch 99–101, 117
bird, on seal 212
birds' heads 108, 168; *107*; handles 116, 152, 157, 183; on fibulae 138; on ring-headed pins 141; pseudo 165
Black Pig's Dyke 83–88, 226; *48*
blacksmith 17, 22, 27, 147–50
Blackwater, River 82
blades, of swords 141, 143
bloom 148, 149; temperature 149
Boa Island, Co. Fermanagh 186
boar 179; tusk 83
board game, pegged 121
boat 111, 208; *62*; wickerwork 204
body, bog 128, 187–88; **77**
bogs 18, 21, 36, 65, 87, 88, 98, 108, 124, 146, 182–84; ores 147; raised 98, 121

Bohemia 186
Bohermeen, Co. Meath 217; *141*
bone, beads 141, 189, 194, 195; combs 121; decorated 121; flakes, decorated 167, 180; *104*; hilts 142; needles 120; objects 126; scoops 120; *69*
bones, animal 74, 120, 168, 195; human 218
Book of Leinster 14
Bord na Móna 98
bosses, biconical 154; bronze 146; cruciform 201; domed 146; lentoid 166, 168; on ring-headed pins 140; shield 146; sub-conical 154; wood 146
bottle, glass 207; *131*
bovine mask 168
bowls 116, 168; bronze 116, 155, 183; *65*; mixing 10; silver 216
boxes, gold 23; wooden 34
Boyne, River 183, 205, 214; Valley 180
bracelets 22, 23; bronze 30, 141, 201, 212, 213; glass 74, 141, 198; gold 210; Hallstatt 37; *15*; jet 141, 201
Bray Head, Co. Wicklow 209
bread 21
Brega, kingdom of 66
Brennus 9
Bricriu 14
bridges 184
bridle-bits *see* horse-bits
Brigantes 200, 201, 205
Brigantia 200
Britain 13, 17, 27, 28, 61, 127, 139, 140, 157, 210, 214, 219; Druidism 179; imports from 157, 196; La Tène art in 163; Q-Celtic in 206; spearbutts in 144, 204; timber uprights in 186
Brittany 182
Broighter, Co. Derry 111; *75*; **36**; gold boat 111, 208; *62*; hoard 128; necklace 128; torc, buffer 128, 157, 161, 166; *105*; **67**; votive deposit 183, 184
bronze 12, 22, 26, 33, 58, 150; binding of 116; bowl 155, 183; bowl, cremation in 196; bracelet 30, 201; *141*; cake 151, 153; cast 105, 106; fibulae 60, 80, 113, 127, 138, 189, 198, 212; grille 158; hilt-guard plates 142; ingot 151, 153; ladle 217; lathe-finishing 157; locket 141, 194; molten 161; polishing 155; raw 155; repair 158, 159; Roman 58; rosette 201; sheet 22, 29, 115, 144, 153–55, 159, 201; shield boss 146; 'spoons' 158; studs 201; sword-grip 143; tooling 155; torc 128, 201; trumpets 150, 184; tweezers 154, 198; working 58, 151–57; yoke-mount 184
Bronze Age 9, 17; burials 189, 191; cairns 180; Early 41, 67, 70, 128; Iron Age transition 123; Late 18, 24, 27, 30–35, 44, 58, 59, 60, 62, 70, 75, 111–16, 119, 122, 149, 151, 161, 186, 220, 225, 228; Middle 128, 189, 191; mounds 193, 194; ringbarrows 189; torc 210
bronzesmith 112, 150–61
brooches 183; bow-brooch 212; composite bronze/iron 150; Hallstatt 28; Navan type 128, 139, 158; *see also* fibulae
Brown Bull of Cooley 15
Brusselstown Ring, Co. Wicklow 62, 63
buckets 22, 25; escutcheons of 159
bull hunt 125
Burgess, Colin 29
burial, alive 199; chieftains 10, 12; children 195, 199; coins from 215; cremation 25, 68, 128, 189–99; double 199; female 12, 141, 194, 199; foetus 199; inhumation 12, 68, 75, 127, 189, 193, 200; males 195, 199; mounds 41, 67, 68, 69, 80, 217; ring from 157; secondary 192, 194, 195; skulls 183; warrior 141; *see also* graves, tombs
butchery 125

Caesar 9, 10, 12, 16, 57, 178, 179, 204
Caherconree, Slieve Mish 46, 47; **13, 14**
Caherdrinny, Co. Cork 41; *22*
cairns 41, 70, 76; Bronze Age 180; Emain Macha, at 180; Neolithic 180

Caledonians 105
calf-hide, shield 146
Camus 155, 183
cannibalism 204
canoes 111, 118; dugout 22
cape 119; deer-skin 128
Cappagh, Co. Kerry 29; *14*
carburization 26, 149
Carbury Hill, Co. Kildare 127, 128, 191; jet spoon 217; shears *74*
Carlingwark, cauldron 184
Carman 82
Carn Tigherna, Co. Cork 14; *23*
Carnfree, Co. Roscommon 83
Carpathian Mountains 10
Carraig Aille, Co. Limerick 213
Carrickfergus, Co. Antrim 116; tankard **40**
Carrowbeg North, Co. Galway 193; *119, 120*
Carrowjames, Co. Mayo 128, 189; *114*
Carrowmably, Co. Sligo 80
Carrowmore, Co. Sligo 123, 199; skull bones 185; teeth 185
cart 102, 104; *52, 56*; *see also* wagons
carvel-construction 111, 208
Cashel, Co. Sligo (sword) *82*
casting 22, 127, 151, 155, 157; bronze 127; cores (clay) 108, 152; fibulae 138; metal 126; ornament 140
Castleblakeney, Co. Galway 128, 188
Castlestrange, Co. Roscommon *102, 109*
Cathbhadh 14
Cathedral Hill, Armagh 185; **76**
Cathedral Hill, Downpatrick, Co. Down 21, 58
Cato the Elder 10
cattle 21, 125, 126, 204; raiding 88, 125
Cauci 206
cauldrons 64; **37, 38**; bronze 10, 22, 25, 26, 27, 32, 115, 153, 184; Hallstatt 37; iron 32, 114, 115, 149; *17*; poplar 115; repair 159; ritual deposit 184; silver 184; symbol 184
causeway 85
cavalry 29
Cavan 83, 88
Celtic clothing 127, 128; expansion 10; figure sculpture 185; invasion 228; language 12, 223; metalwork 183; migration 223; mythology 115, 126, 182, 184; religion 12, 16; sanctuary 180; society 62, 141, 185; tradition 64, 71; vanity 127; women 11, 127, 128
cemeteries 12, 68, 146; flat 195; Iron Age 182
Cerberus 209
cereals 122, 123
ceremonial centres 180; character 123; objects 24; occasions 110; sites 74, 212
Cernunnos, antlered god 178
chains, suspension 115
Champion, Timothy 29
champlevé 108, 157
chapes 27, 144; Hallstatt 29, 30, 75; openwork 144; scabbard 144; **55**; winged 29; *14*
chaplets 152
charcoal 149; birch 117, 148; oak 148
chariot 11, 12, 104, 105, 106; *55*; burials 105
charioteer 105
Charon, the ferryman 209
chasing 161
cheek-pieces, bone 21
cheek-rings 107, 152, 159
chevaux de frise 45, 61, 62, 228; *33*
chieftains 9
child burials 195, 199
Childe, Gordon 222
chisels 22, 119, 149, 155, 157, 162; iron 162; tanged 32, 34
Christianity 64
chronology, Iron Age 76
chuck-marks 155
churns 116
cire perdue 126, 152
cists 189; long stone 209
Claragh Mountain, Co. Cork 39
Classical writers 10–12, 78, 127, 141, 203–4, 220

Clibborn, Henry 207
clinker-construction 111
cloaks 128
Clogher, Co. Tyrone 41, 48; fibula from 138; *77*; pottery from 58, 213
Clogher Valley 139
Clonbrien, Co. Longford 7
Clondalee, Co. Meath, spearbutt **54**
Clonfinlough, Co. Offaly 19, 22; *5*
Clonmacnoise 14; quern from 167; *73, 104*; torc *see* Knock
Clonoura, Co. Tipperary 117, 120, 146
clothing 186
Cloughmills, Co. Antrim 116
club, magical 87
cobbling 212
coffin 75
coins 12, 105, 210, 214, 215; copper 212; gold 208, 210; Roman 58, 208–13; silver 210, 215, 216
Coleraine, Co. Derry, spearbutt *87*
colonizers 221
combs, bone 121, 127; weaving *68*
compass 15, 168; arm 15; ornament 121, 168, 191; style 167; work 161, 165, 166; *105*
composite artifacts, iron/bronze 150
Conall Cernach 14
concentric circle motifs 165
Conchobhar Mac Nessa 14
Condit, Tom 62, 63
Connachtmen 15
Constantine II 212
Constantine III 216
Constantius II 213, 216
copper, alloy 25, 151; cake 151; coins 210; ingot 208; mining 151, 208; occurrence of 151
coracles 22, 111
coral, red 157
cord, of sinew 188
Cork, Co. 151
Cork Horns 120, 155, 166; *97*; **60, 61**
Corlea, Co. Longford 98, 99, 103, 106, 110, 112, 116, 117, 118, 122, 123; *51, 52, 53, 66, 63, 111*; **24–28**; ard *72*; **42**; carved plank 186, 187; date 226
Corleck, Co. Cavan 185, 186
Cormac, King 66, 69
corn 21
Cornalaragh, mount 157; *63*
Cornashee, Co. Fermanagh 80, 83
Cornwall, tin from 151
Corrib River, Co. Galway, sword *90*
cosmetic bottle 207
Cowen, J.D. 29
Crabtree, J.P. 125, 126
craftsmen 165
crane 18
crannogs 18, 19, 32–34, 184; *18*
cremation 25, 68, 128, 189; pyre 189; Roman 207
Croagh Patrick, Co. Mayo 57
Cromaghs, Co. Antrim 21
cross-dykes 88
'crotals' 25
Cruachain, Co. Westmeath 64, 65, 70–71, 104; **19, 20**; ceremonial centre 180; óenach 82; ringbarrows 189
crucibles 116
Cú Chulainn 14, 15, 127
Cullen, Co. Tipperary 195
cult 76, 126, 178, 186; bear 185; fertility 80, 182; monolith 181; water 115
cup-handle 151
cups 116
Curragh, Co. Kildare 82, 199
Curraghatoor, Co. Tipperary 18; *4*
Cush, Co. Limerick 121, 125; gaming pieces from 167; *104*; **41**; Tumulus I 191; Tumulus II 189–91; Tumulus III 191

Daghda 210
Daithi's Mound 70, 71
Damastown, Co. Dublin 208
Dane's Cast 83, 84, 87, 88

Dangan Lower, Co. Galway 149
Danube 163
death 178, 188
decapitation 11, 195
deer 125; antlers 24; red 17, 125, 126; skin 128, 188; trap 17
defences 12, 57, 44–48; bank-and-ditch 21, 38, 58; *chevaux de frise* 45; multivallate 41, 43, 44, 62; univallate 39, 41
Delphi 10
dendrochronology 7, 76, 97, 99
Derraghan More 99
Derry 147
Derrykeighan, Co. Antrim 162, 166; *105, 109;* **69**
Derryoghil, Co. Longford 2
Diarmait 69
dice 12, 126; bone 195; decorated 121
diet, Iron Age 199
Dijon 183
Dindshenchas 66, 67, 82
discs, Bann 155; bronze 27, 201; gold 23; iron 200; Monasterevin-type 153, 159; *94; 59*
dishes, silver 216
ditch/fosse 25, 66, 84–86; external 46; internal 65, 69, 71, 74, 80, 180
dividers, bronze 212
divination 179
dogs 21, 204; bones 24, 125; size 126
Domitian 210
Donaghadee, Co. Down 198
Donegal 83, 139, 214
Donegore, Co. Antrim 58
Doogarymore, Co. Roscommon 21, 104, 106, 117, 118; *54, 56*
Dorsey, the 63, 85, 86, 88, 97; *49*
dough-board 116
dowelling 103
Down 83
Dowris, Co. Offaly 25; hoard 1; Phase 32, 34, 36
draught-pole 102
draughtsmanship 212
dress 128, 188
dress-fasteners 23; bronze 139, 150; iron 149
drill 119; bow 155, 159
Druids 12, 14, 179
Drumacaladerry, Co. Donegal 17
Drumanagh, Co. Dublin 48, 207; *132;* name 208; pottery from 48, 208, 217
Drumanone, Co. Roscommon, Y-shaped object *61*
Drumlane, Co. Cavan 31, 114; cauldron from 149; *17*
Dublin 228; iron horsebits from 150
Duchcov, Bohemia 183; cauldron from 184
ducks 179
Dümmer 103
Dun Aengus 62; *8;* area 45; *chevaux de frise* 59, 61; date 44
Dún Ailinne 64, 68, 71–74, 80, 108, 113, 116, 118, 119, 120, 122, 125, 126, 180, 212; *38–40;* sword *82*
Dun Concobhair, Inis Mean 41, 45
Dun Dubhcathair, Aran 61
Dun Eochla, Inishmore 44
Dun of Drumsna 86, 88, 226; *50*
Dunamo, Co. Mayo 61
Dunaverney, Co. Antrim 31
Dunbeg, Co. Kerry 48
Dunclaidh 83, 88
Dunfanaghy, Co. Donegal *139;* **48**
Dunlaing, King of Leinster 69
Dunmore East *57*
dyes 117, 119; dying (hair) 127
dykes, linear 65

earrings 127
earthworks 66, 67, 68, 70, 74; date 88; linear 70, 83–89, 103; *47;* parallel 82
Edenderry, Co. Offaly, sword *82*
Eleazar ben Yair 200
elm 99; pollen 122
Emain Macha, Co. Armagh 62, 64, 68, 71, 74–79, 97, 184, 206; circular structure 180;

óenachs 82; Phase 4 180; temple at 180; *see also* Navan Fort
England 48, 128, 168, 216, 225, 226
enamel 151, 157, 158, 193; inlay 144, 157; on fibulae 139; studs 140, 157
enclosures 85, 86; annexed 42, 75; bank-and-ditch 72; Dorsey, the 63; earthen bank 80; hilltop 21, 38, 41, 57, 70, 80; internally ditched 65, 69, 71, 74, 80, 180; ritual 69; stockaded 21; stone 21; Tara, at 66, 67, 70, 71; timber-built 68, 195
entrances, hillforts 39, 44, 45–47; lintelled 45
Eochaid 98
Eogan, George 29
epic tales, Irish 127
escutcheons, bucket 159
Etruscans 9
Europe 185
eye-salve 218

face 108; foliate 177; in art 163, 177
false-relief 162
faunal analysis 126; remains 125
feasting 73, 74, 81
Feerwore, Co. Galway 113, 116, 118, 126; *67;* burial at 141, 195, 199; chisel from 149; Turoe stone at 182
Feigh Mountain, Co. Antrim, hoard of coins 215
felloe 105
female, age 199; burial 194, 199, 207; physique 199
Ferdia 15
Fergus Mac Roich 14
Fermanagh, Co. 83, 150
fertility cult 182, 187
festivals, Celtic 82, 121, 180; Gallo-Roman 183
fibulae 128, 139, 141, 193; *77, 78, 107, 113;* **3, 49;** bronze 60, 80, 113, 138, 189; dating 138; decoration 168; foot-section 138, 139; iron 138; La Tène type 138; leaf-shaped bow 138; manufacture 138; Nauheim-derivative 198; Navan-type 128, 139, 158; **43, 48;** pins on 139; repair 159; rod-bow 138; Roman 74, 201, 212, 213, 217; *139;* with snake head 177; **49**
field boundaries 71; enclosures 125; systems 125
files 149, 154, 155, 157, 162
Findbhennach (white-horned bull) 15
fire baskets 32
fish 18; traps 117
flagons 10, 212
'fleshhook' 31
Flower Hill 215
foetus, burial of 199
Fontes Sequana 183
food production 121–27
Fore, Co. Westmeath *123;* burial 196; lug on bowl 168, 196; *78*
foreshare 123
forge 147–49
Forradh, Royal Seat 67
fosse/ditch 25, 66, 84, 85, 86; external 46, 189; internal 65, 69, 71, 74, 80, 180, 192
fox 126
France 17, 48, 218
Freestone Hill 41, 57, 59, 120, 126; *24, 69, 136;* bronzes from 58, 116; coin from 212; pottery from 58, 116
Fresians 45
fuels 147
fullers 149
furnace, bowl 148; smelting 148, 149; temperature 148
Furness, Co. Kildare 189

Gallagh, Co. Galway 188; *77*
Gallo-Roman carvings 183; festival 183; offerings 183; Samian ware 208
Galway, Co. 139, 144
games 81; funeral 82
'gaming pieces' 121, 167, 195; *70, 104*
Gaul 67, 83, 128, 143, 163, 178, 186, 210
Gauls 9, 10, 11
Geoffrcy of Tours 183

Germany 12, 103; wooden figures in 187
Giraldus Cambrensis 81
Glanbane, Co. Kerry 43
Glasbolie, Co. Donegal 83; **23**
glass 58, 157; beads 22, 74, 127, 141, 189, 193, 194, 195, 212; *113;* bottle 207; *131;* bracelets 141, 198; Continental 198; inlay 212; Roman 68; urn *131*
Glassamucky Brakes, Co. Dublin, weaving comb 68
Glenballythomas 70
glue 117
goat 125, 126, 177
goblets 10, 212
goddess 182
gods 13; torcs worn by 127, 178
Golden, Co. Tipperary 218, 219; *142*
goose 179
goosefoot 123
gorgets 23
Gorteenreagh, Co. Clare, 'lock-ring' *8*
Gortgill, Co. Antrim 111
Gortgole, Co. Antrim, horse-bit *100*
Gortygeeheen, Co. Clare 123; *43*
gouges 22, 119
Grainne 69
Granard, Co. Longford 83
Grange, Co. Sligo, ring-headed pin *80*
Grannagh, Co. Galway 189; *112, 113*
Grauballe 188
grave goods 189–99, 200
graving-tools 155, 157, 165
Great Clare Hoard 25
Greece 10, 224
Greek colonies 9
Greene, David 15, 105
greyhound 126
Grianan Aileach 41
Groningen 188
Gundestrup cauldron 184

habitation 127; enclosed 31; site 32
Hadrian 209
hair, black 188; dying of 127; facial 186
Hallstatt culture 9, 37; in Ireland 26–32, 35, 37, 163, 228; objects 221; *13*
hammers 22, 149, 155, 162
handles 116, 152, 217
Harbison, Peter 62
harbours 200, 206, 208
Harding, D.W. 222
hare 17, 126
hatching 165
Haughey's Fort, Co. Armagh 21, 43, 57–59; date 58; pottery from 58
hazel 18, 33, 99, 117, 122; bands, used in garrotting 188; nuts 123
head, cast bronze 105; cult of the 185; gear 119; horned 155; on horse-bit 177; human 177, 185; three-faced 185
Healy, Patrick 62
hearths 113
Henderson, Julian 198
High King 16, 66
Hill of Ward 82; *see also* Tlaghta
hillforts 12, 38–61, 213, 228; *21–28;* bivallate 43, 44, 62; builders 41, 62; burial mounds at 180; chronology 58; contour 60; culture 58; definition 38; distribution 60; *32;* foreign influences on 61; function 48; multivallate 41, 62; trivallate 43; typology 38; unfinished 44; univallate 38; walled 43–47
hilt, anthropoid 143; *83;* fittings 120, 143; -guard 142, 143; sword 142
Himilco 79
hoards 25, 27, 30, 31, 34, 37, 110, 128, 161, 210; *15, 19;* Broighter 128; *36;* coin 215, 216; Duchcov 183; Llyn Cerrig Bach 179; Roman 214; silver 215, 216; Somerset 151

Hochdorf, Germany 10, 126
honey 126
horns 22, 120, 141; *57*; Cork 155; on idol 186; Petrie Crown 155; *see also* trumpets
horse 21, 27, 105, 106, 108, 111, 125, 126; draught 111, 159; hair 119, 126; harness 110, 119, 149; pendant 151; racing 81; riding 107, 108, 159; sacrifice 81; size 108
horse-bits 107, 108 110, 157, 183, 184, 225; *58–60, 93, 100, 101, 107*; **30–34, 65, 66**; composite, iron/bronze 150; decorated 108, 168; iron 32, 150; La Tène type 104; link-loops 159, 161; mouthpiece 153; repair 158, 159; ring pivots 159; Somerset 151, 161; status symbols 108; three-link 107, 152; two-link 107; unfinished 151, 153
horizontal loom 119
houses, circular 80; rectangular 12; timber-built 21, 113
Hughstown Hill, Co. Kildare 43, 62
human bodies 187; figure 185; form 185–87; head 185; remains 199; sacrifice 179, 199; stylized 143
hurdles 117
huts 21, 32, 41, 73, 74, 75; plans 212; platforms 41, 58; timber-built 113

Iberia 17, 60, 61, 61, 228
imports 10, 106, 128, 157, 161, 200–3; bowl 168; copper 208; enamel 158; Hallstatt 31; mirror 127; Roman 214; swords 143; tin 15; torc 161, 163
inauguration (of kings) 67, 70, 83; sites 80–83, 180; tree (*bile*) 83
incest 204
infantry 29
ingot, bronze 151; silver 215
inhumation 68, 75, 127, 189–99, 209; crouched 195; extended 193, 195, 200; flat 189; flexed 193, 195, 200
inlay, red enamel 144, 157
invasion hypothesis 28, 224, 228
Ireland 13 and *passim*; *1*; perception of 203–6; Ptolemy's map 204; *130*
Irish La Tène style 166
Irish Scabbard Style 165
Irish Sea 208
Irish sources 13–16, 64–97, 141, 178, 181; historical 80
iron 12, 26, 161; bloom 148; fibulae 127; mandrels 149, 154; objects 194; ores 26, 147, 148, 165; slag 148; smelting 26, 26, 28, 35, 37, 117, 148; technology 26, 147–48, 220
Iron Age, chronology 147, 220; and *passim*
Isamnion 205
Island MacHugh, Co. Tyrone 18
Italy 9, 10, 158, 218

Jackson, K.H. 16
janus figures 186
Jarlshof, Shetland Is. 17
jet 22; bracelets 141, 201; spoon 217
jetties, La Tène 184
joinery 212
Jupiter 180
Juvenal 219

Kelly, William 222
Keltoi 9
Kenagh 98
Keshcarrigan, Co. Leitrim 116, 152, 155, 157, 168; *65, 107*
key, iron 213
Kilbeg, Co. Westmeath 118; *67*
Kildare 82
Killeevan, Co. Monaghan 108; *34*
Killucan, Co. Westmeath, horse-bit *59*
Killycluggin, Co. Cavan 162, 182; *109, 110*
Kilmurry, Co. Kerry 31; *15*
Kiltierney, Co. Fermanagh 192; *117, 118*
Kingdom of Leinster 71
Kings of Thomond 83
'Kings Stables' 24

kingship 80, 97
Kishawanny, Co. Kildare 217; **35**
Kluckhohn, Clyde 222
knife-handle 101, 119
knives 22, 119
Knock, Co. Roscommon, torc 128, 161, 163, 184, 225; *76*; **45**
Knockadigeen, Co. Tipperary 43; *25*
Knockans 82
Knockbrack, Co. Dublin 80
Knockdhu, C. Antrim 46; *29*
Knocknalappa, Co. Clare 19
Knocknashee, Co. Sligo 39, 41; *21*
Knowth, Co. Meath 121, 126, 157, 195, 199, 209; *121, 122*

La Tène, art style 162, 226; artifacts 65; burials *3*; cemeteries 141; craftsmanship 128; culture 10, 12, 16, 36, 59, 60, 62, 65, 104, 105, 107, 149, 163, 221–28; *2*; fibulae 128; Irish style 166, 225; late 143; metalwork 177, 184; objects *104, 143*; period 48; ritual site 183, 184; scabbards *84*; site 107, 183–85; votive deposits at 183
ladle, bronze 217; *141*
Lagan, River 205
Lagore, Co. Meath *140*
Lake Neuchâtel, Switzerland 183
lakes 182–84
Lambay Island, Co. Dublin 205, 208, 209; *125, 128*; burials 200; fibula *126*; mirror 127; shield boss 146; sword 143; torc 128; *127*
Lanesborough, Co. Longford 104
language, Irish 62
lathe, pole 155
leaf ornament 140
leather 23, 24, 101, 116, 119, 143; shield 146; tanning 117; thongs 146
Lebor na hUidre 14
Lebor na Nuachongbála 14
Leinster, Kingdom of 71; South 228
Leitrim 83, 155
Lia Fáil 67, 70, 180
Liffey, River 214
lignite 22, 58
linch-pins 105, 106, 107; *57*
Lindow Moss 188
linguists 224
link-loops 159
Lisnacrogher, Co. Antrim 123, 184, 185; crannog 184; mount *107*; ring-headed pins 157; rings 128, 144; *86*; scabbards 144, 159, 165; *85, 103*; **55, 70**; sickle *71*; spear 144, 157; *87*; spearbutts 144, 159; swords 150; *82*; **51, 52**
Littleton Bog, Co. Tipperary 121, 146
Livy 9
Llyn Cerrig Bach, Anglesey 179, 183, 184; *58*
Llyn Fawr, Glamorgan, Wales 27, 28; *12*
locket, bronze 141, 194
'lock-rings' 23; *8*
Longford, Co. 83, 112
loom, horizontal 119; vertical 22; weights 119
lost-wax technique 126, 152
Lough Beg, Co. Antrim 183
Lough Crew, Co. Meath 113, 121, 126, 157; bone flakes 167, 168; *104, 105, 106*; *72*; compass arm 151; in pagan mythology 180; passage tombs 180
Lough Erne 185
Lough Gara 32
Lough Gill, Co. Sligo, sword *14*
Lough Gowna 88
Lough Gur, Co. Limerick 17, 106, 113, 126; yoke mounts 183; *57*
Lough Inchiquin, Co. Clare 184
Lough Kinale 88
Lough Lene, Co. Westmeath 111, 208; *133*
Lough Mourne 31; axe 149; *16*
Lough Ree 104; fibula *79*
Loughan Island, River Bann 155, 183; *98*
'Loughey', Co. Down, burial 198; *124*
Loughnashade, human skulls 184, 185; trumpet 165, 184; *58*
Loughshinny, Co. Dublin 207

Lucan 186
L. Servilius Caepio 183
Lugaid Mac Con 69
Lugh 178
Lughnasa, festival of 82, 121
lugs, suspension 195
Lurigethan Co. Antrim 45
Lyles Hill, Co. Antrim 58
Lynn, Chris 74, 88, 180

MacAirt's Fort, Cave Hill, Co. Antrim 46
McCormick, Finbar 126
Maeatae 105
Magh Adhair 83
Maguires, inauguration site of 83
male, age 199; burial 195, 199; height 199
mallets 100, 101
Mallory, J.P. 16, 58
mandrels 149, 154, 155
maple 117
Marcus Tutianus 218
Marinus of Tyre 205
Marne, France 12
marrow extraction 125
Masada 200
masonry work 212
Maximus of Tyre 76
mead 126
Meare 198
Meath, Co. 66
Medb 15, 70
Medb 15, 70
Mediterranean 9, 10, 12, 17, 127, 203, 228; boat 208, 209; *133*; plate 216; wares 207; world 185
Menapii 206, 208
Mentrim Lough, Co. Westmeath 121; *70*
Mercury 178
metal-workers 163; centres of 165
mid-ribs 142
Midhe, Kingdom of 16
Midir of Brí Leith 98
Midlothian 26
migrations 10, 26
mining, copper 151, 208
mirror 127; disc 207; *131*; handle 166, 193; *107*; iron 201
misy 218
Monaghan 83, 84, 85
Monasterevin, Co. Kildare, discs 153; *94*
monoliths 67, 70, 181–82, 210; decorated 162, 166, 167, 181; *see also* 'standing stones'
Monro, Robert 184
Mooghaun, Co. Clare 43, 44; *27*; **9**
Mooghaun North, Co. Clare 25
mortice 78, 100, 119; -and tenon 102
Moselle, River 12
moulds, clay 22, 32, 116, 152, 155; for bronzes 151, 153; for enamel 158; for spearbutts 144; stone 22
Mound of the Hostages 66, 67; burials at 195
mounds 75, 82, 189–93; burial 82, 180, 189, 191, 193; reuse of 180; 'satellite' 192
mounts 22, 105, 108, 150, 153, 157; bronze 34, 201; openwork 158, 201; spear-shaft 144; *see also phalarae*
Moynagh, Co. Meath 19
Mucklaghs 71, 82
Mullaghmast, Co. Kildare *109*
Mullaghmore, Co. Down 25
multivallation 48, 57, 58, 60; closely-spaced 208
Munster 228
mussels 18
myrrh 218
mythology, Celtic 115, 126, 182; pagan 180

Nauheim-derivative fibulae 198
Navan Fort, Co. Armagh 14, 21, 24, 28, 31, 58, 74, 113, 116, 139; *6, 7, 41–44*; ape from 62, 79, 126; *45*; cattle at 126; central post 101, 180, 186; date 226; ritual construction 180; weaving comb from *68*; *see also* Emain Macha
Navan-type fibulae 128, 139, 158; *79*
neck ornaments 127; gold 128; *see also* torcs
necklaces, amber 34, 127; gold 210; gold wire 128

needles 120
Neolithic 17, 41, 58, 66, 70, 75, 111; cairn 192; mound 195
net, hair 119, 126, 128
Newgrange, Co. Meath 21, 151, 162, 210; hoard 210; Roman coins from 180; *135*; Roman jewellery from 180
Newry, Co. Down, bracelet 141
Nore, River 207

O'Connor, Rory 82
O'Connors, inauguration site of 83
O'Donovan, John 71, 83
O'Kelly, Professor 155
Ó Ríordáin, S.P. 68
oak 18, 70, 97, 102, 116, 117, 119; ards 123; *72*; *42*, *43*; charcoal 148; clearance 122; foreshare 124; planks 98, 101, 208; pollen 122; post 101, 180, 186; shield-grip 146; sleepers 100
oars 22
oats 123
Oberdorla, nr Muehlhausen 187
occupation area 41; platform 32; sites 212
oculist's stamp 218; *142*
óenachs 81, 82
Oengus 64
Oldenburg 103
olla 217
Ollpheist (Huge Worm) 83
oppida 12
Oran Beg, Co. Galway 189
ore, iron 26, 147, 148, 165; bog 147
organic material 100
Orkneys 219
ornament, analysis of 163; arcs 161, 166; basketry 165; bird's head 108, 116, 152, 157, 168; broken-backed curve 166; circles 168; compass 151, 121, 168; concentric circle 165; cruciform 201; curvilinear 10, 12, 108, 152, 154, 155, 163, 165; engraved 144, 161, 165; faces 163; filler motifs 165; fine line 168; geometric 166; goat head 169; hatching 165; leaf 140; local styles 165; Lough Crew-Somerset style 167; mass-produced 213; openwork 157, 158, 201; ornithomorphic 168, 195; palmette 108; plant motifs 162, 165; *pointillé* 210; relief 154, 155; *repoussé* 165; *rocked graver* 144, 149, 157; S-figures 165; scrolls 161, 163, 166; sheep head 168; spiral 140, 141, 154, 163, 165, 166, 198; stamped 213; stippling 165; tendrils 163, 166; three-dimensional 152, 154; triple dot 165; triskele 201; trumpet curve 139, 166, 168; vegetal 165, 166; waves 163, 165
Otherworld 178, 210; beings 180, 186
otter 17
Oughavall, Co. Laois 14

P-Celtic dialect 206
padlocks, iron 212, 213
palisade trenches 74
palisades 19, 66, 72, 74, 75, 85, 88, 97
Palmer, Leonard 224
passage tombs 66, 113, 185, 192; Boyne Valley 180; Lough Crew 157
patera 217
path, log 32
Patricius 216
pegs 99, 100, 101, 113; notched 101
pendants 23, 34; coins as 210; *see also* Y-shaped objects
persicara 123
Petrie Crown 155, 166; *96*, *107*; *57*
Petrie, George 66
phalarae 26, 108
Philemon 205
philology 223
pig 17, 125, 126; bronze 168; cast 168
pins, bone 120; *113*; bronze 34, 139; cup-headed 31; disc-headed 22, 27, 32, 34; gold 23; Hallstatt 28; ring-headed 128, 139, 140, 141, 152, 157, 158, 168; *80*, *81*, *99*; *50*; sunflower 17, 22, 31; 'swan's neck' 27, 31

pitch 155
pits 73, 80, 212; burial 25; cremation in 25, 189, 193, 194, 194; inhumation in 200
placenames 205
plane 119
planking 75
plant motifs 162, 165
plantain 122
plaques, bone 121, 191
platform, viewing 74
platters 216
plough 21; share 147
ploughing, cross 124
podsolization 36
pointillé 210
polis 206, 212
Pollacorragune, Co. Galway 194
pollen, analysis 121, 124; herbaceous 122
pommels 142
Pomponius Mela 204
ponds, artificial 82
poplar 115, 117
Porcupine Bank 217
Poseidonius 16, 163
posts 73, 74, 76, 80
Potterne, Wiltshire 26
pottery, absence of 116; burial 25; coarse 32, 34, 58; Gallo-Roman 48, 208; Gaulish 212; Roman 68, 217; Samian ware 208
pouches 120
pouring gate 151
promontory forts, coastal 45, 48, 207; inland 45-48; *29*, *30*
Propertius 127
prospectors 221
Ptolemy 204-6; map 208, 210, 212; *130*
punch 149, 154, 155; ring- 161
pupall 113
pyre 189

Q-Celtic dialect 206, 228
quenching 26
querns 162; beehive 124, 167, 184, 225, 228; *73*, *104*, *144*; *44*; disc 124; rotary 124; saddle 21, 32, 124
quillon plates, bronze 150

Raffin, Co. Meath 80; *46*
Raftery, Joseph 7, 32
Ralaghan, Co. Cavan 24, 186; *10*
ramparts 39, 44, 58, 82, 85, 86, 97; double 62, 63; earthen 65, 74; stone 46
Raphoe, Co. Donegal, heads 185
Rath 207
Rath Dubh 82
Rath Grainne 69; *37*
Rath Laoghaire 67
Rath na Ríogh 66, 67, 70, 71
Rathcoran, Baltinglass Hill 43, 44, 62; *26*
Rathcroghan 70, 71; *20*
Rathgall, Co. Wicklow 18, 21, 25, 41, 44, 57, 58, 120; *4*, *31*; *4-6*, *17*; date 58; finds from 58; furnace at 148; pottery from 58; straptag from 120, 128, 213
Rathlin Island 217
Rathnagree 62
Rathtinaun, Co. Sligo 19, 22, 32-35; *18*; axehead from 149; *91*; hoard 19, 20
raven 31, 179
razors 22; bifid 34; Hallstatt 28
Red Bog, Co. Louth 121
reeds 101
refugees 209
regia 206, 212
Rhine, River 184
Rhineland 182
reins 105, 106
relief ornament 154, 155
religion 12, 16, 178-79, 188; nature 187
religious assemblies 180; beliefs 178; carvings 185
repoussé 154, 165

resin 155, 161
Richborough, Kent 216
ring-headed pins 128, 139, 140, 152, 157, 158, 168; *80*, *99*; *50*; distribution 141; *89*; export of 140
ring-pivot 159
ringbarrows 25, 70, 71, 189; *112*, *114*
ringforts 38, 71, 74, 116; platform 67; triple-banked 68, 212
rings 128, 168; bronze 157; finger 198, 210; hollow 144; *86*; iron 192; metal 189, 195; suspension 115, 149
ritual 70, 74, 124, 128, 183, 210; cauldron, as ritual object 184; centre 213; death 188; deposit 23; enclosures 69; endocannibalism 204; horse sacrifice 81; offerings 183; practices 25, 183; sites 65, 180, 215; sport 141; totem pole 186
river goddesses 182, 183
rivers, navigable 207
rivet 154, 155; casting 155; holes 154
riveting 157
roads 98, 109
roadways, timber 65, 99
rocked graver ornament 144, 149, 157; 'walked' 165
Roe, River 18
Roman, boat 111; burials 196, 206-7, 209; *131*; carvings 183; coins 58, 208, 209, 210, 212, 213; disc-brooches 210; fibulae 74, 201, 212, 213, 217; *139*; finds 194; *137*; gold 180, 210; influence 203; inscription 216, 218; jewellery 180; necklaces 128; seal, lead 216; settlers 212; statuettes 214; trade 207; traders 209; trading stations 207; visitors 180; world 221; writing 210
Romans 57, 179, 200, 207; in Ireland 206-10, 214
Rome 9
Roscavey, Co. Tyrone, ring-headed pin *80*
Roscommon 83, 86, 225
routeways 66, 69, 88
royal sites 64-65, 79, 80, 103
runners 100, 101
rye, grains 123
Rynne, Etienne 107

sacred groves 179; lakes 179; tree 180, 187
sacrifice 81; human 179, 199
St Adamnán 68
St Anne's Well, Randalstown, Co. Meath 213
St Louis, nr Basle 184
St Patrick 67, 68
St Rúadán 68
salt 9, 126, 127
Samhain 82
Samian Ware 208, 217; *140*
sand-dunes 139
sandhills 113, 215
saw 119
Saxony 103
Scabbard Style, British 165; Continental 165; Irish 165, 166
scabbards 112, 120, 144, 166, 183, 185, 225, 226; bronze 165; iron 10; manufacture 144; plates, bronze 157; *85*; *55*; wood on leather 29, 201
Scandinavia 186
Scarva, Co. Down 84
scoops, bone 120; *69*
Scotland 13, 17, 144
Scott, Brian 147, 149, 150
Scotshouse, Co. Monaghan 88
Scottish National Museum, horse-bit 157
scroll ornament 161, 163, 166
sea eagle 18
seal, lead 212; Roman 216
sealing-strips 154
Seine 183
Sencha Mac Ailella 14
Seneca 183
Senones 9
settlements 12; defended 26; Hallstatt 28; Roman coins from 214

Severn estuary 28
Shannon, River 23, 28, 86, 88, 183, 228; crossing 104; name 183; on Ptolemy's map 205; ring-headed pin from *80, 107*; spearbutts from 144; *87*
shears, iron 127, 192; *74*
sheaths 120
sheep 125; bone 142; head of 168; height 125, 126; wool 128
Sheepen Hill, Colchester, Essex 26
sheet-metalworking, bronze 151, 153
shields 12, 23, 117, 120, 146, 200, 89; *7*; wood and leather 24
ships 26, 79, 111, 208
shirt 127
shoes 22, 119
sickles 22; *71*; iron 27, 123; probable 34; socketed 21
side-links 107, 108
sieves 117
siliquae 216
silk, chinese 10
silver coins 210, 215, 216
skeletons, extended 209
skull, human 80, 184, 185; as depositions 185
sky-god 180
Slaney, Valley 62
slash marks, on shield 146
slate 217
sleepers 100, 101
sleeve-fasteners 23
slings 120, 141
Sloping Trenches, Tara 69; *37*
smith, 146–47; black 17, 22, 27; bronze 17, 27; gold 17, 22, 23
smithy *see* forge
snake head, on fibula 177
soldering 22
Solinus 204
Somerset, Co. Galway 116, 151, 152; *65, 76, 107; 39, 47, 62, 70*; bird's head handle from 168; fibula 159; *79*; ribbon torc 128, 161, 167
souterrains 71
Spain 204, 228
spatulae 120; *69*
spear ferrules 183; fittings 141; *87*
spear-heads, iron 27, 74, 149, 157, 183; *9*
spear point 146
spear-shafts 117, 144
spearbutts 14, 144, 150, 153, 159; *88*; **54**
spears 12, 23, 141, 144
Spinan's Hill 62, 63; *34*
spinning 119
spiral ornament 162, 198; on glass beads 141; on ring-headed pins 140, 154
spiral rings 141
spirals, hair-spring 165; snail-shell 161, 166
spoke-shave 119
'spoons' 157, 167; *104*; **64**; jet 217; Roman 216
springs 183; curative properties of 183
springs on fibulae 138, 139
stag 168, 179; *106*
standing stones 181–82; *102, 109*; *see also* monoliths
steel 149
Staple Howe, Yorkshire 26
statuettes, bronze 214
stippling 165
stone carvings 105, 180, 185; *108*; objects 58
stone circle 182
Stone of Destiny 67, 70, 180; *18*
Stonehenge 76
stoneworking 162
Stonyford, Co. Kilkenny 207, 209, 218; *131*
stop-knobs 107
Strabo 10, 127, 200, 204
strainers 10
'strakes' 208
straptag, bronze 120, 128
Streamstown, Co. Westmeath, horsebits 161; *101*; **65, 66**
structures, timber-built 72, 75

stud 26, 157; bronze 20; rosette 201
Styx 209
supernatural 185
swage 149
swan 31, 179
swan's neck handle 217
sword, blade 141, 142; effectiveness 150; grips 29, 126, 143; pommels 29
swords 10, 12, 16, 23; bronze 28; *9*; Hallstatt, bronze 28, 30; *14*; Hallstatt derivation 28; iron 27, 120, 141–44, 149, 150, 183, 200, 226; La Tène 74, 142; *82, 84, 90*; model, wood 29, 142; *14*; **5**; size 141
Symmachus 204
Synod 82

Tacitus 179, 204, 219
Tailtiu (*Oenach Tailten*) 82
Táin Bó Cuailnge 14–16, 70
Tanderagee, Co. Armagh 186; **75**
tankard 116
tannin 117
tanning 120
tap-slag 26
Tara 64, 65–70, 71, 80, 82, 113, 181, 195; *35–37; 17*; ceremonial centre 180; enamel from 158; padlocks from 212, 213; Roman pottery from 217
tassels (horse-hair) 21
Teach Cormaic (Cormac's House) 67
teeth 199; human 185
Teltown 82; *see also* Tailtiu
temple, at Emain Macha 180
tent 113
terraces, internal 41, 44, 45, 47
terrets 105, 106; *57*
testudo (tortoise) 57
textiles 21, 22, 101, 119, 127; on locket 194
Thames, River 146
Thompson, Francis 112
Tiber, River 9
Ticooly-O'Kelly, Co. Galway, beehive quern *73*; **44**
Timahoe, Co. Kildare 21, 104, 117
timber-lacing 39
tin 25, 151
Tinoran Hill, Co. Wicklow 62
Tipperary 218; chape from 144
Tlaghta, Co. Meath 82; 82; *see also* Hill of Ward
'toilet implements', bronze 212, 217
Tolkien, J.R.R. 228
Tollund, Denmark 188
tongs, iron 149
toolmarks 101
tools 25, 27, 149, 157, 162; graving 155, 157, 165
Toome, Co. Antrim 31; axehead from 149; scabbard from 157; *103*
Toormore, Co. Kilkenny 43, 44; *28*
torcs 186, 225; *135*; **36, 45**; bar 128, 162, 210; beaded 201; *126, 129*; bronze 128, 201; buffer 127, 128; *75*; gold 70; ribbon 128, 151, 161; *76*; terminals 161; votive offerings of 184
totem pole 186; *111*
Toulouse 183
towns, defended 12
trackways 18; *51*; brushwood 21, 99, 103; *2*; *see also* roadways
traders 221
trading 204; Roman 207, 208; stations 207
Trajan 209
transport, land 110; river 110; wheeled 107, 110–11
travel 109
Tray, Co. Armagh 24
trenches 72, 75
tribal expansion 226; gods 178; integrity 180; names 205; power 226
tribes 10, 97
Trier 212
trousers 128
trumpets 22, 25, 112, 150, 154, 155, 165, 184; *95*
Tuatha Dé (*Daghdha*) 87

Tullaghoge, Co. Tyrone 83
Tulsk, Co. Roscommon 70, 71
tumulus 41, 65, 67, 70
tunic 127
Turoe, Co. Galway 162, 166, 181–82; *102, 109*; **65**
tuyère 149
tweezers 154, 155, 198
tyres, iron 105

Uí Néill, inauguration site 83, 87
Uisneach, Co. Westmeath 83, 104, 213
Ulaidh 14, 205
Ulster Cycle 14–16, 125
Ulster, province of 14, 15, 70, 74, 86, 139, 206; capital of 184
Underworld 209
urn-burials 191; glass 207

vehicles 21; wheeled 104, 105
Venutius 200
vessels, bronze 157; drinking 116; leather 116; pottery 22; stave-built 116; wood 22, 33, 34, 101, 116, 119; *66*
villages, defended 57
Vix, France 10
Volcae Tectosages 183
Voluntii 205
votive offerings 128, 181, 183, 184; *see also* ritual, cult

Waddell, John 71
wagons 12, 102–4
Wailes, Bernard 72
Wales, copper mining 208
wall, construction 113; slots 212; wattle 117
Walsh, Aidan 88
Warner, Richard 207
warfare 141–46; cavalry 29; infantry 29
warrior, 12, 105; aristocracy 65, 225; class 141; mounted 111
Waterford harbour 207
Waterman, Dudley 75
wattle, 113, 117
wax 152
weapons 10, 12, 23, 25, 26, 141–46, 185, 200, 201
weaving, combs 119; *121*; **68**; implements 120; tabby 119
wedges, oak 100, 119
wells 182, 183, 213
Westmeath, Co. 139, 155; ring-headed pin 158; *99*
wetland sites 106, 115, 182–84
wheels 21, 180; block 104, 117, 118; *54*; spoked 105
'whistle hole' 186
Whiterocks, Co. Antrim 113
wickerwork, boats 204; fences 19
Wicklow, Co. 23, 63, 151
wild cat 17
willow 99, 116, 117
Wiltshire 26
wine 9, 212
Witham 146
withes 154
wolf 17, 126
wood 23, 24, 101, 143; working 117
wooden structures 180, 184
Wooing of Etain 98
wool 119, 128
Worm Ditch 83

Xenophanes 220

Y-shaped objects 108, 110, 217; *60–61, 92*; **35**; unfinished 151
Yellow Book of Lecan 14
yew 99, 106, 117, 208
yoke 105, 106; *29, 30*; mounts, bronze 184; *57*
Yorkshire 105; scabbards from 165, 226

Zeus 76